New Casebooks

DAVID COPPERFIELD

and

HARD TIMES

CHARLES DICKENS

EDITED BY JOHN PECK

St. Martin's Press

Introduction, selection and editorial matter
© John Peck 1995

First published in Great Britain 1995 by
MACMILLAN PRESS LTD
Houndmills, Basingstoke, Hampshire RG21 2XS
and London
Companies and representatives
throughout the world

A catalogue record for this book is available
from the British Library.

ISBN 0–333–59881–4 hardcover
ISBN 0–333–59882–2 paperback

10   9   8   7   6   5   4   3   2   1
04   03   02   01   00   99   98   97   96   95

Printed in Malaysia

First published in the United States of America 1995 by
Scholarly and Reference Division,
ST. MARTIN'S PRESS, INC.,
175 Fifth Avenue,
New York, N.Y. 10010

ISBN 0–312–12492–9

Library of Congress Cataloging-in-Publication Data
David Copperfield and Hard Times—Charles Dickens / edited by John Peck.
p.   cm. — (New casebooks)
Includes bibliographical references and index.
ISBN 0–312–12492–9
1. Dickens, Charles, 1812–1870. *David Copperfield.* 2. Dickens,
Charles, 1812–1870. *Hard Times.* 3. Domestic fiction, English–
–History and criticism.   4. Family in literature.   I. Peck, John,
1947– . II. Series.
PR4558.D39   1995
823'.8—dc20   94–35204
                                                     CIP

Contents

v

Acknowledgements

The editor and publishers wish to thank the following for permission to use copyright material:

Chris R. Vanden Bossche, for 'Cookery, not Rookery: Family and Class in *David Copperfield*', *Dickens Studies Annual*, 15 (1986), 87–109, by permission of AMS Press, Inc; Virginia Carmichael, for 'In Search of Beein': Nom/Non du Père in *David Copperfield*', *English Literary History*, 54 (1987), 653–67, by permission of the Johns Hopkins University Press; Jean Ferguson Carr, for 'Dickens, *Hard Times*, and Feminine Discourses', *Dickens Studies Annual*, 18 (1989), 161–78, by permission of AMS Press, Inc.; Steven Connor, for excerpts from '*Hard Times*' in *Charles Dickens*, Blackwell Publishers (1985), pp. 89–106, by permission of the author; Simon Edwards, for an excerpt from '*David Copperfield*: The Decomposing Self', *The Centennial Review*, 29, 3 (1985), 328–52, by permission of *The Centennial Review*; Richard Fabrizio, for 'Wonderful No-Meaning: Language and Psychopathology of the Family in *Hard Times*', *Dickens Studies Annual*, 16 (1987), 61–94, by permission of AMS Press, Inc.; Catherine Gallagher, for an excerpt from *The Industrial Reformation of English Fiction, 1832–1867* (1985), pp. 147–66, by permission of the University of Chicago Press; John Kucich, for excerpts from *Repression in Victorian Fiction: Charlotte Brontë, George Eliot and Charles Dickens* (1987), pp. 228–35, 244–51. Copyright © 1987 the Regents of the University of California, by permission of the University of California Press; Margaret Myers, for 'The Lost Self: Gender in *David Copperfield*' in Judith Spector (ed.), *Gender Studies: New Directions in Feminist Criticism*, Creative Writing Program (1986), pp. 120–32, by permission of Bowling Green State University; Mary

Poovey, for excerpt from 'The Man-of Letters Hero: *David Copperfield* and the Professional Writer in *Uneven Developments: The Ideological Work of Gender in Mid-Victorian England* (1988), pp. 89–101, 116–25. Copyright © 1988 by the University of Chicago Press, by permission of Virago Press and the University of Chicago Press.

General Editors' Preface

The purpose of this series of New Casebooks is to reveal some of the ways in which contemporary criticism has changed our understanding of commonly studied texts and writers and, indeed, of the nature of criticism itself. Central to the series is a concern with modern critical theory and its effect on current approaches to the study of literature. Each New Casebook editor has been asked to select a sequence of essays which will introduce the reader to the new critical approaches to the text or texts being discussed in the volume and also illuminate the rich interchange between critical theory and critical practice that characterises so much current writing about literature.

In this focus on modern critical thinking and practice New Casebooks aim not only to inform but also to stimulate, with volumes seeking to reflect both the controversy and the excitement of current criticism. Because much of this criticism is difficult and often employs an unfamiliar critical language, editors have been asked to give the reader as much help as they feel is appropriate, but without simplifying the essays or the issues they raise. Again, editors have been asked to supply a list of further reading which will enable readers to follow up issues raised by the essays in the volume.

The project of New Casebooks, then, is to bring together in an illuminating way those critics who best illustrate the ways in which contemporary criticism has established new methods of analysing texts and who have reinvigorated the important debate about how we 'read' literature. The hope is, of course, that New Casebooks will not only open up this debate to a wider audience, but will also encourage students to extend their own ideas, and think afresh about their responses to the texts they are studying.

John Peck and Martin Coyle
University of Wales, Cardiff

Introduction

JOHN PECK

DAVID COPPERFIELD

David Copperfield was published in 1850; Dickens had by this time written seven novels and there were, if we include the unfinished *Edwin Drood* (1870), to be seven more. Curiously, however, despite its central position in Dickens's career and in the nineteenth century, *David Copperfield* has not until recently attracted much noteworthy criticism.[1] Although critical attention to Dickens has soared over the past 30 years, it has tended to be certain novels, in particular *Bleak House*, that have been central both to traditional and non-traditional criticism.[2] *David Copperfield* by comparison, even in the 1960s and 70s, drew little notice. In the 1980s, however, as critical thinking developed in new directions – in particular, as New Historicist, feminist and psychoanalytic criticism became more established – interest in *David Copperfield* surged. Suddenly, almost from nowhere, it came to be seen as one of the central texts of the nineteenth century. Indeed, it is no exaggeration to say that in the new writing on the novel, and especially in the essays collected in this *New Casebook*, we gain an impression of one of the world's great novels being rediscovered.

Traditional Criticism
Rediscovered by critics, that is; the broader public, of course, did not need to rediscover *David Copperfield*, as it has always been one of Dickens's best-loved novels.[3] Yet it is the very popularity of *David Copperfield* that might, traditionally, have proved its critical

1

undoing. Essentially, *David Copperfield* is a *Bildungsroman*, that is a novel that follows the development of the hero or heroine from childhood into adulthood, through a troubled quest for identity.[4] David starts life in a state of bliss, which is destroyed with the arrival of Murdstone; he then goes through life encountering a variety of strong, weak or amusing characters. He finally finds happiness in his second marriage, to Agnes, but there remains a sense of loss, that the wholeness of his earliest existence will never be restored. The novel is so evocative in its recollections of childhood and so full of memorable characters, that it is tempting to feel that the energy that drives it stems from Dickens coming to terms with his own life, and that this is why *David Copperfield* seems to lack the kind of formal and thematic organisation, and sharp social criticism, that is so evident in several of Dickens's other novels. And this is how it has often been regarded, as an autobiographical novel, hugely enjoyable but with limitations.[5] Indeed, many critics have all but ignored it: a standard pattern in traditional criticism is for the critic to discuss Dickens's youthful exuberance in works such as *Nicholas Nickleby* (1839), see the mature Dickens taking shape in *Dombey and Son* (1848), and then skip over *David Copperfield* as a kind of interlude, proceeding to the three subsequent novels, *Bleak House* (1853), *Hard Times* (1854) and *Little Dorrit* (1857).[6]

But not all critics ignored *David Copperfield*. One influential view, still widely reflected in teaching of the novel, is that of Gwendolyn B. Needham, in a 1954 article 'The Undisciplined Heart of *David Copperfield*'.[7] Needham argues that the whole of David's life story is about his emotional growth; as a young man he is too pliant, too easily influenced, and lacking in self-confidence. He is surrounded by figures such as Aunt Betsey and his mother who have also suffered because of their undisciplined hearts. And even characters such as Steerforth and Rosa Dartle echo the same theme, exemplifying 'the misery to which the undisciplined heart can doom itself and bring innocent victims'.[8] David's love for Dora is the most obvious example of how he allows his heart to rule his head. When, however, Annie Strong, the young wife of Dr Strong, talking about her own life, refers to 'The first mistaken impulse of an undisciplined heart', David begins to take stock; he accepts responsibility for his actions, and attempts to make his marriage to Dora as happy as possible. After her death he wanders, eventually awakening to some sense of beauty in nature before, finally, finding happiness with Agnes.

Needham's thesis seems very plausible, particularly as in her account, which is packed with valuable insights, all the details of the text fuse together to endorse and extend this theme. The reservation one must feel, of course, is that this is an excessively moral reading of David Copperfield, as if the whole intention of the novel is simply to assert a platitude.[9] A further problem with Needham's approach, however, is that, in various ways, it tries to present David Copperfield as the kind of work of moral realism that George Eliot might have produced, and although Needham seems to find an almost Eliot-like subtlety in the novel, most readers, I imagine, would be inclined to feel that such a comparison cannot really be sustained. Barbara Hardy is interesting on this.[10] Like Needham, and indeed like most traditional critics, she accepts the pattern that is almost unavoidable in talking about David Copperfield, the pattern of opposition between waywardness, visible in the conduct of both Steerforth and Micawber, and an idea of control, reflected in the way that David assumes control of his life. Hardy, however, reverses Needham's judgement on the novel when she argues that the unifying function of the idea of the taming of the undisciplined heart is actually a weakness, that David Copperfield offers 'a very neat graph of progress: once David sees that his heart is undisciplined, the path ahead is fairly smooth and straight'.[11] Her point is that David Copperfield is indeed coherently organised to make a moral point, but lacks the degree of moral subtlety that we might associate with novelists such as George Eliot, Henry James or D. H. Lawrence; she suggests that the strength of the novel lies in 'intense and local shafts which strike deep',[12] rather than in the overall pattern.

Hardy seems to offer a necessary corrective to Needham's view, but in fact they work from a common premise: they share the assumption, which is at the heart of traditional liberal humanist criticism, that a successful literary text represents a complex moral statement. The difference between them is that Needham feels that David Copperfield possesses the necessary qualities to sustain this statement whereas Hardy, along with those who regard David Copperfield as a delightful semi-autobiography, feels that it lacks rigour. In the comparison, Needham might seem the less sophisticated critic, but her positive approach is perhaps preferable to that taken by Hardy, who falls into a familiar trap of traditional criticism in being far too ready to reprimand the author for his assumed shortcomings. At one stage, for example, she comments: 'David often reveals – or rather *betrays* – Victorian limitations which the author does not see but which the modern reader certainly does. David's dissatisfaction with Dora's housekeeping, for instance, is very plainly both characteristic of his sex and age, an expectation and a need which it never occurs to him to question or criticise.'[13] The critical strategy here is that Hardy identifies what she feels is the position taken in the text, and then condemns Dickens for the narrower, less than liberal, less than modern aspects of his thinking.

As we shall see, identical assumptions are also brought into play in traditional responses to *Hard Times*. Most criticism of the novel starts with the idea of an opposition: on the one hand, we have the utilitarians, on the other, the imaginative world of the circus. The simplest and most straightforward criticism praises Dickens's condemnation of inhumane values, and salutes him for offering a powerful warning to his age. More complex traditional criticism, however, whilst recognising that Dickens is on the side of the imagination, points out his covert enthusiasm for middle-class order, a fact that betrays itself in his patronising attitude towards the working-class characters in *Hard Times* and his hostility towards trade unionism. Time and time again, traditional criticism makes this rapid leap from analysing the text to ticking off the author, essentially for not being consistently liberal enough in his attitudes.[14] Such criticism is informed by an assumption that the artist should be a kind of superior truth-teller, who can stand outside the values of his or her period, offering a form of timeless wisdom. By contrast, recent criticism, as we shall see, regards the text as a site where the ideological contradictions of a period are exposed, and to some extent examined, but not necessarily contained and judged. What this means in the case of *David Copperfield* is that, rather than following Barbara Hardy's line of censuring Dickens for his blinkered views, critics have taken a positive view of *David Copperfield* as a text that brings to life in a vivid way Victorian confusions and assumptions about gender and personal identity. Such a radical change of emphasis did not, however, really become evident before the 1980s, although there were earlier signs of new approaches to the novel.

A Change of Direction

Around the start of the 1970s, partly influenced by critical theory but also anticipating theoretical innovations, the stance of many Dickens critics began to change. We can see this in the chapter on *David Copperfield* in James R. Kincaid's 1971 book *Dickens and the Rhetoric of Laughter*. As against those critics who focus on David's development, Kincaid argues that the idea of disciplining the heart

> is a terribly reductive formula for a humane and responsive existence, that it is priggish, escapist, ugly, and narrow, that it denies the values that count – those of Dora, the Micawbers, and Mr Dick – and that this 'disciplining' is partly a euphemism for desensitising, falsifying, sentimentalising.[15]

Whereas Barbara Hardy finds fault with Dickens's values, Kincaid suggests that, although David makes the case for prudence, discipline and rigidity, the novel actually encourages us to see the inadequacy of these values. At a simple level, David's growing earnestness has nothing to do with the comic values, and comic characters, that feature so prominently in the novel. Traditional criticism tended to endorse David, and dismiss as foolish or suspect anything or anyone opposed to him, but in Kincaid's reading a far more interesting tension is produced between David, who is drifting towards Murdstonean firmness, and a relaxed and comic world.

Kincaid devotes a considerable section of his chapter to a discussion of Micawber, whom he sees as embodying and expressing values, and speaking in a voice of his own, that run entirely counter to the earnest rigidity that David increasingly adopts.[16] David, who begins the novel 'in full accord with comic values', has by the end, 'become their enemy'.[17] Kincaid works with the same basic opposition as earlier critics, but his scepticism about David enables him to get away from Barbara Hardy's idea that there is 'a very neat graph of progress' in *David Copperfield*. What Kincaid offers is a sense of real conflict, something stronger than a simple thesis about moral growth; the text is repositioned as a complex critique, that examines sceptically the kinds of moves towards conformity that characterise the mid-Victorian period. In particular, Kincaid problematises the whole issue of bourgeois identity.

The importance of Kincaid's argument lies in its break with the circularity of traditional criticism. It is only a slight exaggeration to suggest that, ultimately, most liberal humanist criticism of *David Copperfield* reduces to a tautology: critics recognise that the problem dealt with in the text is bourgeois identity, but the only answer they can offer is bourgeois identity, that the way to cope with the world is to be a responsible, compassionate individual.

Discussion of the novel ceases, therefore, before it really even begins, for David's search for his mature identity is tracked by critics who endorse the liberal humanist notion of the importance of a mature identity.[18] The simple, yet original, move Kincaid makes is to withdraw from this kind of complicity with the overt pattern of personal development in the text. He starts to raise questions about the Victorian concept of self, at the same time allowing the possibility that the novel itself is posing equally uncomfortable questions. In doing this, Kincaid sets the course for modern criticism of *David Copperfield* which, by and large, lingers over the central opposition, taking it apart and seeing its complexity, rather than rushing to extract a moral statement from, or pass moral judgement on, the text.

Despite its originality, however, Kincaid's approach is still in many respects traditional, in that he fastens upon plot, character and relationship, and works with a conventional sense of how we derive meaning from a text. Terry Eagleton contrasts such an approach with one that 'treats characters, events and relations as functions of certain controlling systems of signification'.[19] What Eagleton's words point to is the revolution in reading practices that came along in the late 1960s, in the form of structuralist and poststructuralist ways of reading a text.

Structuralism and Poststructuralism

Stucturalism, taking its lead from Ferdinand de Saussure's work in linguistics, is an analytic method that is less concerned with the unique qualities of any individual example than with the structures that underlie the individual examples.[20] Traditionally, critics have made sense of texts by relating them to life, but the pure structuralist does not wish to move outside the text. Instead, he or she moves in, trying to work out general theories about how texts function; it is a kind of quasi-scientific endeavour to uncover the tacit grammar of texts. As such, structuralism might seem a valid, but rather dull, technical approach to literature. But, in rejecting a conventional interest in life beyond the text, preferring to see every book as a construct working by certain rules, structuralism adopts a position of not seeing things from within the general cultural and value framework of society; the touchstone for critical analysis ceases to be the mimetic 'truthfulness' or lack of 'truthfulness' of a text.

No sooner, though, had structuralism started to make its presence felt in literary criticism than it began to be superseded by poststructuralism. Poststructuralism – the term is a broad one that designates a variety of critical perspectives that, from the early 1970s, developed in the wake of structuralism – was both a development from and reaction against structuralism. Structuralism, in setting itself up in opposition to mimetic criticism, established, perhaps for the first time, a widespread recognition of the manner in which traditional critics create a framework of interpretation and evaluation for a text by relating it to their own view of life. Structuralist criticism attempted to stand back, to separate itself from this kind of imposition of a set of cultural and social values on texts. Poststructuralism takes this questioning of the assumptions a reader brings to the text much further. Deconstructive criticism, in particular, challenges our desire for fixity, for stable and determinate meanings in a text. The procedure of deconstructive critics is to pursue the conflicting forces within the text itself which dissipate and defer meaning, focusing on the multiple and undecidable possibilities of the words on the page.[21]

All of this might become clearer if we consider the idea of the subject and identity. Traditional criticism is largely organised around an idea of coherent identity – the human 'subject'. In *David Copperfield*, for example, the two keys for making sense of the text have always been David as central character and Dickens as author, with clear designs and intentions. Poststructuralism challenges this way of organising experience; in the works of Derrida, de Man, Foucault and Lacan, the reassuring notion of the individual, or subject, is destabilised and disunified.[22] Such decentring of the subject is, however, just one strand in a radical questioning of all systems and structures, a profound scepticism about all-inclusive ways of making sense of the world, that characterises poststructuralism. This scepticism includes a critical attitude towards structuralism, because of structuralism's pretensions to set up a comprehensive grammar of texts. One of the central tenets of structuralism, for instance, is the idea of the binary opposition – for example, between waywardness and control in *David Copperfield* or imagination and facts in *Hard Times* – but the idea of a binary opposition can generate a schematic neatness in a critical reading. Poststructuralist criticism, in reaction, is likely to pursue the ways in which any opposition collapses, contradicts and undermines itself.

It should be apparent by now that every aspect of poststructuralist thinking challenges the old liberal humanist cosy conspiracy with the text, where the pattern of the book was established, where a sense of the 'subject' was always at the centre, and where a view was established of what the author was trying to say. With the advent of poststructuralism, criticism is thoroughly destabilised, but new approaches also contain new possibilities, that dimensions to texts might exist that the old system never noticed. In saying this, however, we need to bear in mind that much of this rereading simply passed *David Copperfield* by.[23] The trouble is that, at face value, it looks like an innocent, even innocuous, old-fashioned plot and character novel. Critics working along new lines in the 1970s were much more attracted by other Dickens novels, especially *Bleak House*, a text that overtly plays with story-telling, the act of writing, and the pursuit and interpretation of mysteries. One notable exception, however, is a 1977 essay by Robert E. Lougy that, in its poststructuralist approach, provides a vivid illustration of how criticism can break with old habits.

Lougy, in 'Remembrances of Death Past and Future: A Reading of *David Copperfield*' (the essay is not included in this collection but is anthologised elsewhere[24]), notes how, at the end of the novel, we feel a dissonance between David's story and life, 'in spite of the novel's attempt to make us see the circle it draws as complete and whole'.[25] It is a similar point to that made by Kincaid, but Lougy then turns to Roland Barthes' proposition that a work of art denies for as long as possible the final moment of stasis, postponing the point when its vision will be compromised or terminated by its form. This is a typically poststructuralist emphasis on the problematics of literary form: much of the essay focuses on images in the novel, such as that of a lunatic's face peering in at a window, that cannot be assimilated within the coherent narrative pattern, for they evoke a terror of separation and discontinuity. In this terror, Lougy argues, the novel confronts a knowledge found in the realms of darkness and dreams; there is, we come to realise, an immense gulf between such interiority and the public order of social structures. Something that soon becomes apparent in Lougy's essay is that he has released himself from the usual stabilising referents of plot and character and, in doing so, discovers just how much there is in the novel that operates beyond our usual reasoning impulses, particularly in the way of irrational forces. The fact that he spots these unnerving elements is in no small measure due to the fact that he adopts a critical approach that does not reach for the usual safe moorings.

What we see in Lougy's essay, therefore, is a critical method that has separated itself from assumptions that tidy up texts, assumptions that force novels to deliver a coherent meaning. Rather than tying things down to a sense of a single meaning generated by the author, the text is seen as plural, seen as conducting an open and subverting debate. It is, indeed, the very notion of stability that is challenged in the essay's emphasis on alienation, madness and death in *David Copperfield*. As radical as Lougy's reading is, however, things might be taken further in a full deconstructive reading. Lougy undermines the comfortable reading of *David Copperfield*, but he does, none the less, offer us a unified reading (in a sense, he has assembled a set of referents, such as madness, which are simply the opposite of our usual referents for establishing a pattern in this novel). A deconstructive reading, by contrast, would be less concerned with establishing a stable overall view; the emphasis would fall, instead, on the ceaseless play of irreconcilable and contradictory meanings in the text. A very good example of this is provided in Steven Connor's essay on *Hard Times*, which appears in this volume.[26] Comparable deconstructive readings of *David Copperfield* do not, however, seem to exist. In fact we have to wait for the next step in theoretical thinking in order to see a substantial body of new work on *David Copperfield*.

New Historicism

Starting in the mid-1980s, critics at last began to pay a great deal of attention to *David Copperfield*. What sparked off this interest was a renewed concern with seeing texts in their historical context. Taking their lead from the work of Michel Foucault, many felt there was a need to turn again to a consideration of the past (one of the most frequently expressed criticisms of deconstruction was that it was ahistorical, that it had no sense of a text in context).[27] The whole line of poststructuralist thinking had, however, raised so many doubts about the interpretative frameworks we generally employ that it was no longer possible to think about the past without being sceptical about the assumptions we bring to history; if texts were to be considered in context, this would have to go hand in hand with rethinking our notions of the past.

This should become clearer if we consider the differences between a traditional historical approach to Dickens and the kind of work being produced today. Readers of Dickens can still derive a great deal of benefit from Humphry House's *The Dickens World*;[28] after a while, however, House's book begins to irritate because of its straightforwardness, as if there were social abuses that needed to be reformed and Dickens's novels were principally effective in drawing attention to these problems. More often than not, traditional literary historians approach the issue in this way, as if texts simply reflect history rather than being produced by it. Whereas a critic like House produces a coherent historical narrative, New Historicists work with a sense of the complex political crosscurrents within a text. History ceases to be a matter of dates, great events and a stable narrative; instead, the key issues become politics, ideology, power, authority and subversion. At the same time, New Historicism is intensely aware of its lack of objectivity, acknowledging that historians reconstruct the past in the light of their own ideological preoccupations and constraints.[29]

A clear example of the way in which a renewed interest in history creates new possibilities in considering *David Copperfield* is provided by the first essay in this collection, 'Cookery, not Rookery: Family and Class in *David Copperfield*', by Chris R. Vanden Bossche. The essay is built upon a sense of opposition in the text, a division between the values of middle-class domesticity, represented by cookery images, and a different set of values associated with the name of David's first home, Blunderstone Rookery: 'Cast out of the Rookery,' Vanden Bossche writes, 'losing his family, [David] seeks to re-establish his identity by finding a new family and a new meaning for Rookery.'[30] This might seem a familiar approach, in that the emphasis falls upon the hero's quest for identity, but whereas traditional criticism tracks David's progress as a disciplined individual Vanden Bossche presents Dickens as occupying a fluid and uncertain position in which he debates the uncertainties of David's life. In part this involves reading against the grain of the text, rejecting the overt pattern of the triumph of the middle-class family, focusing instead on the gaps and contradictions within the pattern. In this respect Vanden Bossche's approach resembles Lougy's, but everything is now seen in an historical context as Vanden Bossche examines how the text reveals the unresolved ideological tensions of the day as it dramatises the process of 'middle-class self-making'.[31] Superficially this might seem to resemble the traditional focus on the development of bourgeois identity, but the difference is that this is now seen as an immensely complex issue with all manner of political, social and sexual implications.

Vanden Bossche draws attention to this 'self-making' process by concentrating on material that is dissonant with the achieved pattern of the story, and by positioning the text in the context of the 1850s, when a new sense of self and domestic order was emerging. The result is that *David Copperfield*, a novel that has struck many as one of Dickens's least complicated, emerges as a multi-layered work, centrally engaged in all the questions the Victorians were asking themselves about society, about the self, about gender roles, indeed about the whole economic and political structure of their world. Such an adjustment in the critical view not only reflects the wide-ranging influence of Michel Foucault on contemporary thinking about the past but also the extent to which established myths of Victorian stability and progress have been replaced by a sense of a fraught and divided age. Far from being a cosy novel about growing up, *David Copperfield* begins to be seen as a novel in which the Victorian age voices its fears and uncertainties, even as it tries to define and understand itself.

New Historicism, Politics, Feminism

The title of the second essay in this collection, by Simon Edwards, is '*David Copperfield*: The Decomposing Self'. As we have seen, traditional critics liked to cling on to the idea of the sensitive individual or self as a moral touchstone in a confusing world. The overt pattern of the text seems to endorse this position: the plan of *David Copperfield* favours David, as the villainous Heep, the dangerous Steerforth, and the unsuitable Dora are defeated or die. Of course, even traditional critics could see problems with the glibness of this pattern, but generally they approved of the hero and his values. Whereas traditional criticism has been ready to accept the pattern of the text, recent criticism, however, has seen only problems, especially in the notion of the 'subject'. In order to understand why we need to consider Edwards's essay together with the third essay in this selection, by Mary Poovey.

Edwards starts by drawing attention to the fact that *David Copperfield* was published in the same year as Thackeray's *Pendennis*, Tennyson's *In Memoriam* and Wordsworth's *The Prelude*. All four works could be said to deal with a buried personal history. Coming out in 1850, they appeared at a point when industrial unrest (as reflected in the Chartist Movement) was becoming a thing of the past, and Britain was emerging as an outstandingly successful industrial society. Central to the emergence of this advanced capitalist society was the coming into being of a new 'self-constructed'[32] individualism. This is a different kind of individualism from that associated with romanticism; the emphasis is on discipline and restraint, a new species of bourgeois individual for a new society. As Edwards points out, while we have long recognised that Dickens stands in a complex relationship to capitalist society, we also need to recognise the complexity of his relationship to this bourgeois individual.

The most obvious problem is that individuals are not inherently disciplined; the presence of Steerforth, indeed the strong emphasis on sexual desire throughout the novel, makes this abundantly clear. Passions, we might suspect, are hidden or subdued in the new social order, or else old patterns of male power reannounce themselves in new ways. The point comes across particularly well towards the end of Edwards's essay, where he focuses on dangerous powers, both social and sexual, within society, including the nature of David's attraction to Dora and his awareness of the seductiveness of Emily. The idea of a responsible, mature individual – content to accept containment and control – begins to seem a flimsy illusion, a myth to support the moral order of society but in reality far from unified or stable.

Mary Poovey also focuses on the idea of the self-constructed subject. She starts by stressing the important function of such a model in mid-Victorian Britain, explaining how 'a psychological narrative of individual development ... both provided individual readers with an imaginative image of what identity was and created a subject position that reproduced this kind of identity in the individual reader'.[33] She then goes on to show, however, how Dickens's text also alerts us to the problems associated with this individualist psychology. For a start, the 'subject' is male, with identity taking 'the form of a physical and emotional development in which the male subject tempers his sexual and emotional desires by the possibilities of the social world'.[34] The bourgeois subject, therefore, is not seen as the natural embodiment of rational values, but as a role emerging in the nineteenth century to serve the needs of a newly industrialised society. There is, for example, an increased stress on 'manliness': the male is associated with the sphere of work, the woman, more than ever before, is associated with the home.[35] *David Copperfield* presents an overall vision of orderly domestic management connected with controlled sexual conduct – an arrangement that underlines and supports male middle-class authority – but at the same time the text cannot totally efface the contradictions that such stable representations seek to repress. As such, the text offers us the rhetoric of class and gender that emerged in the Victorian period, but also makes us aware of the limitations of these constructions. Simultaneously, it contributes to and interrogates the new and developing discourse of bourgeois society.

An obvious characteristic of the essays by Vanden Bossche, Edwards and Poovey is that they are political criticism. Political in several ways. For a start, they look at the whole social picture in the novel, seeing the political implications of the focus upon individualism. Inevitably, therefore, the essays are wide-ranging in their criticism, touching upon a wide variety of issues: they move from the personal to the public, from questions of gender to questions of economics, always making connections, always showing how one feature of mid-Victorian society is interdependent with another. A related way in which such criticism is political is that, in considering these issues, it acknowledges how the text itself is making a political intervention in the society of its day. This goes deeper than the overt thrust of the novel, specifically its overall endorsement of discipline and marriage; it involves a recognition of the broader, more unsettled, debate that *David Copperfield* sustains. Traditional critics, spotting inconsistencies, berated Dickens for flaws in his social, sexual and psychological vision. Rather than regarding such contradictions as signs of failure, recent criticism regards inconsistency as a sign of disturbance, as a sign of a complex debate that cannot be accommodated within a neat pattern.[36] This leads us on to another way in which current criticism is political: in emphasising disturbance, in rejecting the old containing structures, in particular in questioning the values associated with liberal humanism, many critics today reveal their own political radicalism.

One aspect of this that has come to the fore in recent years is the extent to which critics focus on questions of gender. Feminist criticism first began to make a substantial impact in the late 1960s. Initially, as in the work of Kate Millett, the emphasis fell on the misogynist nature of much great literature (there are traces of this in Barbara Hardy's comments on Dickens's presentation of David's dissatisfaction with Dora's housekeeping). Since then, however, feminist criticism has moved on to a broader consideration of the whole issue of gender. Starting from the premise that the structure of society is patriarchal, that is organised on terms dictated by men and to the advantage of men, feminist criticism challenges essentialist definitions of what it is to be a woman: definitions that assume human nature is universal and which refuse to see how culture plays a significant part in constructing and fixing identity.[37] It should be apparent that such thinking gels with much of what has already been described in this Introduction – a rejection of inherited categories, a sceptical look at the discourses that society has employed to define and organise itself – but in the case of feminism, this becomes an attempt to rethink the fundamental issue of gender.

In the 1980s, however, feminism criticism often overlapped with New Historicism. Their common ground is clearly illustrated in Mary Poovey's essay, where she stresses how the Victorian sense of individualism was inseparable from ideas of manliness and patriarchal authority. The ideal partner for David is Agnes, the housekeeper wife, an image of the feminine that became increasingly stabilised in Victorian Britain. Similar issues are explored by Margaret Myers in 'The Lost Self: Gender in *David Copperfield*', essay 4 in this collection. Working from the idea of a male/female split in the novel, Myers argues that David acquires a conventionally masculine demeanour, but at the expense of feminine-identified ideas of selfhood. In this scheme of things, Steerforth represents the worst aspects of indulged cultural manhood. At an opposite extreme is the moral and emotional Tommy Traddles, who suffers greatly in the masculine environment of the school. David, in various ways, is feminine-identified, both at Salem House and later in life, but as he grows older he becomes earnest, rational and hardworking: he 'maculinises his own selfhood'.[38] Inevitably, Myers deals with David's treatment of Dora but, unlike traditional critics, does not condemn Dickens for any implicit prejudice he might be revealing in the novel. On the contrary, she sees the text as deeply involved in examining this culturally-condoned view of women. The author's prejudices are simply irrelevant; what matters is the way in which the text gets inside the contradictions of the ideologies of the day.

Psychoanalytic Criticism

A point Myers raises in the course of her essay is that, alongside those critics who have discussed *David Copperfield* as a *Bildungsroman*, there have always been critics who have seen it as an Oedipal drama in which David quests for an idealised version of his lost mother.[39] Possibly the best traditional psychological reading is Mark Spilka's '*David Copperfield* as Psychological Fiction', published in 1959.[40] Spilka discusses the novel in terms of David's inner life, and sees it as relating childhood anguish in an attempt to ease its pain. David, as he matures, comes to terms with and thereby overcomes his insecurities; it is as if the sickness of his mind is a sickness that the novel can heal. What is apparent about this reading is that it is entirely consistent with other traditional readings of the novel: the emphasis falls upon personal development, upon eliminating weaknesses, presented in this instance as psychological sickness.

A very different emphasis emerges in recent psychoanalytic criticism.[41] To establish a clear picture, however, we need to start with basic principles. All psychoanalytic theory begins with the sense of loss the subject experiences upon its separation from its mother's body. This necessarily affects the sexuality that is the constitutive factor in the construction of the subject. A full account of psychoanalytic criticism would involve paying due attention to Freud and Jung, but modern psychoanalytic criticism starts with Jacques Lacan,[42] who argued that Freud and his followers laid too much stress on the controlling 'ego', the conscious or thinking self, as separate from the 'id', the repressed impulses of the unconscious. By contrast, Lacan saw the ego as a carrier of neurosis: there can be no such thing as a coherent, autonomous self. Lacanian criticism, taking its lead from such thinking, engages with the entire idea of the structure of the self and its relation to the social.

Examples of the ways in which psychoanalytic theory converts into critical practice are provided by essays 5 and 6 in this collection, by Virginia Carmichael and John Kucich. Virginia Carmichael starts by drawing attention to an Oedipal reading of *David Copperfield*, but then embarks upon a reading that is 'culturally and critically more inclusive'.[43] First, however, she has to establish two key terms in Lacanian thinking: the Symbolic Order, and desire. The child in the early stages of psychosexual development moves from the pre-linguistic, or 'imaginary', stage to the symbolic stage. At this point the child begins to grasp such linguistic oppositions as male/female, father/son: this symbolic realm of language is, in Lacanian theory, the realm of the law of the father. The child in this Symbolic Order is driven by desire for a lost and unachievable object; because it is unachievable, the self is forever lost in an endless chain of displacements in the quest for meaning. As in a number of the essays referred to so far, there is a sense of a fragile subject in a world constructed along patriarchal lines.[44]

In Carmichael's essay, events in David's life echo his transition from the pre-linguistic Imaginary Order to the Symbolic Order. To some extent *David Copperfield* shows David being 'mastered'[45] as he writes, but it also the case that 'his writing itself bespeaks a problematic accession to the Symbolic Order'.[46] As with so much modern critical thinking, the real focus of Carmichael's essay is, therefore, language. David encounters a series of men (Mr Micawber, Mr Dick, Uriah Heep and others) all of whom have a particular, and odd, relationship to language, as they attempt to master the world. The most obvious example is Mr Dick's compulsive writing of the King Charles Memorial as his way of managing intrusive desires and failures from the past. David, by contrast, learning shorthand, establishing himself as a writer, works out a productive relationship to language. But it is the dominant discourse of his society that David studies and absorbs. This idea of a dominant, male, middle-class discourse, that organises experience in terms of what it admits and what it denies, and which marginalises all other discourse, runs as a fairly consistent thread through all the essays in this volume. What critics focus on are the stresses and strains that become apparent in this discourse even as it is in the process of establishing itself. Carmichael, for example, picks out David's problems with sexual bonding, his sense of himself as an awkward third party in groups of three, and more generally, his search for what he lost on entering the Symbolic Order.

Although Carmichael's essay is cast in psychoanalytic terms, she consistently expands the discussion, investigating how David's sense of insecurity reflects a whole society's insecurities about sex, gender and the self. There is a similar sense of the broader cultural and political implications of a psychoanalytic model in John Kucich's essay, the last on *David Copperfield* in this collection. Like other critics, Kucich is interested in the nature of Victorian subjectivity; his particular stress falls on David's 'self-divided' interiority.[47] He starts by asking why David is the only character in the book who is allowed to take a second partner in marriage without this being seen as, in some way, wrong. The answer is that, in David's case, a contradictory emotional balance is achieved. Initially his love is connected to illicit and self-destructive passions, but by the end, in marrying Agnes, the coherence of his identity is established; he has, in a sense, triumphed over time. What Kucich emphasises, however, is not the neatness of the resolution but the problems that still make themselves felt even in the ending. The stress falls upon David's inward self-conflictual tension. Kucich not only conveys well the fragility of this inward state, but in the process makes us adjust our sense of Dickens, for in emphasising the interiority of *David Copperfield*, he makes us aware of a writer with a very odd and uncomfortable relationship to the social world.

There are many similarities and areas of overlap in the essays on *David Copperfield* collected in this volume, but Kucich's essay strikingly illustrates how the tradition of recent criticism does not impose uniform readings upon the novel.[48] On the contrary, the ground is prepared for new insights, for it is a central aspect of current criticism that it does not seek to control the text or pin it down; the interest is always in the possibilities of the text rather than in a circumscribed meaning. The effect on *David Copperfield* has been enormous; a novel that for years was virtually ignored by critics has escaped from traditional judgements about its limited scope, and is now seen as a text that explores in an astonishingly complex way questions about the self and society in Victorian England. In the process, *David Copperfield* has moved from the margins to the centre of Dickens studies; all the signs are that it will stay there.

HARD TIMES

David Copperfield was followed in 1853 by *Bleak House* and a year later, in 1854, by *Hard Times*. It is a short novel by Dickens's usual standard, and in various ways can be described as uncharacteristic. Writing about the industrial North of England, Dickens is far away from his favoured London settings, and the brevity of the book imposes severe restraints upon his familiar expansive inventiveness. It also more single-mindedly argues a case than his other novels, targeting for attack the ideas of the utilitarians. If *David Copperfield* has always been one of Dickens's best-loved novels, the same cannot be said of *Hard Times*,[49] yet over the past 30 years it has become one of his most studied works.[50] There are obvious reasons for this. Any general survey of literature course must include a Dickens novel, and *Hard Times* seems to lend itself to such courses. It is relatively short, and also appears to be extremely teachable, primarily because a very clear issue can be identified in the text: it is easy to grasp that Dickens opposes the regimentation of the utilitarians, something that comes across in the opening scene in the school, and that he advocates a kinder alternative, primarily associated with the circus. The utilitarians are cold, unfeeling and unforgiving, whereas the circus folk are tolerant, generous and loving. The clarity of the contrast means that a reader who might be overwhelmed by the complexity of, say, *Little Dorrit* is likely to feel in control with *Hard Times*. Critical work on the novel then becomes largely a matter of showing how Dickens brings to life the world of Bounderby and Gradgrind, and the opposed world of Sleary; moral appreciation of the force of Dickens's theme – approval of his support for humane values – combines, therefore, with aesthetic appreciation of how effectively he conveys his case. This, in all essential respects, is the approach taken by F. R. Leavis, the critic who, above all others, must be credited for drawing attention to a once neglected novel; Leavis praises the social critique in the work, and is equally eloquent on Dickens's skill in bringing his vision to life.[51]

Leavis's defence of the novel did, however, raise an issue that has affected subsequent discussions of *Hard Times*. Criticism of literary texts is, for the most part, interpretative; there might be an implicit or explicit evaluation of the text, but critics are primarily concerned with constructing a reading. Discussions of *Hard Times*, by contrast, move quickly towards evaluation; more than with most novels, critics feel compelled to declare whether they consider it a successful or unsuccessful work. Leavis, in fact, regarded it as Dickens's masterpiece, but many disagree.[52] There are those who offer an aesthetic reservation, feeling that Dickens is at his best on a broader canvas, but more common are critics who cavil at his stance in the novel. Specifically, the criticism is that although Dickens presents himself as an opponent of rigid order, when we look closely we see the extent to which he aligns himself with middle-class notions of order; this is reflected in his patronising attitude towards the working-class characters and in his hostility towards trade unionism.[53] The issue is returned to again and again in traditional criticism, with some critics attacking Dickens for his limitations of vision and others defending him, often on the grounds that the importance of what he has to say excuses any inconsistencies.[54]

My own view is that much of this is an unproductive and misdirected wrangle. One of the most positive features of recent work on *Hard Times* is, indeed, the fact that it moves beyond the old arguments about the correctness or incorrectness of Dickens's perspective. The reason it can do this is because of the widespread acceptance by critics today that every text will be marked by internal inconsistencies, inconsistencies which reflect conflicts within the period when the book was published. Rather than authors being regarded as all-seeing sages, who should be able to rise above their age, texts are now generally regarded as sites where a culture expresses its contradictions and confusions. Consequently, modern critics writing about *Hard Times* are likely to be more concerned with thinking about the implications of the central opposition in the text (the values of the utilitarians versus the values of the circus) than with evaluative judgements about Dickens's vision.

Deconstructing Hard Times

We can see this in the way that critics have rejected the idea of *Hard Times* as 'a moral fable'.[55] This phrase was used by Leavis to describe the way in which he felt *Hard Times* was written to a predetermined thesis, without the variety and diffuseness we might expect to find in a realistic novel. The view of *Hard Times* as a fable is the starting point for Steven Connor's essay (no. 7), the first on *Hard Times* in this collection. It is taken from Connor's book *Charles Dickens*, from a section entitled 'Deconstructing Dickens'. The book appeared in 1985; as with *David Copperfield*, significant new work on *Hard Times* only really began to emerge in the mid 80s. (This is perhaps a convenient moment to point out that readers interested only in *Hard Times* might, none the less, find it helpful to read the first part of this Introduction, where some attempt is made to discuss terms such as deconstruction which are used without explanation in these pages on *Hard Times*.) Connor starts from the fact that *Hard Times* is, or appears to be, a rhetorically assertive novel, dominated by a persuasive voice. It also appears to be fairly simple in structure, as it is based on a rigid binary opposition of fact and fancy. What Connor does is look at how language is used to convey the opening positions, at how Gradgrind, for example, wants to define and control the world through language. His speech is dominated by metaphor, as he strives after equivalences between things, almost in the manner of a mathematical calculation. The circus people, as one might expect, use language in a different way: their speech is often inefficient and indistinct. The opposition in the text, therefore, is between different kinds of language.

But there is more to the text than this basic opposition, as Connor demonstrates. The complication is that Dickens, rather like the utilitarians, wants to convince us of equivalences (for example, between the educational philosophy of Gradgrind and the economic theory of the new industrialism). Moreover, Dickens, like Gradgrind, often resorts to metaphorical equivalence. It is as if he pretends to associate himself with the world of fairy tale, but in order to get his thesis across he needs, in a forceful way, to assert his presence. Consequently, *Hard Times* can be seen as 'recommending an openness of interpretation which it must itself resist in order that the recommendation may be made in the first place. Or, to put it another way, the text has to be strictly systematic in order to construct its condemnation of system.'[56] Yet, at other points, as in the speech of Mrs Gradgrind, the text subverts itself perhaps more than it intends.

In what ways does Connor redirect thinking about *Hard Times*? The first point is that he does not condemn Dickens for the rigidity of the binary opposition in the book, nor does he condemn Dickens for inconsistencies within the pattern. Indeed, Dickens himself has really got nothing to do with it. Traditional critics always wanted to move away from the text to a sense of the author's position, but Connor looks at the contradictions as inherent within the novel form itself, as serving to reflect and reveal conflicts within the ideologies of the day. Apparent problems in the text are seen not as shortcomings but as symptoms of deeper and more profound tensions: *Hard Times* is examining the notion of freedom within a capitalist, industrial economy, and rather than offering a fairy-tale liberal answer of everybody being nice to everybody, both thematically and in its language and structure expresses the problems of the relationships between freedom and authority, the individual and society. In its lack of stability, its metaphoric undoing of itself, it both analyses and embodies issues of power and identity.

Much of this, in fact, remains implicit in Connor's account, which might strike some readers as very dense and technical. It is possible to read the essay feeling that there is a next step that it fails to take, that of relating the narratological discussion to the broader social issue. But, in fairness to Connor, it has to be said that this is just one section from a book on Dickens which works through a variety of theoretical approaches. Indeed, the chapter ends by pointing out that the issues touched on 'are more than just linguistic issues; they are related to fundamental questions about the nature and formation of identity in society and to specific questions of authority and power'.[57] The remaining chapters in Connor's book, on *Great Expectations* and *Our Mutual Friend*, expand the discussion in just this direction and are essential reading for anyone who wants to consider more fully questions of the relationship between critical theory and Dickens's novels.

From Deconstruction to New Historicism

The second essay on *Hard Times* (no. 8) in this collection, by Catherine Gallagher, makes the leap from deconstruction to New Historicism. Gallagher starts with factual material about industrial society in the North of England and goes on to discuss how Dickens proposes that social cohesion can be achieved by introducing the sort of co-operative behaviour found in private life into the public realm. She then, however, examines how the novel finally confronts the fact that the family is isolated from the larger society. Critics have complained about Dickens's retreat into middle-class family values, but Gallagher argues that *Hard Times* and Elizabeth Gaskell's *North and South*, by 'advocating the integration of public and private life and then dissociating the two ... reproduce the paradox of the ideologies that inform them'.[58] Like Connor, she sees contradiction as being at the very heart of the novel form:

> English novels are characterised by a structural tension between impulses to associate and dissociate public and private realms of experience. The tension, however, is unusually noticeable in these two industrial novels because they emphasise thematically the very thing they cannot achieve structurally: the integration of public and private life.[59]

Once more, the emphasis shifts away from criticising Dickens for inconsistencies in the novel. On the contrary, the centre of interest is relocated in the way that the novel positions itself within, and reflects irreconcilable ideological and formal tensions of, both the Victorian period and the novel form. Like Connor, Gallagher goes beyond, or behind, the surface 'flaws' of the novel, identifying the fundamental tensions of Victorian society that underlie the surface difficulties. She offers us a sense of predicaments in the social project of Victorian fiction that are mirrored in the structural characteristics of the novel form. In short, the text is produced by a crisis – the advent of an industrial society, the separation of private and public – that the text itself cannot resolve. Indeed, it cannot even 'speak' this crisis directly or objectively, for the text itself is a product of, and therefore part of, the crisis.

A number of Gallagher's premises are similar to Connor's: there is, for example, a similar emphasis on the function of metaphor in the novel (although the things she says about the role of metaphor differ from what Connor says), and a similar emphasis on how the narrative stance, for all its talk of fancy, is in fact at odds with fancy. She also stresses the manner in which *Hard Times* calls in question its own narrative practice. But Gallagher goes further than Connor in discussing the political implications of the evidence examined, especially the ways in which the text questions the notion of paternalist reform and uncovers deep-seated problems in the ideological values of capitalist, industrial Victorian Britain. At the heart of the essay lies a very sophisticated critical and linguistic argument, but at the same time there is something very straightforward about the case made, for Gallagher is dealing with such central issues as the relationship between private and public life in Victorian Britain, with the relationship between family life and people's working lives, and with how individuals survive, cope, accommodate themselves – indeed, live and die – within a complex society. Consequently, the essay offers us an illuminating sense of the 1850s (in particular, how issues that still concern us were confronted at the time) while at the same time conveying a sense of how the novel form, specifically the language of fiction, attempts to deal with conflicting impulses in the period.

Feminism, Psychoanalysis, New Historicism

Looking at the ways in which Victorian society structured and organised itself, looking at how people saw and defined themselves in this society, leads, as it did with *David Copperfield*, to the issue of gender. The most obvious thing to note about the 'fact' world of Bounderby and Gradgrind is that it is male and aggressive. Jane Ferguson Carr, in 'Writing as a Woman: Dickens, *Hard Times* and Feminine Discourses', the third *Hard Times* essay (no. 9) in this collection, takes up the challenge of examining the sexual politics of *Hard Times*, a topic that necessarily involves a consideration of the broader sexual politics of Victorian Britain. She begins by looking at an essay by George Henry Lewes (George Eliot's partner for many years). Writing about Dickens, Lewes betrays many of the characteristics of his age in using a language that attempts to control literature and, more specifically, control 'women's emergence into more public spheres'.[60] Dickens, in the judgement of Lewes, is seen as having attitudes that resemble those of women, particularly in his emphasis on domestic affection and ordinary sympathies. Carr takes up the point, but argues that Dickens made a recurring exploration of discourses usually identified as feminine. By aligning himself with terms and values associated with women, Dickens investigates what is challenging, transgressive or resistant in society. Viewed in this light, *Hard Times* becomes a novel that both analyses and challenges the structure of power in Victorian society.

Carr pursues the implications of this with great subtlety, eventually arriving at a sense of how Dickens is a critic and outsider, but one who, ironically, capitalises on his status as an outsider; he speaks against those who possess power, but revels in his own power as a novelist. The essay could have become a rather myopic examination of the contradictions of the novelist's position, but as handled by Carr it becomes an expansive consideration of power in Victorian England, particularly as constituted in gender roles. As such, the essay provides a further illustration of how feminist criticism and New Historicism frequently intertwine: by its end we have a clear idea of the significance and role of gender in *Hard Times*, but this is part and parcel of a larger analysis of the complex crosscurrents in Victorian Britain and how the novel, as an art form, copes with such issues.

But there is more to Carr's reading than this. Traditional criticism always seemed intent on pinning novels down, on saying the final word about them. It strove to master and control texts; it seemed intent on displaying its power over texts. By contrast, an essay such as Carr's opens things up, indicating the range and complexity of the issues that are embodied in the text. And this is the case with all the essays in this volume; that although the informing assumptions of deconstructive, feminist, psychoanalytic and New Historicist criticism have much in common, the criticism produced is immensely varied, the theoretical base providing an opportunity rather than holding the critic back. This point is particularly well illustrated in the last essay in this collection (no. 10), by Richard Fabrizio. Discussions of *Hard Times*, as one might expect, by and large run in a different direction from discussions of *David Copperfield*, for obvious reasons: *David Copperfield* is a novel that focuses on the issue of identity, and consequently most modern discussions of the novel focus on the construction of the subject in a bourgeois society. *Hard Times* is evidently a social novel, so the emphasis falls upon the contradictions of industrial society, with a particular emphasis on the place of the family in such a society. The fact is, however, that *Hard Times*, as a novel produced in the 1850s, also has a great deal to say about the self, a point that Fabrizio makes clear in his essay on language and the psychopathology of the family in *Hard Times*.

It is an essay that ranges adventurously over many of the issues touched upon in this Introduction. Fabrizio starts with the proposition that, rather than being a satiric portrait of industrialisation, *Hard Times* is 'a keen description of the psyche forged out of socio-economic conditions'.[61] What complicates matters is that Dickens is part of what he seeks to analyse: 'Dickens had to describe a psychic condition with a vocabulary that itself was a symptom of the disease.'[62] The central focus of Fabrizio's essay is on the domestic family under industrial capitalism, with an emphasis on just how many of the relationships are distorted and perverted. Minds are affected by industry; there is even the emergence of a new personality type in the lobotomised Bitzer. It is a world in which family life is in dissolution, where there is desire but never fulfilment. In the course of the essay, the narrow, thesis-dominated *Hard Times* that critics used to write about is transformed into a novel that is infinitely richer, that contains far more than critics in the past ever noticed. At its best, current criticism, building upon a theoretical base, time and time again creates just this kind of expansion of our sense of classic texts.

But more than this, at its best it changes both our reading practice and our sense of what we are reading. For Fabrizio, *Hard Times* is not just another 'social' novel without any implications for the 'subject'. Far from it. Just as critics of *David Copperfield* have come to see the novel as profoundly political in its concern with the subject, so criticism is coming to see that the political world of *Hard Times* has equally important consequences for the subject. It is this kind of rereading of Dickens that recent criticism has brought about that shapes the direction and purpose of this collection.

NOTES

1. It is necessary to make a distinction between praise for *David Copperfield* and interesting criticism of the novel. As Angus Wilson writes, in *The World of Charles Dickens* (London, 1970), when he was a boy (around 1930), 'If critics were asked to name an English novel worthy to stand among the great fiction of all time – *War and Peace* and so on – *David Copperfield* was very likely to be their choice. This great admiration had been handed down from Victorian times'

(p. 213). But such admiration of *David Copperfield* did not stimulate much in the way of substantial criticism of the novel.

2. Theoretically inspired criticism of *Bleak House* begins with J. Hillis Miller's Introduction to the Penguin edition of the novel (Harmondsworth, 1971), pp. 11–34. A good impression of the ways in which recent criticism 'has given *Bleak House* a higher and higher placing amongst Dickens's major novels' is offered in Jeremy Hawthorn, *Bleak House* (London, 1987).

3. Dickens referred to *David Copperfield* as his 'favourite child': 'Of all my books, I like this the best. It will easily be believed that I am a fond parent to every child of my fancy, and that no one can ever love that family as dearly as I love them. But, like many fond parents, I have in my heart of hearts a favourite child' (Preface to the 1867 edition in the Penguin edition [Harmondsworth, 1966], p. 47). Philip Collins comments on the popularity of *David Copperfield*, in *Dickens: The Critical Heritage* (London, 1971): 'It immediately became, and remained a general favourite. Not all admirers were as categorical as Tolstoy: "If you sift the world's prose literature, Dickens will remain; sift Dickens, *David Copperfield* will remain; sift *David Copperfield*, the description of the storm at sea will remain" (quoted in *The Dickensian*, 45 [1949], 144). But there was widespread agreement that *Copperfield* was his masterpiece ...' (p. 242).

4. *David Copperfield* can, to be more precise, be described as a *Künstlerroman*, that is a novel dealing with the education of an artist.

5. Angus Wilson, for example, in *The World of Charles Dickens* (London, 1970), acknowledges that *David Copperfield* is 'a sort of masterpiece. And yet at the end of it, I think, there is a disagreeable sense that this most inner of Dickens's novels is the most shallow, the most smoothly running, the most complacent – indeed, in the pejorative use of that word, the most Victorian' (p. 215).

6. Edmund Wilson's view, in *The Wound and the Bow*, is not untypical: '*Copperfield* is not one of Dickens's deepest books; it is something in the nature of a holiday' (quoted in Q. D. Leavis's interesting essay on *David Copperfield* in F. R. and Q. D. Leavis, *Dickens the Novelist* [London, 1970], p. 65). J. Hillis Miller, in *Charles Dickens: The World of His Novels* (Cambridge and London, 1958), a book that is still perhaps the best overall introduction to Dickens, offers less than ten pages on *David Copperfield* before a 65-page chapter on *Bleak House*. As Norman Page writes, in *A Dickens Companion* (London, 1984): 'Critics and common readers have generally agreed that this novel contains some of Dickens's most vivid portrayals of character ... However, the novel has attracted the attention of recent critics less than some others; and although many readers of earlier generations would have concurred in regarding it as their favourite, its merits have

seemed less indutiably outstanding to most recent commentators' (p. 161).

7. *Nineteenth-Century Fiction* , 9 (1954), 81–107. The article is reprinted in part in the Norton edition of *David Copperfield* (New York and London, 1990), pp. 794–805. See note 3 of John Kucich's essay (p. 152 of this volume), where he contrasts the approach taken by Needham and that taken by James R. Kincaid.

8. Ibid., p. 799.

9. Needham seems to have been the first critic to argue that the novel is about the progress from an undisciplined heart to a disciplined heart, but the number of critics we encounter subsequently saying something rather similar suggests just how widespread this kind of moral view of fiction was in the 1950s and 60s. For example, Harvey Peter Sucksmith in *The Narrative Art of Charles Dickens* (London, 1970) asserts that 'If a single theme in *David Copperfield* is worked out through the structure of the novel, then it is "the first mistaken impulse of an undisciplined heart." The novelist shows how David grows through various stages of self-deception towards a mature experience of love' (pp. 58–9); Edgar Johnson, in his biography *Charles Dickens: His Tragedy and Triumph* (New York, 1952), makes a very similar point about the subordination of the impulses of the past to the prudence of the present (p. 700); and K. J. Fielding, 'Dickens and the Past: The Novelist of Memory', *Experience in the Novel: Selected Papers from the English Institute*, ed. Roy Harvey Pearce (New York, 1968), comments that 'by self-mastery a man may live down what might have harmed him ... The direction of Copperfield is toward fulfilment' (p. 110).

10. Barbara Hardy, *The Moral Art of Dickens* (London, 1970), pp. 122–38.

11. Ibid., p. 130.

12. Ibid., p. 129.

13. Ibid., p. 124.

14. George Orwell, in his essay 'Charles Dickens', from his 1940 collection of essays *Inside the Whale*, perhaps initiates the tradition of criticising Dickens for the middle-class stance of his novels. The essay is reprinted in Stephen Wall (ed.), *Charles Dickens: A Critical Anthology* (Harmondsworth, 1970), pp. 297–313.

15. (Oxford, 1971), p. 163.

16. Kincaid quotes G. K. Chesterton's comment that Micawber defies critical explanation: 'All the critics of Dickens, when all is said and done, have only walked round and round Micawber wondering what they

should say. I am myself at this moment walking round and round Micawber wondering what I shall say' (Ibid., p. 177).

17. Ibid., p. 191.

18. An example of liberal humanist criticism at its most bland is Trevor Blount's introduction to the Penguin edition of *David Copperfield* (Harmondsworth, 1966), pp. 13–39.

19. General Editor's Preface to Steven Connor, *Dickens* (Oxford, 1985), pp. iv–v.

20. Useful introductions to structuralism include Terence Hawkes, *Structuralism and Semiotics* (London, 1977) and Jonathan Culler, *Structuralist Poetics* (London, 1975).

21. Guides to deconstruction include Jonathan Culler, *On Deconstruction: Theory and Criticism after Structuralism* (London, 1983) and Christopher Norris, *Deconstruction: Theory and Practice* (London, 1982).

22. Representative works include Jacques Derrida, *Of Grammatology* (Baltimore, 1976), Paul de Man, *Allegories of Reading* (New Haven, 1979), Michel Foucault, *Madness and Civilization* (London, 1976), and Jacques Lacan, *Ecrits: A Selection* (London, 1977).

23. As late as 1984, Philip M. Weinstein could write: 'A few words are in order on *David Copperfield's* present disrepute. Its surface serenity attracts scant attention in a critical climate that still finds in *Dombey and Son* the first masterpiece, then jumps to *Bleak House* and the subsequent darker novels. When assessed, *David Copperfield* tends to elicit brief and condescending comments, if not an occasionally outright dismissal ...' (*The Semantics of Desire: Changing Models of Identity from Dickens to Joyce* [Princeton, 1984], p. 24). The only other essay from the 70s to set alongside Kincaid and Lougy is Robin Gilmour's 'Memory in *David Copperfield*', *The Dickensian*, 71 (1975), 30–42, which rather like Kincaid's piece looks beyond the novel's official morality of the disciplined heart.

24. The essay originally appeared in *Dickens Studies Annual*, 6 (1977), 72–101. It is reprinted in Harold Bloom (ed.), *Charles Dickens's 'David Copperfield'* (New York and Philadelphia, 1987), pp. 47–66.

25. *Dickens Studies Annual*, ibid., p. 73.

26. See pp. 155–70 below.

27. For introductions to Foucault's ideas and influence, see Alan Sheridan, *Michel Foucault: The Will to Truth* (London, 1980), Simon During, *Foucault and Literature: Towards a Genealogy of Writing* (London, 1992), Peter Burke (ed.), *Critical Essays on Michel Foucault* (London, 1992), and Lois McNay, *Michel Foucault* (London, 1994).

28. (London, 1941).

29. For an introduction to New Historicism, see Harold A. Veeser (ed.), *The New Historicism* (London, 1989); and Don E. Wayne, 'New Historicism', in *Encyclopedia of Literature and Criticism*, eds M. Coyle, P. Garside, M. Kelsall and J. Peck (London, 1990), pp. 791–805.

30. See p. 31below.

31. See p. 33below.

32. See p. 62 below.

33. See p. 81 below.

34. See p. 82–3below.

35. For a complementary consideration of Victorian manliness, see Eve Kosofsky Sedgwick, *Between Men: English Literature and Male Homosocial Desire* (Cambridge, 1982).

36. In addition to Foucault, another critic who has had a tremendous influence on current practice, specifically on the current approach of seeing texts in their historical context, is Raymond Williams. Relevant works include *The English Novel from Dickens to Lawrence* (London, 1970) and *The Country and the City* (London, 1973).

37. Guides to feminist critical thinking include Catherine Belsey and Jane Moore (eds), *The Feminist Reader: Essays in Gender and the Politics of Literary Criticism* (London, 1989), and Mary Eagleton (ed.), *Feminist Literary Criticism* (London, 1991).

38. See p. 114 below.

39. For an interesting discussion of the Oedipal dimension of *David Copperfield* see Dianne F. Sadoff, *Monsters of Affection: Dickens, Eliot and Brontë on Fatherhood* (Baltimore, 1982). See also Gordon D. Hirsch, 'A Psychoanalytic Rereading of *David Copperfield*', *Victorian Newsletter*, 58 (1980), 1–5.

40. *Critical Quarterly*, 1 (1959), 292–301. The essay is reprinted in part in the Norton edition of *David Copperfield* (New York and London, 1990), pp. 817–26.

41. A good, concise introduction to psychoanalytic criticism is Elizabeth Wright, 'Psychoanalytic Criticism', in M. Coyle, P. Garside, M. Kelsall and J. Peck (eds), *Encyclopedia of Literature and Criticism* (London, 1990), pp. 764–76.

42. Good guides to the thinking of Lacan and his impact upon literary criticism are Jane Gallop, *Reading Lacan* (Ithaca, 1985), and Shoshana Felman, *Jacques Lacan and the Adventure of Insight: Psychoanalysis and Contemporary Culture* (Cambridge, 1987).

43. See p. 126 below.

44. Cf. Poovey pp. 82–3 below.

45. See p. 127 below.

46. See p. 127 below.

47. See p. 145 below.

48. There are those who see the matter differently, who feel that modern critical approaches do impose a uniform response. See, for example, Jerome H. Buckley's essay, 'The Identity of David Copperfield', in James R. Kincaid and Albert J. Kuhn (eds), *Victorian Literature and Society: Essays Presented to Richard D. Altick* (Ohio, 1984), pp. 225–39, in which he makes the case for a more traditional approach to the novel.

49. As Philip Collins points out, in *Dickens: The Critical Heritage* (London, 1971), 'F. G. Kitton did not include *Hard Times* in his *Novels of Charles Dickens* (1897) but relegated it to the companion-volume, *The Minor Writings* (1900). This typifies a widely-held estimate of its merits and importance' (p. 300). George Gissing, quoted in George Ford and Sylvère Monod (eds), *Hard Times*, Norton edition (New York, 1966), wrote: 'Of *Hard Times* I have said nothing; it is practically a forgotten book and little of it demands attention' (p. 330).

50. One measure of the popularity of *Hard Times* as an academic text is the catalogue of the academic publisher Norton, where it is grouped with *Pride and Prejudice, Wuthering Heights* and *Jane Eyre* as one of the four 'most widely assigned novels'.

51. '*Hard Times*: The World of Bentham', in F. R. and Q. D. Leavis, *Dickens the Novelist* (Harmondsworth, 1970), pp. 251–81. The essay was first published in *Scrutiny* in 1947, and also included, as an appendix, in Leavis's *The Great Tradition* (London, 1948).

52. Two critics who take issue with Leavis are John Holloway, in '*Hard Times*: A History and a Criticism', in *Dickens and the Twentieth Century*, ed. John Gross and Gabriel Pearson (London, 1962), pp. 159–74, and David M. Hirsch, '*Hard Times* and Dr Leavis', *Criticism*, 6 (1964), 1–16.

53. John Lucas, in *The Melancholy Man: A Study of Dickens's Novels* (London, 1970), who dismisses *Hard Times* as 'an unsuccessful novel', complains that Dickens is 'entirely contemptuous of Slackbridge, the man who tries to bring the men out on what would seem to be a perfectly justifiable strike' (pp. 254–5). Similar reservations inform David Craig's Introduction to the Penguin edition of *Hard Times* (Harmondsworth, 1969), pp. 11–36. David Lodge, in *Language of Fiction* (London, 1966), offers the criticism that 'Dickens could only

offer a disembodied and vaguely defined benevolence as a cure for the ills of Coketown' (p. 146).

54. As recently as 1985, D. W. Jefferson, in 'Mr Gradgrind's Facts', *Essays in Criticism* , 35 (1985), 197–212, is still complaining that the central contentions of *Hard Times* 'so confidently urged will not bear critical inspection, and it must be condemned for its distortion of truth. Its relegation to a minor place among Dickens's writings could only do good' (p. 211). If Jefferson represents one kind of old-fashioned approach, an equally old-fashioned approach is evident in Allen Samuels's *Hard Times*, in the Critics Debate series (London, 1992), where the informing attitude seems to be that Dickens's intention excuses any shortcomings: 'What he did offer, with all its faults, was a broad-purposed, generous, humane critique of a society obsessed by ideology' (p. 94). Samuels's book as a whole is a, now rather uncommon, expression of a liberal humanist position.

55. F. R. and Q. D. Leavis, *Dickens the Novelist* (Harmondsworth, 1970), p. 252.

56. See p. 165 below. Another essay, influenced by theory, that breaks away from old ways of judging *Hard Times* is Roger Fowler's 'Polyphony and Problematic in *Hard Times*', in Robert Giddings (ed.), *The Changing World of Charles Dickens* (London, 1983), pp. 91–108.

57. See p. 169 below.

58. See p. 173 below.

59. See p. 173 below.

60. See p. 198 below.

61. See p. 219 below.

62. See p. 220 below.

1

Cookery, not Rookery: Family and Class in *David Copperfield*

CHRIS R. VANDEN BOSSCHE

> 'Why Rookery?' said Miss Betsey.
> 'Cookery would have been more to the
> purpose,if you had any practical idea of
> life, either of you.'
>
> (*David Copperfield*, 1:5)

Aunt Betsey's question about the name of the Copperfield home creates a division between two sets of values. Mr Copperfield had tried to set himself up as a country gentleman by calling his home Blunderstone Rookery; to Aunt Betsey, this idea is as empty as the rooks' nests out in the yard. To the rookery, she opposes her own practical middle-class domesticity, represented by cookery. The rhyming conjunction of rookery and cookery never occurs again in the novel, but the two words do re-appear. Coming as it does, on the eve of David's birth, Betsey's comment directs the search for social legitimacy that constitutes the course of his career. Cast out of the Rookery, losing his family, he seeks to re-establish his identity by finding a new family and a new meaning for rookery. Like his father, he seeks the legitimacy of the country gentleman, and, in the subtitle of his autobiography, claims the title 'David Copperfield the Younger of Blunderstone Rookery'. But, by the time he completes his search for family and identity, the meaning of rookery has changed a great deal because he has accepted the values of cookery.

Dickens's novels always demonstrate the linkage between class and family, and *David Copperfield* can be read as a story of the triumph of the middle-class family.[1] Like so many novels, *David Copperfield* depicts a search for a family, but the family finally discovered sets this novel apart from eighteenth-century novels and even from an earlier Dickens novel like *Oliver Twist*. In *Twist*, as in *Tom Jones* or *Humphrey Clinker*, the orphan discovers his social identity, his place in the world, by discovering his familial origin.[2] Only within the notion of the aristocratic family does origin matter because this family defines itself in terms of lineage.[3] Oliver's notoriously correct English accent is his patrimony. Even so, when he discovers his parentage, his social origin, he also recovers his birthright and, most importantly, a complex of family relationships that reveal that Rose Maylie is his aunt: 'A father, sister, and mother, were gained, and lost, in that one moment.'[4] Even though the novel insists upon Oliver's basic human value, it finally affirms that that value rests upon his social origin; Jack Dawkins and Charley Bates, for whom no such discovery is possible, cannot escape from the den of thieves into middle-class respectability. *Great Expectations* returns to the same issues, but has Pip discover that his origins are criminal, that the basis for his status as gentleman is not owing to his natal origin (the motif of misidentification at birth), but to crime and money. It carries out what *David Copperfield* commences, an analysis of the naturalisation and legitimation of social status.

David Copperfield establishes an intermediate position between these two novels. Whereas Oliver moves with naïve certainty from his childhood in the workhouse into the middle-class world of the Brownlows, David Copperfield, though born and raised in a gentleman's home, never feels certain that he belongs among gentlemen as we are constantly reminded by his fears that servants and other social inferiors can see through his pretences to that estate. Discovery of social position in family origin has become just as impossible as it is to be in *Great Expectations*. David already knows where he was born and who his parents were, but this is of little use to him in his future life. Nor does the novel reveal an original family or crime; it is not a novel of origin but of destination. In this regard it may considered every bit as devastating in its critique of society as *Great Expectations*. While the substitution of social destination for social origin still aims to naturalise social status, legitimising middle-class self-making, this novel also provides us with reasons to doubt that David has always been destined by providence to achieve this end.

David Copperfield begins with an initiatory loss of family and status, and its plot portrays David's quest to regain social legitimacy through the discovery of a family. In the process, he discovers three types of families, which while presented as alternatives, define a complex structure of class relations in which no single one could exist without the others. Only his journey through the first two makes it possible to enter the family he discovers at the novel's end. These three family types correspond to the three major loves in his life: Emily, Dora, and Agnes.

I

The novel's retrospective narration, the story told from David's destination as middle-class novelist and contented family man, reinforces the notion that *David Copperfield* is a novel of destination. This provides us with a way of understanding why the happy ending of *David Copperfield* differs from many other Dickens novels in that the family resides in London, not in a pastoral setting. For, in a significant way, the pastoral, though not depicted, makes the final scene of domestic bliss possible. In order to explain why, we must go back to the domestic and pastoral idylls of Blunderstone and Yarmouth presented in the beginning of the novel.

Blunderstone, before Murdstone arrives, is a self-enclosed community composed of David, his mother, and Peggotty. The idyllic nature of his childhood there is largely retrospective; indeed, it is already so in his childhood. The opening chapters, though presented as comedy, portray a series of childhood anxieties: Aunt Betsey's frightening arrival on the night of his birth, his fears of the ghost of his father, even a tyrannical Peggotty.[5] And already in chapter 2 Murdstone intrudes upon the scene. The most idyllic scene occurs only after he has been sent away to school (ch. 8), a brief moment that David describes as a last taste of his idyllic childhood, but this former life is already a creative memory, the product of his resistance to Murdstone and Creakle.

His idyllic representation of this moment places it in the same space as Yarmouth. David presents his first visit to Yarmouth as an extension of the early childhood idyll into a timeless dimension. He gives it special force precisely because his visit means the end of that life; he has been sent there to be out of the way while Murdstone usurps his place. The idyll of Blunderstone is limited to the domestic sphere, but Yarmouth is full-blown pastoral, a lively pre-industrial community that, as Peggotty says, is 'the finest place in the universe' (3:25). David describes it as Edenic: timeless, classless, and innocent of the knowledge of good and (future) evil. The immediacy of the sea – the Peggottys live in a boat that has often sailed on it and that now lies on the sands close by it – makes this place seem a part of nature. Dickens's representation makes us want to call it a village rather than a city in order to emphasise what seems to be its natural order; the model is not the industrial midlands, but the agricultural village, its principal activity, fishing, like farming, being the provision of food. Furthermore, it does seem to be classless; the fishermen have no masters, and we see neither boat-owners nor the merchants who take the fish to market. Finally, both the boat-house and the town possess that element of neatness and busy snugness, that elementary but unfussy order, that so often characterises idyllic spaces in Dickens. The very smallness of the boat-house makes it a child's paradise, as does the ingenuity and simplicity of its conversion to that purpose. And the town, crammed full of 'gas-works, rope-walks, boat-builders' yards, shipwrights' yards, ship-breakers' yards, caulkers' yards, riggers' lofts, [and] smith's forges' would seem to be the Wooden Midshipman of *Dombey and Son* unpacked into its more lively pastoral origins (3:25).

Yarmouth represents David's first desperate attempt to find a family, the loss of which is symbolised by his displacement by Murdstone. When he first enters the boat-house, which becomes his fundamental emblem of the domestic idyll, 'the perfect abode' (3:26), he sees a family that does not really exist. In an ironic reversal of the discovery of father, mother, brother, and sister that closes novels like *Oliver Twist*, David finds that the occupants of the boathouse whom he sees as husband, wife, son, and daughter do not fit his preconceived categories. Yet he continues to identify them as a family precisely because their solidarity comes from the communal relationships that motivate Mr Peggotty to gather this group together under his roof, not simply from the fact that they share the same dwelling or name. By falling in love with little Emily, David expresses his desire to enter into this family that, because it remains outside of time, will remain an essential stage in his search for family. Even when he begins to feel his class difference and can no longer desire Emily herself, she and her family represent one aspect of the family he would ultimately create for himself.

But in making Yarmouth an idyll, he blots out all the problematic elements of the place: the sea, representative of its naturalness, also signifies death, and has 'drowndead' two fathers and a husband in this group alone. (Later, we will be introduced to Yarmouth's other principal family, that of Omer and Joram the undertakers.) David's sense of equality is illusory for he is treated with deference, and Emily wants to be a lady, demonstrating her own recognition that Yarmouth exists in a class-bound society. David's failure to recognise these problems only emphasises the fact that he wants to make Yarmouth an idyll. He never wants the real Yarmouth life, but a life that would fulfil his desires. It represents something that he desires and remains always as a representation, for he already expresses his distance from Yarmouth when he complains of its dreary flatness upon first arriving there (3:24). In fact, his experiences there make him conscious for the first time of his own social position and, as much as anything, cause him to resist the loss of social status incumbent upon being sent to the bottle factory.

This new awareness of social status, more than Murdstone's shove down the social scale, makes David feel he has been deprived of any secure and legitimate social position. David's anxiety has a real social basis, for social mobility runs in both directions: even as many were arriving in the middle and upper classes others were being proletarianised, their position as lower gentry threatened by the changing structure of economic relations. David does not mind the work so much as the degrading company it forces him to keep, and the passage in which he describes the 'secret agony of [his] soul' as he 'sunk into this companionship', with its disparaging comparison between Mick Walker and Mealy Potatoes on the one hand and Traddles and Steerforth on the other, betrays a well-developed class consciousness (11:133). Indeed, the passage shows such emphatic disregard for his fellow workers that, taken from their point of view and not that of the boy suffering the angst of social displacement, it comes as a shocking display of class violence. Yet he never recognises the similarity between his alienation from the Peggottys and from these boys, and continues to idealise the Peggottys' condition even as he deplores the warehouse.

II

London represents David's exile from home, the city being the antithesis of the pastoral idyll. There he identifies not with his fellow
mistreated workers, but with the Micawbers, who feel, like David,
that they have been displaced from their proper social station. Just
as David has lost his family, Mrs Micawber claims to have lost
hers. The Micawbers are a comic version of the aristocratic family
David idealises, the Steerforths. Mrs Micawber constantly refers
to her 'family' in order to insist upon her pretension to gentility in
the face of their actual situation (11:136; 12:146; 17:222–3;
57:689–91). But the Micawbers are never able to ally themselves
with her always absent and therefore functionally fictitious family.
We believe so much in their social status that we readily accept that
Mr Micawber's attempts to enter commerce as a corn factor and a
coal seller are inappropriate. His (great) expectations that 'something will turn up' are a parody of the plot in which the orphan's
true identity finally returns him to his proper place in society. This
adult orphan still awaits the return to social origins no longer possible in this novel, and, in the meantime, remains a bankrupt.
Resisting a decline, whether real or imagined, into the status of
middle-class tradespeople or the working class, the Micawbers
insist that they belong to and are destined for the gentry just as
David clings to the images of Blunderstone and his upper-class
school chum, Steerforth.

When, after he has completed his schooling in Canterbury, he
takes a journey to 'look about' for a profession, he soon encounters
the image of his desire, Steerforth, who introduces him to a new
family that represents social legitimacy, the next family that David
seeks to enter. The Steerforths, like the Peggottys, are fragmented, a
bachelor, widow, and orphan, but here the fragmentation divides
the family, as every member fights against the others. Nonetheless,
whereas Mr Peggotty immediately disabuses David of his vision of a
family, the Steerforths insist that they are one. Family here does not
represent communal values, but social status. Rosa speaks for her
family when she asks if it is true that the Peggottys, because they
are mere rustics, have no feelings (20:251), and Mrs Steerforth
speaks from this point of view when she insists that it would be impossible for her son to marry Emily (32:400). Most significantly,
Rosa insists that only a real family, one that lays claim to that title
through its legitimate lineage, can have a home; to her, only the

Steerforth home, not the Peggotty home, is laid waste by the elopement of Emily and Steerforth (50:614–15). These attitudes, along
with their style of living, cause us, like David, to associate them
with the aristocracy even though they apparently possess no titles.
This family merely asserts its social status by claiming to be a
special kind of family. David always seems shocked by their attitude, but he never rejects the Steerforths or submits them to the
comic satire with which he represents the same pretensions of the
Micawbers. He seems unaware that his sense of the Peggottys as
unselfconscious country folk lies very close to the Steerforths' view
of them as simply insensitive.

Although he takes the Steerforths as his model, he does not fall in
love with Rosa Dartle, though he considers the possibility, but with
another apparent representative of the gentry, Dora Spenlow.
Aware that his social situation locks him out of the Steerforth
world, he nonetheless aspires to it and accepts a career at Doctors'
Commons upon Steerforth's assurance that they 'plume themselves
on their gentility there' (23:293). Mr Spenlow lives up to this characterisation, claiming that 'it [is] the genteelist profession in the
world' (26:331), and David's determination to fall in love with his
daughter before he has ever met her indicates that he desires the
social legitimacy of gentility as much as Dora's charms. Indeed,
Dora's charms themselves simply signify her social status: flirta-
tiousness, silliness, guitar playing, even curls, all mark her class
identity. Almost immediately, David fantasises living with her in
Highgate, the neighbourhood where the Steerforths reside, and
which he associates, therefore, with gentility.

David's representation of this stage of his career satirises the aristocratic economy that he had embraced in order to signify his allegiance to that class. His amorous exploits are marked by these
aspirations, and, like Steerforth, who can afford to buy a boat and
take jaunts whenever he wishes, he becomes wasteful in his pursuit of
Dora. Entertaining extravagantly, which incurs Agnes's disapproval,
he spends a large portion of his allowance to become a dandy, buying
shoes that are, like Dora's housekeeping, uncomfortable. He wastes
time seeking a chance encounter with Dora, and when he is not doing
that he is pursuing a career in Doctors' Commons where the principle
of gentility is allied to the most wasteful of legal operations. With
Aunt Betsey's bankruptcy, he undergoes a major transformation. Still
motivated, as before, by the goal of attaining Dora, he embraces a
totally different economy as a means of attaining her, replacing the

show of indolence with dreams of industry. The time he had spent wandering the streets in search of Dora, he now spends as Doctor Strong's secretary, in his spare time working at shorthand to produce a surplus of literal and symbolic capital for his future.

But how can we explain this sudden abandonment of gentility in favour of what would seem to be the more mundane claims of the middle class? When he had previously been threatened with social displacement, it was precisely the aristocractic model that had motivated his escape. When he decided to flee London and the warehouse he turned to Peggotty only for a loan, feeling that she could do no more than this for him. Betsey Trotwood, his father's aunt, had been his only hope for restoring his social status.

Though he feels he has succeeded, Dover and Canterbury do not represent gentility but the middle class. David encounters all the virtues of middle-class life there: Aunt Betsey's common sense and prudence, Dr Strong and Annie's companionability, and, above all, the domestic virtues of Agnes Wickfield. He encounters tradespeople and professionals – teachers, lawyers, clerks, butchers – not gentry. Corresponding to the chance meeting with Steerforth that led him to choose Doctors' Commons, his chance encounter with Traddles now provides another model for his new means of attaining Dora. Although David always regards him with condescension, Traddles's steady accumulation of furniture and other capital – each step in his professional progress is a 'pull' – in order to marry his Sophy parallels David's more melodramatic visions of self-improvement. Whereas, earlier, David had prided himself on Dora's accomplishments relative to Sophy's, he now seems to wish she had more of Sophy's household experience. Dora, for her part, almost instinctively fears both Traddles and Betsey Trotwood as representatives of an alien way of life (41:513–14). In Mr Spenlow he comes to see economic failure caused by the attempt to emulate gentility. Indeed, the middle-class economy defines itself as a rejection of the style of living that it considers a wasteful economy. But this sets up a comic conflict between David and Dora, the occasion of their first dispute in their courtship, and, as he himself points out, their first marital discord. The conflict arises when David announces to Dora that he has become poor, and asks her if she would try to learn about accounts and read a cookery book. We can recognise that in making this suggestion he is drawing on what he learned at Dover, because cookery was first introduced into the novel by Aunt Betsey.

Considering his objectives, David would undoubtedly have given Dora one of the many cookbooks aimed at 'the middle class of society'.[6] Eliza Acton's *Modern Cookery in All Its Branches*, considered the first cookbook especially designed for the middle class, appeared in 1845 and remained the most popular cookbook until the appearance of *Beeton* in 1861. Alexis Soyer's popular *The Modern Housewife or, Ménagère* (1849), published the same year as *Copperfield*, specifically claimed to aim at the 'moderate scale' of the middle class, 'leaving the aristocratic style entirely to its proper sphere'.[7] Along with the cookery books came a panoply of domestic manuals. The title of the most famous of the nineteenth-century cookbooks, Isabella Beetons's *Book of Household Management* (1861), expresses the claims of cookery books themselves to provide much more than mere recipes. This book, which combined features found in many earlier ones, sold more copies than any Dickens novel. Other manuals – corresponding to our popular 'how-to' books – offered specific domestic advice on the 'servant problem', health, child-rearing, budget management, accounting, and all aspects of housekeeping, as well as the more edifying moral economy laid out in Sarah Ellis's tetralogy, also aimed at the middle class, *The Women, The Daughters, The Wives,* and *The Mothers of England* (1839, 1842, 1843, 1845).

While the contents vary widely, all of these books align themselves with what their authors prefer to call 'domestic economy', the science of creating a 'comfortable' home.[8] Nearly all of the domestic manuals instruct wives on how to budget their income and how to keep accounts of what they spend so that they can stay within their budget. Micawber understands the middle-class rule of domestic economy well. His famous advice, 'Annual income twenty pounds, annual expenditure nineteen and six, result happiness. Annual income twenty pounds, annual expenditure twenty pounds ought and six, result misery' (12:150) merely repeats a commonplace of the manuals regarding the basic budgetary process.[9] But Micawber finds this 'advice so far worth taking' that he 'has never taken it himself' (12:149) because he lives within the aristocratic economy, and like Dora, cannot really comprehend this middle-class one.[10]

The principle of economy extends far beyond income and expenditure. Even the style of cooking comes under this heading since the menus and recipes usually eschewed a complex style, beyond the capabilities of the serving staff of a middle-class household, in favour of fresh ingredients, simply and sensibly prepared. Beeton standardised measurements and provided precise information on how many people each recipe would serve and how much it would cost to prepare. Class distinction can even be found in the basic rules of cooking: 'The object, then, is not only to *live*, but to live economically, agreeably, tastefully, and well'.[11] Beeton distinguishes her middle-class audience from the working class by awarding them a diet that goes beyond mere subsistence while at the same time proscribing excess; no scrap of food, right down to the drippings, can be wasted.[12] As Soyer's Mrs B. insists, 'I managed my kitchen and housekeeping at a moderate ... expense compared with some of my neighbours, who lived expensively, but not so well as we did'.[13]

If the novel represents Yarmouth as the scene of the tragic fall (both in terms of nostalgia for the lost pastoral realm and its destined effacement through the seduction of Emily, linked together by David's class awareness and his complicity with Steerforth), David's courtship of and marriage to Dora belongs to its comic-satiric strand. Writing from the point of view of his final allegiance to the middle class, David makes himself as well as Dora and the Micawbers the object of gentle but insistent satire. Yet he does not satirise their ambitions or their desire for a special social position, only what he now deems to be a wasteful and irrational economics. From the time of his 'conversion', when he rejects the aristocractic economy, the centre of the comic scenes shifts from his own antics to Dora's inability to comprehend domestic economy, presenting the comedy of her 'irrational' and 'impractical' response to house-keeping (37:461; 41:516).

Dora's failure can be keyed precisely to a lack of understanding of domestic economy. As the domestic manuals demonstrate, this economy is not only monetary, but spatial, temporal, emotional, and moral. In fact, Dora does not make extravagant purchases, except perhaps the pagoda, and her housekeeping never seems to endanger their overall budget. Rather, David feels 'uncomfortable' because she is so inefficient. The pagoda bothers him, not because of its expense, but because it wastes the very limited space of their cottage, as does the rest of the dining room clutter. Because 'nothing ha[s] a place of its own', Traddles must squeeze himself in at the table amidst Dora's flower-painting, the guitar case, and the irrepressible Jip. Contrast this with the tranquillity of the Wickfield drawing room, or with the Wooden Midshipman where each navigational instrument has its own box perfectly fitted to it, the

ultimate expression of the adage 'a place for everything and everything in its place'.[14] Similarly, Dora wastes time because she cannot
command her servants to get dinner ready on time, not because she
is simply indolent. And, although she does not get into debt, she
does waste money because she does not know how to market,
choosing lobsters that are all water and unrecognisable joints of
mutton, and buying a 'beautiful little barrel' of unopened oysters,
making her choice on aesthetic rather than economic grounds
(44:548). Because she does not know enough about cooking, her
roasts turn out burnt or underdone; because she does not keep her
accounts, tradespeople overcharge her for butter and pepper and
servants charge cordials to her; and because she does not keep the
pantry locked, the servants steal from her. Had she been able to
endure the cookery book, it would have advised her on all of these
matters.

If David finds Dora impractical and irrational, she finds his insistence on early rising and hard work 'nonsensical' and 'ridiculous'
(37:464). Since Dora's sense of economy is so totally foreign to his,
it is only appropriate that the cookery book makes her head ache
and ends up a play thing for Jip. In it she would have found the
same complaints made by David without his mitigating charms.
When he decides that she is already 'formed' and simply will never
comprehend his understanding of economy, he gives in to their
warnings that the education of daughters is crucial to their future
abilities as wives and housekeepers, crucial precisely because it will
form their attitudes towards home and family.

Dora's absolute incomprehension of David's pride in his poverty
comes from a completely different code of behaviour corresponding
to an aristocratic economy. These economic codes do not correspond, however, to actual economic differences between classes.
This representation of the different economies originates from
middle-class sources and a view of the national economy in which
the symbolic, political, and economic capital of the aristocracy was
felt to be steadily declining as that of the middle class was just as
surely accumulating. Dora's code demands her total ignorance of
money, while David would impose one that makes the housewife
the keeper of the account book. From David's point of view, Dora
lives within an open-ended economy that has driven her father to
bankruptcy, an economy that employs leisure talents, like guitar
playing and flower-painting, to represent its success by displaying
the extent to which one can appear not to have to economise. For

Dora, allegiance to this code is absolutely necessary if she is to marry, as her father had obviously planned, into the gentry. Whenever she endeavours to act the role of the middle-class house-keeper, however, she soon becomes weary, bored, and frustrated. Her most serious attempt at housekeeping is simply 'make-belief ... as if we had been keeping a baby-house for a joke' (44:553). This childish and playful attitude towards housekeeping is entirely in keeping with her training and her other talents. She cannot work hard because her identity is formed by a notion of delicacy and or-namentation and her ability to charm with these talents.

The writers of the domestic manuals would have blamed all the problems of Dora's household on her, and on her parents for failing to make her better able to cope with them. Sending a daughter to school was itself suspect since the daughter would likely fail to learn household skills, and might furthermore learn values that would make her unwilling to do so. They argued that education should prepare young women for the role of housewife, both through training in domestic skills and by inculcating the sense of self-effacement necessary to motivate them to always consider the comfort of others.[15] Manuals like *Economy for the Single and Married*, for those like Dora and David whose income ranged between £50 and £500, complain that the education of women 'in the middle classes' is 'simply *ornamental*', rendering them 'indolent, useless, and a disgrace to their connexions'.[16] Nor was this attitude limited to these manuals; Ruskin criticised the middle class for bringing up their girls 'as if they were meant for sideboard orna-ments'.[17] So we should not be surprised when David complains of Dora that she 'seemed by one consent to be regarded like a pretty toy or plaything' (41:515–16).

Because female education had for some time focused on the 'refined accomplishments' identified with leisure activities (drawing, playing the piano, and French conversation), it is criticised for failing to prepare young women for their role as middle-class wives. Sarah Ellis bluntly charges that this sort of education is meant to re-inforce the values of the aristocracy, its products learning, 'for the future guidance of their future lives, the exact rules by which the outward conduct of a *lady* ought to be regulated' but not conduct appropriate to their own station in life.[18] Ellis does not object because she regards this sort of education as pretentious social-climbing but because she believes in the moral superiority of middle-class life. While arguing that the schools fail to prepare young women for domestic duties, she and her fellow writers seem more concerned with the bad moral economy of a system in which these girls lose 'the influence of household life and know as little how to cook a dinner as to cure a cold'.[19] Consequently, Catherine Beecher, in a *Treatise on Domestic Economy*, suggests that less time be spent at school and more in domestic employments,[20] an argument undoubtedly welcome to those who could hardly afford to send their girls away to school anyway.[21] The ideal, of course, is the wife who combines housekeeping efficiency with more refined accomplishments; after all, part of her role of creating a comfortable environment is aesthetic, and Soyer's Mr B. is proud of his wife who was 'first acquainted with the keys of the store-room before those of the piano'.[22]

For the purposes of defining one's class status, the moral economy outweighs the economic one. David never complains about the actual economic consequences of Dora's housekeeping; despite the examples of the Micawbers and Mr Spenlow, he seems confident that his industry will keep them ahead of their creditors. In portraying the comic 'Ordeal of Servants', David stresses his public humiliation rather than the financial cost. On their comfortable income (already when they get married he is apparently making £350 which would put them at the top of the middle-class income level),[23] he is not as concerned with the loss of money itself as with the public display of wastefulness. He is ashamed, a feeling that he expresses obliquely when he complains that their housekeeping 'is not *comfortable*' (44:544, emphasis added). The domestic manuals, like David, are much concerned with comfort, whether it be comfort of shoes or the home; through the notion of comfort, the more mundane aspects of domestic economy are transferred to the moral sphere. In *How I Managed My Home*, Mrs Allison's friend Bertha insists on finding a way to dispose of stale bread because she is concerned with the moral, not the negligible monetary, significance of wasting it. At this point, domestic economy becomes socially significant as well because one's commitment to its morality signifies one's values and class loyalty. David does not care about the physical discomforts of Dora's housekeeping so much as the 'something wanting' that pervades his life, the emptiness of that signifier, 'David Copperfield the Younger of Blunderstone Rookery', which was to have been filled up by his marriage to Dora, but persists throughout it (48:594). He learns that Dora's gentility is only another empty signifier, and this ultimately generates his desire for the home-maker, the woman designated upon her first appearance in the book, when still a child, as a 'housekeeper' (15:191).[24]

III

The cookery books and household manuals that would only have hurt and baffled Dora would tell Agnes what she already knew. If she read them, she would not go to them for information but for reinforcement of her identity in a world that had always based social legitimacy upon values other than her own. By implicitly telling women that they should educate their daughters to be home-makers, not idle and decorative, these books created an opposition to the aristocracy that helped define the new realm of the domestic.

The domestic manuals also dealt with the 'servant problem', and David and Dora's 'Ordeal of the Servants' must be understood in the context of books like *Home Difficulties; or Whose Fault Is It? A Few Words on the Servant Question* (1866).[25] The solution of the manuals is that good wives must start out by being good servants.[26] Agnes, who has dedicated herself to maintaining the comforts of her father's home since childhood, is the ideal woman to replace Dora.

The basket of keys is the sign of the housekeeper's household authority, and Agnes, like Esther Summerson, wields them with confidence and skill. The keys are symbolic sceptres of their sovereignty, yet their subjects, the servants, are seldom permitted on stage. Although she must have them, Agnes seems to have no servants in her house, and there is no mention of them in the household described at the end of the book. She has no servant problem because she is herself a housekeeper. She and Esther wave their keys like magic wands that produce order and comfort through selfless devotion alone. (When Aunt Betsey moves into David's quarters after her financial failure, Agnes noiselessly transforms his rooms so they resemble her Dover home [35:440].) In her attempt to be domestic, Dora takes charge of the keys, but for her the magic does not work; although she goes 'jingling about the house', the places to which the keys belong are left unlocked – an invitation to the servants to steal – and the keys become, like the cookery book, a plaything for Jip. Murdstone had forced David's mother, who was equally incompetent, to hand her keys over to Jane Murdstone

(4:42). In effect, when David transfers his affections from Dora to Agnes, and already when he feels that emptiness in his life that only Agnes can fill, he does the same thing.[27]

Out of the creation of the domestic idyll, David hopes to erect his new social identity. In turning the home into an idyll, in marrying the angel in the house, he seems to find an alternative to both the working-class family and the aristocratic family, but, at the same time, the identity of the middle class depends on his belief in these other family forms against which he defines the superiority of his own. His narrative creates an entire mythology of the family, a history and a geography, through which one can distinguish family forms. It accounts for the creation of the middle class by distinguishing between past and present forms of both the gentry and the working class.

The aristocracy represents social legitimacy because it had once deserved its powerful position. To come from a 'good family' means that you belong to the ruling class, but also suggests ethical superiority. But the aristocracy's moral and literal bankruptcy – represented by the financial failure of Spenlow and the moral one of Steerforth – forces it to relinquish this position. The world of the Micawbers and Doctors' Commons gives way to that of Betsey Trotwood, Tommy Traddles, and David Copperfield.

Similarly, he splits the working class between Yarmouth and London, a geographic distinction that corresponds to the historical realities of. But, while urbanisation and industrialisation are historical facts, nineteenth-century representations of these social phenomena create a history that does more to justify and legitimate the middle class than explain the condition of the working class. Just as the middle class finds the basis for its power in the precedent of the aristocracy, it finds the model for the home in the pastoral image of the rural working class – the Peggottys – while distinguishing itself from the nearby urban proletariat – the rookeries inhabited by the likes of Mealy Potatoes and Mick Walker. Like David's depiction of Yarmouth, these depictions of the communal family, extremely common in the nineteenth century, usually present it as a lost pastoral idyll. The notion of the communal values of the extended family forms the basis for the values of domesticity, and sets the middle-class family apart from the urban working class with which it co-existed.[28]

Embracing the home and the *work* ethic, David attempts to re-produce the communal values represented by the older working class while asserting his difference from the new one. His family performs the communal function that the Peggottys, driven apart by the course of events, can no longer perform. In order to claim this realm for the middle class, Gaskell and others depict the pastoral ideal as something that is passing away if not altogether vanished. David, of course, spatialises this by representing the passing order of things in terms of rural Yarmouth, the future as his own London. But he also deals with it temporally, and Dickens himself seems to have preferred things that are 'old-fashioned rather than old'.[29] While he frequently satirises affection for 'the good old days', he sentimentalises 'old-fashioned' Paul Dombey, and makes old-fashioned furnishings a part of the charm of Bleak House. Old-fashionedness does not belong to the past, to be exhibited in museums; it belongs to the present, an anachronistic transcendence of history. This old-fashionedness sets apart both the Peggotty family, as part of the passing rural era, and the home of the Wickfields, with its 'quaint' diamond panes, its 'wonderful old staircase', 'old oak seats', and 'old nooks and crannies' filled with 'queer' furnishings (15:190–1). When David Copperfield senses a distance between himself and Emily, he suggests that the Yarmouth order of life is no longer viable in the modern world he inhabits, but also asserts that it can be recovered in middle-class domesticity.

The middle class absorbs the pastoral, the family as communal unit of production. While the homeless contemporary working class must constantly struggle to survive, the middle-class domestic sphere reconstitutes the lost sense of community. Agnes with her brood of children, gathered around David, reproduces Mr Peggotty's generosity in gathering in orphans and widows in his boat-house.

Consequently, the conclusion of *David Copperfield* does not require a pastoral setting. The home becomes the urban version of pastoral, a bit of the country within the city.[30] Esther's room in old-fashioned Bleak House represents its own idyllic nature in pastoral scenes of 'ladies haymaking, in short waists, and large hats tied under the chin'.[31] As the title of Ruskin's 'Of Queens' Gardens' suggests, the middle-class family specifically associates itself with the pastoral ideal embedded in this representation of the family; the home 'is the place of Peace; the shelter, not only from all injury, but from all terror, doubt, and division' and in 'so far as the anxieties of the outer life penetrate into it, and the ... hostile society of the outer world is allowed ... to cross the threshold, it ceases to be home'.[32] It is a garden of Eden kept by a queen, a refuge for those kings who, as the companion essay's title ('Of Kings' Treasuries') suggests, spend their days in the counting house.

The home, as pastoral refuge of communal labour, depends on the selfless devotion of the housekeeper. The warlike economic forces that threaten the family pervade the male domain outside the home, and the threshold between inside and outside is a place of social transformation. Just as David refuses to see the Peggottys as part of the modern working class, allied to Mealy Potatoes and Mick Walker, he seeks to evade the problematics of this division between domestic and commercial worlds that even affects the form of his narrative. David needs the city even as he idealises the country, and this produces a tension between the commercial act of writing his history and the domestic realm that he records through that act.

IV

If the family and its domestic milieu enables the middle class to define a neat structure of classes and social relationships, of upper and lower, inside and outside, these structures themselves cannot entirely enclose society, and they are not able to put everything neatly into place. After defining the roles of men and women through the opposition of home and workplace, Ruskin runs into difficulties, his argument self-destructing in the nearly indecipherable tangle of metaphor that concludes his essay.[33] Both the division into private and public domains, and the even more fundamental division of urban and pastoral upon which it depends, produce disturbing contradictions that may make us feel less than content with the final vision that David offers us.

The home as an enclosed and protective space can also be stifling. The boat-house appeals to young David because its scale is closer to his, its rooms are so neat and snug, its curving walls resembling the womb. And if one of the prime functions of the home is to isolate one from the outside world, what better means than the self-contained boat at sea? Even on land, it lies on the shore apart from the town, giving it a suburban aspect transferable to a cosy cottage in Highgate. The appeal of the ship as home certainly has much in common with our fascination with life on spaceships and space stations. But, as Fredric Jameson has pointed out, this pleasure runs against the almost certain monotony of sensory deprivation, isolation, and the limited society of a small space crew.[34] In transforming his pastoral idyll into a domestic one, David builds his home around one of those women whom Alexander Welsh calls 'angels of death', a woman who reminds David of a saint in a stained glass window.[35]

The division between the private home, peaceful sphere of the angelic woman, and the public world, sphere of conflict and the economic activity of the man, also betrays fundamental contradictions and discontinuities. The problem of gender, dividing the world into masculine and feminine spheres, becomes a problem of the binary division itself that creates an ambiguous threshold between the two domains, the necessity of crossing this threshold constantly threatening the division itself. Ultimately, we find that the realms are interdependent and implicated within one another: try as Wemmick (of *Great Expectations*) may to rigidly separate Walworth from the City, the walls around his castle possess an all too ominous resemblance to those of the Newgate prison. Recent analyses of the family have argued persuasively that by accepting this separation of home and commerce we fail to see the way in which they reinforce one another.[36] Beneath this opposition of home and commercial world lies their basic identity: the desired reconstitution of the home as idyllic unit of production.

The notion of 'domestic economy' itself should remind us that the home is a site of commercial activity, but, at the same time, it also implies its distinctness from the non-domestic economy. The idyllic portrayal of the home implies the concept of unalienated labour, a labour of love rather than necessity. For the nineteenth century, labour, which is always alienated and performed within the warlike conditions of the marketplace, must take place outside of the home if the home is to maintain its idyllic status. Women's work within the home has wrongly been considered non-work simply because child-rearing and housekeeping, which have important economic functions, are not remunerated with wages. But if we consider the ideological necessity that the home remain unpolluted by the alienated labour of the marketplace, we can begin to see an underlying reason for this attitude.

The notion of unalienated labour suggests that work is not really work because one's relationship to it is fundamentally different than that of the factory worker. This accounts for how the domestic manuals treat housework. Their insistence on self-sacifice and consideration for others suggests that women perform their work out of love, without any motive of profit.[37] This also accounts for why the actual work of housekeeping is disguised by descriptions of the basket of keys, descriptions that conceal the real work. Ellis proscribes bustling about in a manner that makes your housekeeping obtrusive, and Eliza Warren advises the wife to conceal all signs of her labour before her husband returns from work.[38] Not only do Agnes's servants remain invisible, so does the scrubbing, dusting, and mending that she or they must perform.

This desire to find an unalienated form of labour that does not participate in the violence of the marketplace and can resume its place within the home defined as unit of production produces further discontinuities when the husband crosses the threshold. In *Dombey and Son*, Dickens had presented the problematics of the separation of home and work in the separation between Dombey's house and his 'firm'. David attempts to reunite them when he rejects the work assigned to him by that advocate of 'firmness', Edward Murdstone, in favour of writing, a more genteel profession that seemingly enables him to regain control of the means of production as an author who can work at home. Traddles too combines work and home, in the reverse direction, when he 'unprofessionally' moves his family into his law office.

The work ethic, that David embraces so fervently, evokes the pastoral ideal embodied in Caleb Garth of *Middlemarch* and the beehive of activity in the village of Yarmouth, but not washing bottles in London.[39] The difference between washing bottles and writing novels is not just the wages, but where one works, the warehouse or home. Working as a secretary he earns about four times as much (£70) as he did in the warehouse, but the symbolic payoff is much greater than if he had earned the same amount at a menial occupation. For, at the same time that he believes he will find his place through hard work, he believes that only the elect can reach it. Although this paradox employs the theological language of Calvinism, which urges hard work yet insists that salvation cannot be earned, the problem need not be considered in the theological terms it borrows; it belongs to economics, and extends to the nature of domestic economy.[40] In secular terms, domestic economy legitimises the middle class: the work ethic displays its superiority to the wasteful aristocracy while the theory of the elect, translated as unalienated labour, distinguishes their labour from that of the factory operative. This legitimation is essential in a world in which unrestricted self-making – the ability of just anyone to achieve 're-spectability' – would destroy the class structure that the middle class only wishes to re-arrange.

The paradox of the work ethic, however, produces discontinu-ities within the role of the writer. Even as the writer himself enters the home, writers are represented in terms of the woman who crosses into the marketplace: the philanthropist and the prostitute. In 'Of Queens' Gardens', Ruskin argues that the only appropriate activity outside the home for middle-class women is philanthropy, as an extension into the public realm of their domestic duties of se-curing 'order, comfort, and loveliness'.[41] Philanthropic endeavours, like the home, are non-profit organisations, motivated by selfless regard for others. Women who profit by their economic activity prostitute themselves. In contrast to Agnes and Esther, we have Nancy (of *Oliver Twist*) and Martha Endell. Or Edith Dombey, whose marriage of convenience is clearly marked as prostitution.

Dickens, and David, would like to think that authors too are philanthropists. Dickens works at producing the excess of language that will give joy to his readers as Sleary's circus does, and he attacks social misery with the same aims as the philanthropists. While completing *David Copperfield* he started his weekly *Household Words*, with its obvious allusion to hearth and home, as a vehicle for social reform. During this time he was also helping Angela Burdett-Coutts establish an institution for 'fallen women', advising that these women should be trained in home-making.[42] His instinct that these women must yearn for a home suggests that he identifies with them as well in their role as 'street-walkers'. Significantly, David does most of his street-walking during his ex-travagant courtship of Dora, and only walks through London when led there by a street-walker (he apparently also walks to think about his writing, like Dickens, but sticks to the suburbs). Martha, whose last name, Endell, suggests the end of life in the dell, has left the rural idyll of Yarmouth to become an urban street-walker in London. Writers, whatever their intentions, must sell their work, and it, like the banknote, is mere paper.

These divisions of pastoral/urban and private/public also produce discontinuities between David Copperfield and Charles Dickens, between the world of the novel's domestic fiction of wedded bliss and its excluded domestic frictions. We find in this novel a clue to some of Dickens's desires: his desire for social legitimacy and his distaste for Catherine Dickens's reported indolence. But, whereas

David Copperfield achieves the comfortable home with surprising ease once he sets his mind to it (compared to Traddles for example), Dickens found himself at this time distressed by an apparently loveless marriage.[43] His home was not comfortable, yet what would he have done with an Agnes even if she were able to bear up to being constantly pregnant while managing the household better than Catherine Dickens did? (Perhaps Dickens did acknowledge the impossibility of his desire by associating Dora's fatal illness, which causes her to remain inactive, with childbirth.)

Dickens was always most at home when he was at work. His compassionate portrayal of prostitutes, as well as his interest in philanthropic endeavours to aid them, suggest his strong identification with the symbolic anti-domestic impulse that they represent. Rather than bringing his work into the home, he constantly fled to Broadstairs and Brighton, even to the Continent, more at home in the streets where he gathered material for writing and worked through its problems, and where he could carouse with friends in a most undomestic way. 'Nurses, wet and dry; apothecaries; mothers-in-law; these, my countrymen, are hard to leave', he wrote in tongue-in-cheek response to an invitation from Stanfield, Maclise, and Forster in 1844: 'But you have called me forth, and I will come'.[44]

Because the author works for joy and not merely to accumulate capital, he paradoxically produces an excess within the literary work that defies domestic economy. The parsimony of Dickens's miserly characters must be contrasted with his own extravagance with words and with David's ability to produce both comedy and melodrama. Yet, though David Copperfield returns his work to the home, he does not bring the rest of the family into the workforce as Mr Peggotty had done; Agnes's role is to take care of the house, and Dora's assistance with the pens – a parody of the family as unit of production – comes only as compensation for her inability to keep house. Furthermore, the form of David's autobiography reinforces the division of the world into public and private realms, constraining the autobiography within the realm of the domestic and private (he never meant it to be published on any account) while excluding his writing activity and its unwritten *Kunstlerroman*. The excess involved in artistic production might endanger the household economy; to discuss his writings would be to bring his commercial activity into the home. If Dickens's fictional autobiography, representing his progress towards achieving middle-class status, reduplicates the cookery books, his novels would seem to belong to another realm.[45]

From *Dickens Studies Annual*, 15 (1986), 87–109.

NOTES

[Chris R. Vanden Bossche's essay focuses on the hero's search for social legitimacy and how David aligns himself with a middle-class domestic economy that is also seen as a moral economy. In a skilful way, the essay examines an aspect of the novel that we might take for granted: the nature of middle-class domestic life. This was something the Victorians were in the process of creating, defining it by its differences from both aristocratic or gentry values and working-class codes. The class theme is, of course, just one element in the text, but Vanden Bossche's essay shows how all other aspects of the novel are interdependent with it; the text becomes a mirror of self-understanding and self-analysis, in which issues such as the family, gender and work are only comprehensible in relation to the idea of the evolution of a Victorian middle-class world. The essay, as it develops, adopts an approach that is very common in recent criticism, in showing how the argument being conducted in the novel is echoed in other, non-fictional texts from the period – in this instance, cookery books and manuals of domestic economy. By the end of the essay we have a clear sense of how *David Copperfield* promotes a middle-class idyll of the home, yet also how the text forces us to consider shortcomings in this vision of domestic order (for example, how, given the division between the public sphere of work and the private sphere of the home, women's work has to be seen as a form of 'non-work').

Vanden Bossche's approach, and that of the next two essays, can be described as New Historicist: the critic focuses on the development of a bourgeois ideology, identified by its distinctive discourse (which is set against competing discourses in the society). The interest is in power relations, how a certain group, in this instance the middle class, is defining its values as normative, and excluding the behaviour and values of others as aberrant. The essay (and the same is true of the next two essays) could, however, equally well be described as an example of Cultural Materialist criticism. This approach, most closely associated with the British Marxist critic Raymond Williams, also looks at how texts operate in an historical context, but, whereas New Historicism focuses on power relations, Cultural Materialism is concerned in a more overtly political way with how texts are conditioned by the material forces in a period: Vanden Bossche, for example, is concerned with the notions of production, work, and alienated and non-alienated forms of labour. A further difference between the two critical positions is that whereas New Historicism tends to represent texts as almost totally complicit with the ruling values of a society, Cultural

Materialist criticism emphasises the subversive role of a text. Vanden Bossche's essay, for example, focuses on the dissonant voice in the novel, and how the text questions and resists the imperatives of its overall position. All references to *David Copperfield* in this essay are to the Clarendon Edition, ed. Nina Burgis (Oxford, 1981). Ed.]

1.   My discussion of the Victorian family is indebted to a number of sources. In addition to the social history of the family to be found in the works of Aries, Goode, Laslett and others (see below), I am especially indebted to those who have studied the family as an idea or ideology. Among the latter are Leonore Davidoff, Jean L'Esperance, and Howard Newby, 'Landscape with Figures: Home and Community in English Society', in *The Rights and Wrongs of Women*, ed. Juliet Mitchell and Ann Oakley (Harmondsworth, 1976); Jeffrey Kirk, 'The Family as Utopian Retreat from the City: The Nineteenth-Century Contribution', *Soundings: An Interdisciplinary Journal*, 55 (1972), 21–41; and Patricia Branca, *Silent Sisterhood: Middle Class Women in the Victorian Home* (Pittsburgh, 1975). On the developing history of the word family, see Raymond Williams, *Keywords* (London, 1976), pp. 108–11, and Jean-Louis Flandrin, *Familles, parenté, maison, sexualité dans l'ancienne société* (Paris, 1976), pp. 10–15. Finally, on the sociology of cookery, see Jack Goody, *Cooking, Cuisine, and Class: A Study in Comparative Sociology* (Cambridge, 1982).

2.   As one of the most familiar plots of romance, this plot precedes the novel by centuries. But, this only further reaffirms the argument that this form of discovery of family is linked to the aristocracy, for whom romances were initially written.

3.   The history of the word 'family' demonstrates this. Its earliest meaning indicated household, but by the Renaissance, it was defined in terms of lineage and descent, as in the term 'the royal family'. See Williams, *Keywords* and Flandrin, *Familles* above.

4.   *Oliver Twist*, ed. Peter Fairclough (Harmondsworth, 1966), p. 463.

5.   *David Copperfield*, ed. Nina Burgis (Oxford, 1981), 2:13–14. Chapter and page will hereafter be cited in the text.

6.   *The Housewife's Guide: Or, A Complete System of Modern Cookery* (1838). Cited in Eric Quayle, *Old Cook Books: An Illustrated History* (New York, 1978), p. 164. These books often were specific about their audience, and others were implicitly designed for the middle class. They first began to appear around the turn of the century. See Maria Rundell's *A New System of Domestic Cookery: Formed Upon Principles of Economy, and Adapted to the Use of Private Families* (1806), which she claimed was unlike anything available in her early years.

7. I cite the first American edition (New York, 1850), p. 6. Soyer also wrote *The Gastronomic Regenerator* (1846), aimed at his Reform Club clientele, and a *Shilling Cookery for the People Embracing an Entirely New System of Plain Cooking and Domestic Economy* (1854).

8. See Isabella Beeton, *The Book of Household Management* (1861; fasc. rpt New York, 1969), pp. iii, 17.

9. See, for example, Beeton, *Household Management*, who cites Judge Haliburton as writing: 'No man is rich whose expenditure exceeds his means, and no one is poor whose incomings exceed his outgoings' (p. 6). See also Soyer, *Modern Housewife*, pp. 1–6, and Catherine Beecher, *A Treatise on Domestic Economy* (1841; fasc. rpt New York, 1977), pp. 41, 176. Beecher's American version of domestic economy, despite its emphasis on the needs of American women, follows the English manuals in its basic principles.

10. On the more positive side, his exuberance and wasteful extravagance demonstrate his adherence to the economics of unlimited expense. This is what endears him to us, of course, and is clearly allied to the comic excess that makes him so important in James Kincaid's reading of the novel in *Dickens and the Rhetoric of Laughter* (Oxford, 1971), pp. 162–91.

11. Beeton, *Household Management*, p. 39.

12. See Mrs Eliza Warren, *How I Managed My House on Two Hundred Pounds a Year* (London, 1864), p. 50.

13. Soyer, *The Modern Housewife*, p. 1.

14. See Warren, *How I Managed ...* , p. 45.

15. Sarah Ellis, *The Wives of England* (London, 1843), vol. 2, chs 1–4, on 'Domestic Habits'.

16. By 'One who "makes ends meet"' (London, 1845), p. 44. See also Soyer, *Modern Housewife*, who uses almost exactly the same language (p. 338).

17. 'Of Queen's Gardens', in *The Works of John Ruskin*, ed. E. T. Cook and Alexander Wedderburn (London, 1905), pp. 18, 132.

18. Ellis, *Wives*, pp. 164–5.

19. *The Hand-Book of Woman's Work*, ed. L.M.H. (London, 1876), pp. 6–7, cited in Branca, *Silent Sisterhood*, p. 24.

20. Beecher, *A Treatise*, p. 26.

21. Branca, *Silent Sisterhood*, pp. 45–6.

22. Soyer, *Modern Housewife*, p. 4. Consequently, the manuals don't positively discourage education. Ellis even argues for it rather vigorously.

Mrs Allison of *How I Manage on £200 a Year*, sees with chagrin that her heroic friend Bertha has managed the perfect combination while she has let her own skills in music slip away.

23. I presume that 'when I tell my income on my left hand, I pass the third finger and take the fourth to the middle joint' (43:535) means that he is making £350, a reasonable, though extremely fortunate, increase from the £70 per annum with which he began as Dr Strong's secretary (36:446). Branca argues that the middle-class income ranged between £100 and £300.

24. The fact that Agnes and her housekeeping double, Esther Summerson, take up their duties when so young corresponds to the need for early formation of character, since household economy comes about not merely through mathematical calculation but as a result of identification with the values of domestic economy.

25. See N. N. Feltes's excellent essay, '"The Greatest Plague of Life"; Dickens and Servants', *Literature and History*, 8 (1978), 197–213, Branca, *Silent Sisterhood*, pp. 30–5; and Leonore Davidoff, 'Mastered for Life: Servant and Wife in Victorian and Edwardian England', *Journal of Social History*, 7 (1974), 406–28.

26. Warren, *How I Managed ...*, pp. iv–vi, 52–5, 67.

27. The comparison between Dora and Clara has been noted frequently, but one must also make distinctions. Murdstone marries Clara in order to 'form' her (4:100); David is confused about why Dora is formed in such a way as to make housekeeping impossible. Jane Murdstone is the frugal housekeeper carried to the negative extreme, always suspecting the servants of plots and keeping a parsimonious eye on all goods, in contrast to the benign talents of Agnes and Sophy Traddles. At the same time, this depiction is also relevant to the problems inherent within domestic economy that will be discussed below.

28. In fact, extended families are just as likely to be found today as in the past. See John Goode, *World Revolution and Family Patterns* (London, 1963), and Peter Laslett, *Household and Family in Past Time* (Cambridge, 1972). My point is that this history of the family reflects the nineteenth-century view of the family. Numerous writers, including Ruskin, Carlyle, and Engels, evoke an idealised view of the extended family as do the works under discussion. A central document, one on which Engels drew, is Peter Gaskell's *Artisans and Machinery: The Moral and Physical Condition of the Manufacturing Population with Reference to Mechanical Substitutes for Human Labour* (London, 1836); Gaskell's analysis of the problems of industrialisation and urbanisation focuses on their effects on the family. For an argument that the extended family increased in importance, rather than decreased, see Michael Anderson, *Family Structures in Nineteenth Century Lancashire* (Cambridge, 1971).

29. *Bleak House*, edited by Norman Page (Harmondsworth, 1971), p. 116.

30. Kirk Jeffrey, discussing the American family, makes this clear when he compares the family to nineteenth-century utopian ventures. The utopians often did attempt to reproduce what was felt to be an older, more communal social structure, which usually meant a rural setting as well as experimentation with social structures, and Jeffrey argues that the formation of the nucleated family was a similar venture accommodated to the needs of urban life.

31. *Bleak House*, p. 116.

32. Ruskin, 'Queen's Gardens', p. 122, emphasis added. This passage has become the *locus classicus* of discussions of the importance of home to the Victorian middle class, but in most cases the analysis simply accepts the Victorian explanation of the division between home and the world rather than trying to discover its structural significance. The following is a far from exhaustive list of those who cite the passage: Walter E. Houghton, *The Victorian Frame of Mind* (New Haven, 1964), p. 343; Carol Bauer and Lawrence Ritt, *Free and Ennobled: Source Readings in the Development of Victorian Feminism* (Oxford, 1979), p. 16; Jenni Calder, *The Victorian Home* (London, 1977), p. 10; Susan Casteras, *The Substance or the Shadow: Images of Victorian Womanhood* (New Haven, 1982), p. 14; Erna Olafson Hellerstein, Leslie Parker Hume and Karen M. Offens (eds), *Victorian Women: A Documentary Account of Women's Lives in Nineteenth-Century England, France, and the United States* (Stanford, 1981), p. 278; Christopher Wood, *Victorian Panorama: Paintings of Victorian Life* (London, 1976), p. 59: Eli Zaretsky, *Capitalism, The Family, and Personal Life* (New York, 1976), p. 51.

33. Kate Millett partially untangles it in 'The Debate Over Women: Ruskin vs Mill', in *Suffer and Be Still: Women in the Victorian Age*, ed. Martha Vicinus (Bloomington, 1972), pp. 121–39.

34. Fredric Jameson, *The Political Unconscious: Narrative as a Socially Symbolic Act* (Ithaca, 1981), pp. 217–18.

35. Alexander Welsh, *The City of Dickens* (Oxford, 1971), ch. 11.

36. Zaretsky, *Capitalism*, p. 27 and passim; Rayna Rapp, 'Household and Family', 175–8, in Ellen Ross Rapp and Renate Bridenthal, 'Examining Family History', *Feminist Studies*, 5 (1979), 174–200; and Michèle Barrett, *Women's Oppression Today: Problems in Marxist Feminist Analysis* (London, 1980), ch. 6, 'Women's Oppression and "the Family" '.

37. See Ellis, *The Wives of England*, II, chs 1–4.

38. Ellis, *The Wives of England*, pp. 239–40, and Eliza Warren, *A Young Wife's Perplexities* (1886), p. 35, cited in Calder, *The Victorian Home*, p. 111.

39. On the relationship between family and pastoral in *Middlemarch*, see Anthony G. Bradley, 'Family as Pastoral: The Garths in *Middlemarch*', *Ariel*, 6:4 (1975), 41–51.

40. For a very useful discussion of the work ethic in Dickens, see Welsh, *City of Dickens*, pp. 75–84. The relationship between Evangelical religion and middle-class values is explored in Catherine Hall, 'The Early Formation of Victorian Domestic Ideology', in *Fit Work for Women*, ed. Sandra Burman (London, 1979), pp. 15–32.

41. Ruskin, 'Queen's Gardens', p. 136.

42. Edgar Johnson, *Charles Dickens: His Tragedy and Triumph*, 2 vols (New York, 1952), II, pp. 714–18, 593–4, 621.

43. Ibid., p. 494.

44. Ibid., p. 494.

45. To a certain degree this process of exclusion reverses Dickens's own practice. While David excludes his novels from his domestic autobiography, Dickens excludes his domestic life from his novels. At this point, one could follow another trajectory than that I have followed here, and examine how Dickens attempts to differentiate his representation of the family from that found in the domestic manuals and social histories. Placing himself outside of the novel's domestic realm by injecting it with humour, sentiment and linguistic excess, just the converse of David's attempt to put his art outside of his autobiography, Dickens attempts to distinguish the economy of his novel from the taut economies of the middle class. But this division between the novelistic and the domestic is tenuous at best, and in Eliza Acton's cookery book, Dora would have found a recipe for 'Ruth Pinch's Beef-Steak Pudding'. The cookbook writers were quick to employ the means of the novelist, recognising its appeal to the housewife: Soyer's book is in the form of an epistolary novel, Eliza Warren's domestic advice is written as an autobiographical novel, and Isabella Beeton originally published her cookbook in twenty-four monthly parts. This sort of analysis has been carried out in other discussions of Dickens: see D. A. Miller, 'Discipline in Different Voices: Bureaucracy, Police, Family and *Bleak House*', *Representations* (1983), 59–89, and Catherine Gallagher, 'The Duplicity of Doubling in *A Tale of Two Cities*', *Dickens Studies Annual*, 12 (1983), 125–45.

2

David Copperfield: The Decomposing Self

SIMON EDWARDS

I

This essay attempts a reading of *David Copperfield* in the context of English literary culture in the mid-nineteenth century, and more especially considered with other autobiographical fictions of the same period. It is also concerned with some of the ambiguities inherent in the notion of *accounting* in bourgeois society, the problem of balancing books as conceived by economists and literary critics alike. While I hope to suggest that *David Copperfield* is a novel full of a good deal of playful creativity, I focus as well on certain historical determinants in order to offer something more than an interpretation, even to suggest some of the historical constraints under which *play*, as it were, *labours*.

It is no more than a remarkable coincidence that Wordsworth died in 1850. His death meant the publication, for the first time, of his long autobiographical poem, *The Prelude*. It also meant that Tennyson got the job as Poet Laureate. In part a reward for 'early promise', that post was also reward for his publication in the same year of *In Memoriam*. Subtitled 'The Way of the Soul' that poem is, of course, a profoundly (as well as overtly) autobiographical text, dealing with a buried personal history, just as Wordsworth's personal history had remained a 'buried' text. The period of its immediate gestation (1849–50) coincides with the writing and completion of both *David Copperfield* and Thackeray's *Pendennis*.

These are also the years immediately following the revolutionary political events that spiralled outward from Paris to every major European capital.

From a bourgeois perspective, 1848 meant that certain problems and contradictions had been met or recognised and countered, if not overcome. Nowhere did this happen more swiftly than in Britain, the initiator of the bourgeois mode of production. 1851 was the year of the Great Exhibition. The Workshop of the World was displayed in the transparent Crystal Palace – the architectural apotheosis of the new forms of industrial production of identical and interchangeable parts. The Great Exhibition was a very specific invitation to the whole world to reproduce itself in the image of the bourgeoisie.

These autobiographical texts, then, accompany and articulate a passage in historical time from crisis to triumph. They were accompanied, in turn, and this at a time when historical and fictional narrative were far more closely implicated, by the publication of Macaulay's *History of England*, which classically reinscribed the centrality of the non-violent Glorious Revolution of 1688. That this, and not the English Civil War, should be central was important in any model of the progress of the bourgeois state as *evolutionary* rather than *revolutionary*. The demented Mr Dick's preoccupation with King Charles's head in *David Copperfield* may be bizarre testimony to some of the difficulties of historical interpretation and historical authority to be engaged in the passage from potential madness to sanity.[1]

II

If history and fiction were in some sense competing forms, it is important also to recall the relative status of poetry within the public domain – the artistic-financial *coup d'état* represented by Tennyson's poem in recentring certain kinds of poetic discourse. It is from within a nexus of related transformations of private and public discourse that I want to describe some aspects of *In Memoriam* before discussing *David Copperfield* in more detail.

It is possible to read the central drama of *In Memoriam* as the child's separation from its mother and the struggle to recover the primal circle of feeling through the art of *sympathy*. The most influential theory of sympathy as a function of moral philosophy on the Cambridge circle of Apostles, to which both Arthur Hallam and Tennyson had belonged, was found in Adam Smith's *The Theory of Moral Sentiments* (1759).[2] In so far as this separation and struggle anticipate the experience of loss and the imagination of death, both personal and social, they are accompanied by the deep anxieties which characterise the poem.[3]

Central to such a reading is section XLV:

> The baby new to earth and sky,
>   What time his tender palm is prest
>   Against the circle of the breast
> Has never thought that 'this is I':
>
> But as he grows he gathers much
>   And learns the use of 'I' and 'me',
>   And finds 'I am not what I see,
> And other than the things I touch'.
>
> So rounds he to a separate mind
>   From whence clear memory may begin.
>   As thro' the frame that binds him in
> His isolation grows defined.
>
> This use may lie in blood and breath,
>   Which else were fruitless of their due,
>   Had man to learn himself anew
> Beyond the second birth of Death.

There is, of course, a farther factor in this drama, signalled by section CXXIV, where Tennyson now confronts his earlier doubts with images, which, although displaced, clearly echo those of XLV:

> A warmth within the breast would melt
>   The freezing reason's colder part,
>   And like a man in wrath the heart
> Stood up and answer'd 'I have felt'.

Scepticism is overcome in an act of manly aggression. The erectile *warmth* is now in his *breast* and implicitly directed against the frozen source of maternal warmth. ('The freezing reason's colder part' is continuous with a whole chain of images of barren hemispheres throughout the poem – frozen fonts, fountains, etc.) The gesture does not quite suit, however.

> *No*, like a child in doubt and fear:
>   But that blind clamour made me wise:

> Then was I a child that cries,
> But, crying, knows his father near.
> (italics mine)

This is more reconciliation than rage. The erstwhile remote and alien father – God/Old Man Tennyson/the Oedipal tyrant – becomes a reassuring figure, and the farther/*father* comes *near*. Enshrined in such an Ideal Family, the *clamour* dies away, and it might after all be possible to arrive at one's own uncomplicated masculinity through an act of identification. The reconstruction of the bourgeois family tends always to place great emphasis on *quietness* at home.

This paradoxical liberation (paradoxical because it will involve the reproduction of many of the old constraints) is better understood as a *legitimation*, legitimation of, amongst other things, the bourgeois state apparatus as ideology and not as direct repression. Section CXXIV's closing stanza is startlingly specific. Reproduction is guaranteed, if in a somewhat mystified way:

> And *what I am beheld again*
> *What is*, and *no man understands*   ·
> And *out of darkness* came the hands
> That reach thro' nature, moulding men.
> (italics added)

The hands here may well be busy writing novels and poems to take their place alongside the other institutions of bourgeois culture and education that contribute to the *moulding* of ideal subjects.

The poem ends with a celebration of Christian marriage and with it the knowledge of the reproduction and renewal of the family. It may indeed have been Tennyson's wife, whom he married that year, who not only suggested the title but also persuaded him to publish the poem which had hitherto merely circulated privately as a number of fragmentary lyrics. In the context of the poem's persistent concern about both personal and *genetic* survival, such an ending may also serve as guarantee of the survival of the human species itself. If so, it is a guarantee of evolutionary purpose in the universe without the disfiguring revolutionary break threatened by the events of 1848. Within such a scheme Hallam becomes the 'noble type' of a coming race of Christian gentlemen who will be ready to supervise future developments.

The events in France are alluded to in section CXXVII, a section that chronicles the politics of the Great Exhibition: a masterful

Anglocentric irony beaming over a disintegrated Europe. This bloody class-conflict, which echoes the earlier species struggle of the primal dragons 'that tare each other in their slime', is a product of social repression. But this revolutionary conflict may also be read as one between fathers and sons, in a contest of *authority*, for access to the maternal flow of material well-being. A new order of family life is necessary to minimise such conflict (and we don't need radical psychiatry to tell us that it certainly stepped it up), just as a new political order is intended to heal over divisions between traditional aristocratic interests and those of the fully formed bourgeoisie. So, Tennyson, the vicar's son, will receive a peerage...

There is another side to this. *In Memoriam* is haunted not only by its homophilia (a term to be carefully distinguished from any implication of homosexuality, repressed or otherwise), but by greater doubts about its feminine irrelevance or indolence, its possible *barrenness* in the absence of any active, *activating* masculine principle.[4] In section XXI Tennyson speaks of 'private sorrow's *barren song*' as he imagines a series of criticisms accusing him of, precisely, social irresponsibility. Later (XLVIII) he personifies that same barren Sorrow as the female creative source of the poem, as well as its material substance. Although apparently about the processes of birth, the lyric's syntactical complexity carries also a powerful erotic charge with its talks of lays, parting and proving, lips, sports, 'the deepest measure from the chords'. It implies a female sexuality as characteristic of the earlier lyrics, that is at once both fecklessly promiscuous and haughtily remote. This ambivalence will be rescued by a combination of wholly genital male sexuality and vaginal orgasm, within the institution of productive married love.

III

The social construction of mid-Victorian Britain – whether industrial production, sexual reproduction or literary production – after the menace of organised labour had been overcome, was predicated upon the possibility of self-construction. Imagining the process of such a construction is a central element in the autobiographical texts of these years. Self-construction was indeed an essential part of the ideological core of *laissez-faire* individualism around which the social order was formed. It was an individualism, however, which, unlike the earlier excesses of 'romanticism' and the hitherto disorderly achievements of the writers in question, was now to be constrained by the appropriation of patriarchal authority and responsibility. A reconciliation with the father was necessary if new sons were to be disciplined.[5]

1850 is the moment when the dandy style of the metropolitan *parvenu* – clean shaven and sexually ambiguous – is translated into the new type of dark-bearded bourgeois paterfamilias. Certain clothes – trousers, white shirts and dark frock coats, which had been latently revolutionary at the beginning of the century – became the basis of a rigid new uniform. The umbrella replaced the sword and defined a new relationship and a new space between Christian gentlemen. The gradual fusion of style and manners between aristocracy and bourgeoisie jelled in a new order. The unlikely camaraderie between the fatly feminine, but womanising 'Prinny' (later George IV) and Beau Brummel – the Ideal couple of the Regency – had looked forward to the inception of this regime of stiffly upright, separate, discrete but identical males. These are the Lords of humankind, whether at home, up at the mill, down in the counting-house, on the landed estate or out in the farthest flung posts of the Empire. The dangerously unruly coiffure of the early nineteenth-century male, which had replaced the powdered wig and announced an equality of rank to be discriminated only by the measurement of phrenological lumps, is disciplined by top-hat and clipped sideboards. The ghost of Lord Byron, aristocrat and radical iconoclast, best-selling poet and unpatriotic seducer of women, was finally laid. Such was its frightening potency that it would later reappear as Dracula where it hadn't continued to enjoy a disturbing expatriate existence as Captain Ahab.[6]

Carlyle may have been the earliest to diagnose Byron's role as the first English writer to dramatise and mythologise his own life. A corollary of such a diagnosis would be the new impersonal/personal myths sanctioning the distance travelled by the bourgeoisie in the half-century since 1800.

Not the least of these attempts to exorcise the Byronic legacy is the death of James Steerforth in *David Copperfield*. Like Shelley, he too drowns at sea, his private pleasure boat overturning in a storm. The itinerary of the runaway couple, Steerforth and Little Em'ly, not surprisingly, includes Switzerland and Italy. The relation between David and his former mentor (whose name, Steerforth, suggests a dimension of heroic wilfulness) is, I think, merely one (probably the most frequently noted) of the ways in which the novel negotiates the problematic issue of male authority, the achievement of an appropriate identity and the coming into one's proper inheritance.

Perhaps ideally *David Copperfield* should be discussed together with Thackeray's *Pendennis* as well as *In Memoriam*, for all three texts share the same marks of ambiguous *institutionalisation*. Yet *David Copperfield* may remain the most absorbing, not least because it has attracted so much of the wrong kind of critical attention. At best it has been regarded with the kind of doting affection which Dickens himself appears to invite when he described it in the Preface of 1867 as his 'favourite child'. It often becomes a mere tool of literary criticism, a source-book for Dickens's obsessions and contradictions, useful in interpreting the rest of the work in some 'biographical' or 'holistic' terms. At times it gets beaten over the head by the more 'mature' novels, especially *Great Expectations*, which is less snobbish and so on (though personally I find the disillusioned quietism of *Great Expectations* rather jarring). Again it becomes the victim of a special moral pleading, more or less perverse.[7] Most of these approaches, to say nothing of the self-delighting 'fairy-tale' readings, are essentially *unhistorical*.

Tennyson throughout *In Memoriam* probes questions of writerly responsibility and the writer's relations with his or her readership in ways I have tried to suggest. The studied casualness of Thackeray's apparently infinite recollections of 'times past' in *Pendennis* also incorporates theoretical discussion between its two writers – Pen and Warrington. Such discussions can be very frank.

> 'I am a prose labourer,' Warrington said: 'you, my boy, are a poet in a small way, and so, I suppose, consider you are authorised to be flighty. What is it you want? Do you want a body of capitalists that shall be forced to purchase the works of all authors who may present themselves manuscript in hand? Everybody who writes his epic, every driveller who can or can't spell, and produces his novel or his tragedy – are they all to come and find a bag of sovereigns in exchange for their worthless reams of paper? Who is to settle what is good or bad, saleable or otherwise? Will you give the buyer leave, in fine to purchase or not? ... Rags are not a proof of genius; whereas capital is absolute, as times go, and is perforce the bargain master. I have a right to deal with the literary inventor as with any other; – if I produce a novelty in the book trade, I must do the best I can with it.'
> (*Pendennis*, ch. 32)

There is none of this commentary in *David Copperfield*. We learn nothing of David's understanding of the relations between his art and his life and society. If he has a view of his art, it is a curiously functional one – the novels just get written. He could be on the literary production line of the Workshop of the World, only half-absorbed in a semi-skilled manufacturing process, with the women, like his 'child bride', Dora, anxiously looking on, holding or sharpening his pens at night when he prefers not to go to bed. It's a job that manages to seem both heroic and banal at the same time.

Yet outside the novel and during its composition we find Dickens actively addressing himself to these questions. In March 1850 he launched *Household Words* and in the 'Preliminary Word' wrote:

> We aspire to live in the Household affections, and to be numbered among the Household thoughts, of our readers. We hope to be comrade and friend of many thousands of people, of both sexes, and of all ages and conditions ...
>
> The mightier inventions of this age are not, to our thinking, all material, but have a kind of soul in their stupendous bodies which may find expression in Household Words.

This passage very specifically identifies his work as a novelist with the material gains of industrialisation. Meanwhile he was setting up the Guild of Literature and Art, of which he wrote:

> I do devoutly believe that this plan carried, *will entirely change the status of the literary man in England*, and make a revolution in his position, which no government, no power on earth *but his own*, could ever effect.
>
> (italics mine)

The new centralised role for the 'literary man', to be achieved *autonomously*, is echoed too in the launching, later that year, of his *A Child's History of England* which marks, as much as anything, his claim to the role of guardian of the national culture (as well as an affinity with that earlier knight of literary industry, Walter Scott).

IV

I want here to explore what in the novel is an apparent split between its presentation of David's turbulent personal history and the unexamined bases of an artistic/literary achievement which, for anything we are told to the contrary, may be simply the tool of his self-aggrandisement. We *are* told often enough in the closing chapters that David has been wrestling with his 'undisciplined heart'. Daniel Peggotty's persistent dropping of his aitches should remind us that *heart* and *art* are synonomous in this novel: both are overcome as it concludes. Those dropped aitches are very literal/literary marks of a potential indiscipline, in so far as David's gentility would be irreparably damaged were he to adopt the working-class Peggotty as a father-figure: a defeat of art by, precisely, heart.

Whatever critical response there is to David's *work* in the novel takes the form of a number of jokey throwaways. There are the observations of the bedridden undertaker, Mr Omer, a compulsive reader after years of making coffins.

> 'And since I've taken to general reading, you've taken to general writing, eh, sir? ... What a lovely work that was of yours! What expressions in it! I read it every word – every word. And as to feeling sleepy! Not at all!'

The closeness of Mr Omer's reading, 'every word – every word', takes place in that transitional zone between sleeping and waking which so preoccupied Dickens throughout his work, and to which he alludes in the Preface of 1850. It is as though he has been transcribing a dreamwork. In this process, when complete, 'an Author feels as if he were dismissing some portion of himself into the shadowy world, when a crowd of the creatures of his brain are going from him for ever'. Dickens's grasp of the mutual implication of conscious and unconscious activity deeply informs his writing practice, but perhaps nowhere more than in this novel.

Further there are the anxieties of Mr Chillip, the surgeon who presides over David's birth and who reappears much later in the story expressing his concern over David's 'trying occupation',

> 'Now, sir, about that brain of yours, if you'll excuse my returning to it. Don't you expose it to a great deal of excitement, sir?'

The irony is overtly at the expense of the timid Mr Chillip, but we should note that he has a good deal of experience with mental derangement. Not only is he telling David how the second Mrs Murdstone has been driven 'nearly imbecile' by her tyrannical husband, but he is also in London to give professional evidence before a Commission of Lunacy.

The wry amusement suggested by these remarks hardly corresponds to the *real* anxieties felt by Dickens in the first part of his literary career: the sleepless nights in the manic scramble to meet deadlines; bullying and playing off one publisher against another; the expansion and consolidation of his markets and his social and financial status; the campaigning to change the copyright laws to get hold of his American royalties. If we tend to see these now as creative opportunities rather than disabling hazards in the work of a professional artist in the early Victorian market economy, they are evident in *David Copperfield* in only a very oblique way.

An appreciation of those pressures under which the young novelist worked has been reinforced by literary criticism's recent emphasis on the importance of the 'rupture' of 1848. Indeed, a concern with those events has confirmed that long-standing critical model of Early Dickens and Late Dickens. *Dombey and Son* (1846–7, as a book in 1848), however, has attracted most investigation of the transformations in Dickens's artistic method. The novel which immediately followed has all too often been seen as a mere sport or holiday, a solipsistic proliferation from the suppressed autobiographical fragment. Without the formal constraints that came from Dickens's winding his bourgeois readership up and down, probing and cajoling them in equal measure, *David Copperfield*, of all his novels, may most embarrass us by its unconscious snobberies and its repulsively coy treatment of sexuality and marriage. At times we may be forgiven for reading it as a manual in the art of a social self-defence: how to keep up appearances before your social inferiors – dubious old friends, uppity law clerks, churlish waiters, overbearing menials, and a silly wife.

An adequate critical account will do well to bear in mind John Lucas's insistence (in *The Melancholy Man* [1970]) that we regard each of Dickens's later novels as a unique project, experimental in both structure and effect, rather than as a virtuoso variation on certain recurring themes. I want to describe some of the distinctive structural qualities of *David Copperfield*, though not, I should add, to offer some rigid alternative frame from which to hang the novel.

How should we place this novel in Dickens's development as nineteenth century literary speculator and entrepreneur? We may at least begin with a crude model of his continuing exploitation of the mechanical reproduction of interchangeable parts, each packet of soap opera with a miraculous new ingredient guaranteed to remove the stains from the unloving reader's heart. Dickens was indeed as able a market-researcher and publicity officer as he was a producer, a writer whose own brand loyalty led him to name his own republished works of 1869 as *The Charles Dickens Edition*.

From *Pickwick Papers* to *Martin Chuzzlewit* the work is characterised by a ferocious comic energy and inventiveness, at once the legacy of 'Romantic' spontaneity and the equivalent of the resourceful individualism of the first phase of industrial capitalism whose cutthroat competitiveness is suggested by the suicide of Robert Seymour, his former collaborator in *Pickwick Papers*. These novels are offensive to the canons of organic form which were to emerge after 1848 as central to liberal bourgeois aesthetic and social theory. Dickens's working methods were hardly conducive to any deeply mediated formal unity. Such methods culminate in *Martin Chuzzlewit* with its gigantic excrescences, Mr Pecksniff and Mrs Gamp. For the first time, however, Dickens confronted falling sales and, exhibiting all the initiative of an early industrialist seeking new raw materials and markets, he packed his characters off to the States. If this move to a certain extent enabled him to cut his losses, the real recovery came from his decision to write *A Christmas Carol* and thus create a consumer identification between Dickens and Christmas which was to last seven years and see him through the crisis.

Another response to this crisis was the new compositional technique put to work in *Dombey and Son*, the inception of 'Late Dickens'. Here he emerges as the wholly conscious artist, planning, organising, controlling, attempting to integrate plot, character, theme and symbol. The new solidity of achievement, the new confidence and purposefulness are marks of that new artistic order which was the corollary of the new economic and social order that the novel also tries to trace and comprehend. 'Late Dickens' is one of the supreme artists of that new order; his art poised to take as a given a fully formed social system where full and methodical *realisation* also performs the task of analysis. The novelist is now a kind of social psychologist, showing how society holds together, how it incorporates and modifies, as much as it derives from, individual and collective behaviour. The early work was improvised around the theme of the fundamentally decent human heart in an infinitely corrupt world; the later work shows systematically the heart itself corrupted in the labyrinthine networks of Victorian institutions and ideology.

Fiction during the 1840s is analogous to the railway system developed in the same decade and which *Dombey and Son* describes. It is a dynamic communication system enabling the national integration and institutionalisation of industrial capitalism.

In a brilliant essay on *Dombey and Son*, Gabriel Pearson has shown how, in changing the form of the work he was producing, Dickens was also involved in reconstituting his own role and personality, endowing himself with a new identity – that of a wholly respectable bourgeois – very close, in fact, to the novel's own repulsive and repressive eponymous central character, Father Dombey.[8] The identification is, of course, ambiguous; and it is important to realise that the firm of Dombey and Son, which literally organises the world of the novel, is an increasingly outmoded business enterprise. Dombey's mistrust of the railway system is symptomatic of his inability to adapt to the dominant tendencies within the capitalism of the period, the replacement of individually managed companies by publicly-funded enterprises capable of, precisely, integrating new social and economic elements. So was Dickens seeking to seal new relations with a broader base of readers, to remove the element of risk. I don't want to examine, here, how this motive actually enters into *Dombey and Son*, distorting the tone of its critique and mechanising its comedy, but rather to suggest that *David Copperfield* represents a further and more confident stage in that process of self-reconstruction, a public floating of a hitherto private company.

The mystique of the bourgeois individual – that 'theology of persons' – is the necessary accompaniment of the making of capitalist society. My contention would be that in *David Copperfield* Dickens shows himself in as complex a relation to the former as, most criticism would agree, he stands to the latter. If the former lineaments of the rest of Dickens's later work enable us to comprehend the depth and grandeur of his critique of Victorian Britain, so some indication of the structure of *David Copperfield* should reveal shapes as shadowy and disturbing as those half-seen through the yellowing light of the pages of *Bleak House*, suggesting something of the *anomie* and failure of both human language and relation enclosed in *Little Dorrit*, and generating, even, something resembling the under-developed organisms and entropic mutations that belong to the primal slime and industrial effluvia which make up the River Thames in *Our Mutual Friend*.

Of *Martin Chuzzlewit*, Dickens made the fairly unconvincing retrospective claim that it was organised around the principle of 'how selfishness propagates itself' (Preface, 1844). In spite of the new rigours applied in *Dombey and Son*, *David Copperfield* might be understood as a throwback to the old spontaneity of selfish propagation. I think we can reach its complexity only by dispersing our usual critical figures for dealing with Dickens, the way in which the symbols of our symbolism, as it were, are invariably *spatial* (just as Freud is credited with an architecture of the psyche). That pictorial/moral vision so characteristic of Dickens may descend indeed from his great eighteenth century mentors, Fielding and Smollett, together with both their and his indebtedness to Hogarth.[9] This legacy needs in turn to be set against his other line of descent from Richardson, a line that descends also into the dark cave of interiority. I can only note in passing here how a marriage other than that between David and Agnes is resolved in *David Copperfield*, a marriage between the fictional representations of the two paradoxical strains of the bourgeoisie's originating ideologies – those of the Enlightenment and of Romanticism. (American readers will, I suspect, recognise much of this in Poe. Equally, Poe's attempt at a musical organisation of prose, as in, for example, 'The Fall of the House of Usher', anticipates a number of the themes I want to score.) Allusions to that prototypical fictional *account* of renaming, *Robinson Crusoe*, and the tidy shelves at the back of its hero's Lockean island cave, are plentiful throughout the novel, not least in the whole conception of the Yarmouth boat-house. David's childhood reading in Fielding and Smollett is persistently recalled. Also instrumental in Dickens's development of these resources was Scott's combination of topographical range and enquiry into the nature of historical, temporal process. There is further the contribution of De Quincey's mediation of the paradoxes of Romantic idealism in the first great fragment of bourgeois autobiography, *The Confessions of an English Opium Eater*. Finally, it is the figure of Sterne, that most articulate of the de-articulators of relations between time and space who is written over in the opening pages. The note struck by the midnight chimes of the first paragraph is a distinctly Shandean one.

> Whether I shall turn out to be the hero of my own life, or whether that station will be held by anybody else, these pages must show. To begin my life with the beginning of my life, I record that I was born (as I have been informed and believe) on a Friday, at twelve o'clock at night. It was remarked that the clock began to strike, and I began to cry, simultaneously.
>
> (ch. 1)

The tears of Tristram and the beginning of time coincide in Sterne with the moment of conception. David's submission to the blows of time – 'the clock began to *strike*' – in Dickens's more urgent art, starts, in an almost umbilical loop, at the moment of *recording* (rechording), an act that is both to write and to remember. (He remembers here what has been 'tolled'.) Yet the greater urgency of the particular historical moment may coincide with an act of repression, in a novel where the sexual basis of conception cannot be discussed. No more will the conception of David's own novels be discussed. David, a posthumous son, is a would-be self-conception, the author of himself, the Author Himself, a self-made bourgeois man. Thus it is only through an impersonal passive construction that his birth 'was remarked'. The construction confirms the absence of the father, as the verb itself, *re*-mark, suggests the beginning of life over again as an *inscribed* one, authorised only by the writing, fathered only by the text. Nor, perhaps most importantly, is this opening question merely rhetorical, for the character of David will be developed from the presentation of a set of possibilities, a choice of 'sibling' rivals – Traddles, Ham, Steerforth, Uriah Heep, etc. *Station* becomes a suggestive term with its connotations of 'station in life', and thus David's rejection of a number of class alternatives, as well as that of *stasis*, the moment and site of a completed journey, a point of arrival that will guarantee a hitherto doubtfully heroic status. We should remember that the first train into any newly built railway terminus in Victorian Britain was invariably greeted by a band playing 'See the Conquering Hero Come'.

The vein of Shandean improvisation continues to be tapped:

> I was born with a caul, which was advertised for sale, in the newspapers, at the low price of fifteen guineas. Whether sea-going people were short of money about that time, or were short of faith and preferred cork-jackets, I don't know; all I know is, that there was but one solitary bidding, and that was from an attorney connected with the bill-broking business, who offered two pounds in cash, and the balance in sherry, but declined to be guaranteed from drowning on any higher bargain. Consequently the advertisement was withdrawn at a dead loss – for as to sherry, my poor dear mother's own sherry was in the market then – and ten years afterwards the caul was put up in a raffle down in our part of the country, to fifty members at half-a-crown a head, the winner to spend five shillings. I was present myself, and I remember to have felt quite uncomfortable and confused at a part of myself being dis-

posed of in that way. The caul was won, I recollect, by an old lady with a hand-basket, who, very reluctantly, produced from it the stipulated five shillings, all in halfpence, and twopence halfpenny short – as it took an immense time and a great waste of arithmetic, to endeavour without any effect to prove to her. It is a fact which will be long remembered as remarkable down there, that she was never drowned, but died triumphantly in bed, at ninety-two. I have understood that it was, to the last, her proudest boast, that she never had been on the water in her life, except upon a bridge; and that over her tea (to which she was extremely partial) she, to the last, expressed her indignation at the impiety of mariners and others who had the presumption to go 'meandering' about the world. It was in vain to represent to her that some conveniences, tea perhaps included, resulted from this objectionable practice. She always returned, with greater emphasis and with an instinctive knowledge of the strength of her objection, 'Let us have no meandering'.

This might be intended as a piece of familiarly whimsical irrelevance, except that the old lady has, like us, acquired the first *serial* part of *David Copperfield*, the caul preceding the head out of the womb and thus separable from the unifying source of consciousness (these are not yet David's *memories*). Her reiterated complaint, 'Let us have no meandering', speaks the expectation of Dickens's post-*Dombey* readership for orderly narration, and thus the whole absurd digression is recuperated for the novel's purpose and meaning. The passage alerts us to the identity of man and book. It obeys, in the writing and reading, an impulse towards shapelessness (as David, in his life, will yield to random chance) yet in doing so becomes a statement of shapely intention.

The old lady also holds out against 'the impiety of mariners and others' while she drinks her *imported* tea. This act serves to justify the importance of creative *meandering*, just as it returns us to the historical moment. Only in full possession of what is brought back from the expeditions of the imagination can we comfortably claim the assurances of aesthetic and social order. The image from international commerce is appropriate to Dickens's newfound artistic authority within England's own role at the hub of world trade: the Workshop of the World. A magical, phantasmagoric display of solid objects and the dazzlingly persuasive power of *narration* may both here meet to conceal and reveal the real processes of their making in the *actual* social relations of mid-Victorian Britain.

V

With the aid of a by now familiar passage from Marx's *Capital*, I
want to leap across seven hundred pages or so of text.

> A commodity appears at first sight an extremely obvious, trivial thing.
> But its analysis brings out that it is a very strange thing, abounding in
> metaphysical subtleties and theological niceties ... The form of wood,
> for instance, is altered if a table is made out of it. Nevertheless the
> table continues to be wood, an ordinary sensuous thing. But as soon
> as it emerges as a commodity, it is transformed into a thing which
> transcends sensuousness. It not only stands with its feet on the
> ground, but, in relation to all other commodities, it stands on its
> head, and evolves out of its wooden brain grotesque ideas, far more
> wonderful than if it were to begin dancing of its own free will.[10]

Clearly at one level the great forward thrust of the novel is the
spurious teleology of bourgeois individualism. As the last images of
the novel fade, an explicitly religious transfiguration is accomplished.

> And now, as I close my task, subduing my desire to linger yet,
> these faces fade away. But one face, shining on me like a Heavenly
> light by which I see all other objects, is above them and beyond them
> all. And that remains.
>   I turn my head, and see it, in its beautiful serenity, beside me.
>   My lamp burns low, and I have written far into the night; but the
> dear presence, without which I were nothing, bears me company.[11]
>   O Agnes, O my soul, so may thy face be by me when I close my
> life indeed; so may I, when realities are melting from me, like the
> shadows I now dismiss, still find thee near me, pointing upward!
>   (ch. 64)

The materially prosperous David here converts into a Prospero-like
super-ego, 'subduing my desire'. His meanderings from home to
home are resolved at the point where the novel's meanderings are
over. The passage from Marx invites us to ask whether it is a
'*Heavenly* light' by which he sees 'all other objects'. It may be that
the source of light and transcendence lies in the objects themselves.
Some odd shadows are cast by the last fading reality of the fiction
describing Traddles's rather than David's home.

> Traddles, exactly the same simple, unaffected fellow as ever he
> was, sits at the foot of the large table like a Patriarch; and Sophy
> beams upon him, from the head, across a cheerful space that is
> certainly not glittering with Britannia metal.

Not only has the table acquired a *head* and a *foot*, it has become a spiritually charged zone. Here the bourgeois *Patriarch* (but, ideally continuous with his former 'simple' self – '*like* a Patriarch', merely) is transfigured by the light emanating from solid silver tableware so sacred it cannot even be named as such.

It's Traddles who ought to be cheerful, but he takes his place rather as one of the *things* that fills 'cheerful space'. This is a literally brilliant image, reflecting the bourgeois compulsion to stuff the space around itself with solid objects. The 'Britannia metal' alludes back to Traddles's potentially disastrous personal history in which objects had acquired such enormous sentimental significance. There was not only his and Sophy's attempt to accumulate the simplest eating utensils, but also his pathetic endeavours to retrieve from pawn the flowerpot and marble-topped table they had bought together. These objects had a human-sensuous quality that was related to real human needs. The radiance of this last collection of objects with merely *exchange* value is so bright we can hardly penetrate it sufficiently to locate the actual source of light. It is endlessly mirrored between Sophy, Traddles and the things themselves – all bound in a vibrant dialectic. There is no need to speak of the *sterling* qualities in Traddles's character.

Turning this image inside out is to align it with the novel's train of enquiry into the nature of the role of material objects in the appropriation of identity. At the other end of the social scale is the taciturn Mr Barkis, who appropriates Clara Peggotty's name in a silent courtship that consists only of the exchange of objects. For all that 'Barkis is willin' ' his identity lies not in existential will but in the black box that he keeps in the wagon that trundles endlessly, by equine instinct rather than will, between Blunderstone and Yarmouth. Legendarily it is the possession of a Mr Blackboy and is 'to be left until called for'. As Barkis's life ebbs slowly out with the tide, in Peggotty's ghastly yet moving account, he claws with his stick, like Beckett's Malone, the box closer and closer to the bed in which he is dying. At the moment of death, the problem of identity overcome, he holds the box in a tight embrace: Mr Blackboy has come to collect. Barkis had also claimed that the box was full of 'old clothes' which links the device with the long artistic/literary one of the *Totentanz*, which had been classically reactivated for the nineteenth century by Carlyle's *Sartor Resartus*. David himself is stripped of his clothes on the same Dover road followed by Lear and Gloucester. He recovers at Aunt Betsey's, 'a sort of bundle' of outsize clothes. These he must learn to fit, just as he must cast off those which are inappropriate through Betsey's insistence on regarding him as a girl. 'Pretty boy' and 'poor boy' she calls him – in that order (ch. 13).

Gender confusion accompanies class confusion as the novel's major concern. So complex are the family bonds between the 'creatures' of Dickens's brain that they cannot be unravelled here. Such an unravelling would be inappropriate anyway, a pointless exercise in idealising or reifying the text. The opening remarks on the historical parameters of the resolution of the social/sexual/productive crisis in relation to Tennyson are intended to govern these concluding observations on the novel.

I cannot begin to describe the sheer range and variety of the novel's treatment of family life, of parents and orphans. Narcissistically self-fertilised by the crossing of fatherless male and motherless female – David and Agnes (that troubled brother–sister relation) – it spawns an extraordinary world of intractable aunts, uncles and surrogate parents. The gentle order of family life it imagines is imposed on the anarchic uncertainties of alien and subversive sexualities, is defined against the losses and distortions to which Victorian women in particular were subject. Its opening chapters speak of wretched poverty and deprivation, as well as tyrannic sadism personified in Mr Creakle and the 'tough shit' of Mr Murdstone. But its later development is around the shapes of homosexual and incestuous desires, impotence, frigidity, vampirism and onanism. It is stalked by insanity: its most potent comedy is that of the manic-depressive philoprogenitive Mr Micawber: its moral double-agent, the 'volatile' dwarf, Miss Mowcher. We need only think of the reciprocal desire between Steerforth and David ('Daisy' as Steerforth calls him) enabling the former to seduce David's own 'sister', Little Em'ly, by proxy, as it were, (for) David himself. Alternatively there is the 'marriage' between the ironically named Mr Dick and his anxiously impotent efforts to get King Charles's head back up, and the 'gentlemanly' Betsey Trotwood, in repressed recoil from the drooling oralcy of her drunken husband, and her very specific judgement of men as 'weak'.

The clearest illustration of the novel's extraordinary record of the relations between class and sexuality, the immense power and delicacy of its knowledge of the *libido* and creativity as historical constructs with a set of mutual determinations witnessed by the ideological practices of *writing*, may be seen in the relations between David and Uriah Heep.

Steerforth's name suggests a set of abstract imperatives which David, as he is attracted by them, must overcome. Another surrogate brother, Ham, suggests a timidly undersexed source of productive labour to be denied while it is dignified and exploited. So both Ham and Steerforth die in a mutual embrace on the sloping social sands of Yarmouth beach that are contrasted so sharply by the sheer Dover cliffs from which David will take his final identity. Uriah Heep's name, both parts of it frankly excretory in suggestion – a paradoxical heap of piss challenging the discipline of the constipated Murdstone – hints also at a set (you–or–I) of undifferentiated, unconscious desires. Like Steerforth, his dangerous destructive energy is countenanced by an over-affectionate mother. It is at once David's blessing and burden that he has lost his own.

Both Uriah and David are adopted into the Wickfield *ménage* where they share an incestuous longing for their 'sister' Agnes. While their own sexuality is ambiguous, neither they nor we can be sure that it is not for each other. If Uriah vampires away Mr Wickfield's life blood, Agnes performs a similarly Poe-like operation on David's first wife Dora as she cunningly infiltrates the Copperfield household, nearly as disorderly as the Wickfield's.

Uriah and David watch each other, literally, through the pages of the text. The chapter in which Uriah appears is titled, with real significance, 'I Make Another Beginning'; the next chapter, 'I Am a New Boy in More Senses than One'. This is their first encounter.

> It so happened that this chair was opposite a narrow passage, which ended in the little circular room where I had seen Uriah Heep's pale face looking out of the window. Uriah, having taken the pony to the neighbouring stable, was at work at a desk in his room, which had a brass frame on the top to hang paper upon, and on which the writing he was making a copy of was then hanging. Though his face was towards me, I thought, for some time, the writing being between us, that he could not see me; but looking that way more attentively it made me uncomfortable to observe that, every now and then, his sleepless eyes would come below the writing, like two red suns, and stealthily stare at me for I dare say a whole minute at a time, during which his pen went, or pretended to go, as cleverly as ever. I made several attempts to get out of their way – such as standing on a chair to look at a map on the other side of the room, or poring over the columns of a Kentish newspaper – but they always attracted me back again; and whenever I looked towards those two red suns, I was sure to find them, either just rising or just setting.
>
> (ch. 15)

Towards the end of that passage David tries to objectify himself through those two quintessential agents of bourgeois political economy, a *map* and a *newspaper*. It is clear, however, that the intimacies are felt as too great, and even 'poring over the columns' is a curiously suggestive gesture. Enclosed in the 'little circular room' at the end of 'a narrow passage' – the site, in fact of a new *birth* – we/David are made conscious of Uriah's 'sleepless eyes ... below the writing'. This image looks forward to David's own later habit of writing on solitary, sleepless nights, and thus suggests Uriah as a co-creator as much as a joint creation in this 'new beginning'. Uriah, David, and the *reader* are caught on an impenetrable web of writing, *framed in suspense* for the outcome ('which had a brass frame on the top to hang paper upon'). All *three* observers *read* each other, but *underneath* the text itself, Uriah, as a copyist, resembles David's later manifestation as a shorthand writer at the law courts, transcribing, as here, an existing text. The plot of the novel hangs on the writing which divides the two ('rising and setting suns (sons)'), but through which they peer at each other under our *gaze* (gauze). It is a story of how each will try to complete their books or accounts to best effect. Micawber's exposure of Heep is based on his discovery of the rigged accounts that Heep has kept. The rights/rites/writing of passage are not granted to everyone. Already Uriah's technique, 'his pen went', anticipates the strange spontaneity of David's own. The qualification 'or pretended to go' raises more doubts about the authenticity of such activity than the passage itself can resolve, but in that sense is symptomatic of the novel's own dual status as both a life and a representation of one – a fictional pretence.

'Though his face was towards me, I thought, for some time, the writing being between us, he could not see me.' The attempt to achieve distance, separation *through* writing, simply seems to implicate the two more closely. Heep is a very proximate subtext and we should note the detail further on:

> But, seeing a light in the little round office, and immediately feeling myself attracted towards Uriah Heep, who had a sort of fascination for me, I went in there instead. I found Uriah reading a great fat book, with such demonstrative attention, that his lank forefinger followed up every line as he read, and made clammy tracks along the page (or so I fully believed) like a snail.

Stephen Marcus's study *The Other Victorians* (1966) has clearly indicated the source of the 'clammy tracks: left on *this* great fat book'. Heep's repulsive appearance results from the fact that he is, as one might say, a wanker. David's physical recoil from him, wanting later to run him through with, of all things, a 'red hot poker' (ch. 25), is in part a guilty disavowal of his own nocturnal activities, whether directed at Agnes or Uriah, or even the fear that Uriah's may be as directed as much at him as they are at Agnes.

Finally Uriah moves into David's old room at the Wickfield's (this after he has insinuated himself into spending an uneasy night on the floor of David's London room). When David hears this he blurts out, 'I wish I had the ordering of his dreams!' (ch. 35). There should be no more need to gloss this than the equally agonised ejaculation of Steerforth's, on the verge of seducing Little Em'ly, 'David, I wish to God I had had a judicious father these last twenty years!' (ch. 22).

It is the role of 'judicious father' which the buoyantly hetero-sexual Mr Micawber otherwise unaccountably assumes when he exposes and exorcises Uriah Heep.

I have already noted Dora's contribution to David's earlier writing career. She comes downstairs from her lonely bed to hold and sharpen his pens, while his flying fist races to fill the empty pages (ch. 44). It is creativity as dangerously and non-productively pleasurable from which David must be rescued. The relation with Agnes must be made fully conscious in order to guarantee a healthy fertility. She must be turned (a tight corner, this one) from sister to wife. Equally, the seductiveness of Little Em'ly, the more insidious appeal to the reader's pleasure (her name recalling the most seductive of all Dickens's earlier heroines, Little Nell, in that astonishing nexus of voyeuristic sex and commerce, *The Old Curiosity Shop*), must be replaced by a wise, mature relation between 'equals', in which *reader* and *writer* may properly and responsibly fertilise each other.

I have implicitly queried throughout the notion of uncovering the real/ideal structure of the novel. There is, however, a fairly straight-forward piece of improvised aesthetic balancing so characteristic of even the earliest novels. There are a number of older siblings against whom David must take his measure. One I have not yet mentioned, unsurprisingly adored by and adoring his mother, evap-orates at precisely the moment Uriah Heep appears and whom he in some sense anticipates. I mean Mr Augustus Mell, one of the *dé-classé* pupil teachers at Creakle's vicious Salem House. David hears him playing his flute, always badly it seems, in those shadowy night-time moments, when he feels his own pre-adolescent sexuality most intensely.

> When he had put up his things for the night he took out his flute, and blew at it until I almost thought he would gradually blow his whole being into the large hole at the top, and ooze away at the keys.
>
> (ch. 5)

The tragic artistic and personal aspirations of Mr Mell it is the purpose of *David Copperfield*, man and book, to deliver.

From *The Centennial Review*, 29 (1985), 328–52.

NOTES

[The opening words of Simon Edwards's essay offer an important key to its subject: it attempts 'a reading of *David Copperfield* in the context of English literary culture in the mid-nineteenth century'. What some readers might find confusing, at least initially, is the diffuseness of the essay, the way in which it deals with a great many authors and leaps from topic to topic. For example, the essay seems to deviate from Dickens into the issue of 'accounting in bourgeois society' as conceived by both economists and literary critics. The apparent eclectic nature of the essay is, however, something that is not unexpected or unfamiliar in criticism in a New Historicist or Cultural Materialist mould (see pp. 52–3 for an explanation of these terms), for such criticism seeks to establish connections between the patterns seen in literary texts and those seen in all other areas of life at the time, especially the economic life of the country. The particular focus of Edwards's essay is on the construction of the self in a bourgeois society, specifically the complex post-1848 world. The individualism of this period is distinct from the earlier excesses of romanticism; it is an individualism 'constrained by the appropriation of patriarchal authority and responsibility'. At the same time, there is a tension in the period between the need for control and discipline and more wayward impulses, waywardness that is reflected in the 'manic depressive' personality of Micawber, the many images of madness in the novel, and the intense focus on irregular sexual desires. Indeed, Edwards's essay, in its meandering construction, in its playful, punning manner and, more generally, in its refusal to conform to an orderly set of rules, is itself an illustration of this issue at the heart of the essay. At the end, however, Edwards brings together the issues of the self, bourgeois society, sex and class in a fascinating consideration of Uriah Heep's place in the novel. Ed.]

1. There is no space to discuss this aspect of the novel here. A pupil at Doctor Strong's Academy calculates that the dictionary Mr Dick is

helping to compile will be completed only after one thousand six hundred and forty-nine years: i.e. the exact date of the beheading of Charles I.

2. It was also, of course, Smith who elaborated the theory of the division of labour in his later work *The Wealth of Nations* (1776).

3. I am indebted to listening to and discussion with Steve Bamlett for some of these approaches to the poem.

4. For further discussion of this see an article by Terry Eagleton, 'Tennyson: Politics and Sexuality in *The Princess* and *In Memoriam*', *The Sociology of Literature: 1848* (Essex, 1978).

5. A full account of this process would need to consider the classic female autobiographical fiction of the period: Charlotte Brontë's *Villette* (1850) and Elizabeth Barrett Browning's *Aurora Leigh* (1856).

6. But Melville's novel was to go underground in the USA too.

7. A relatively healthy example of this may be Q. D. Leavis's chapter on the novel in F. R. and Q. D. Leavis's *Dickens the Novelist* (London, 1970). A more strained attempt to show just how well David behaves towards Dora is to be found in Geoffrey Thurley, *The Dickens Myth* (London, 1976).

8. G. Pearson, 'Towards a Reading of *Dombey and Son*', in Gabriel Josipovici (ed.), *The Modern English Novel* (London, 1976).

9. See, for example, the Preface to *Oliver Twist* (1839).

10. Karl Marx, *Capital*, vol. 1 (1867), tr. Ben Fowkes (London, 1976), p. 163.

11. The subjunctive *were* ('without which I were nothing') has an interesting role in this 'metaphysics of presence'. David is literally copulating with/in the supplement, in so far as his marriage to Agnes is consummated in the final dual-part number of the novel in its original serial form of publication.

3

The Man-of-Letters Hero: *David Copperfield* and the Professional Writer

MARY POOVEY

If the nineteenth-century subject was inscribed in and partially constituted by the discourses of medicine and law, then that subject was also less formally – but no less effectively – constructed by another cultural discourse – literature. The historical emergence of 'literature' as a distinct body of culturally valued texts belongs to the late eighteenth and early nineteenth centuries;[1] its social and ideological functions during this formative period were extremely complex, as were its relations to other emergent social institutions, such as literacy, the daily press, and public education.[2] In this chapter, I address only one facet of the ideological work literature performed in nineteenth-century England: I focus primarily on the way in which one writer, Charles Dickens, translated deep structural relations into a psychological narrative of individual development, which both provided individual readers with an imaginative image of what identity was and created a subject position that reproduced this kind of identity in the individual reader. My implicit argument here is that one effect of the 'literary' in this period was the textual construction of an individualist psychology; my explicit argument is that this process was part of the legitimation and depoliticisation of capitalist market and class relations, that the definition (and defence) of the English writer's social role was intimately involved in both, and that stabilising and mobilising a particular image of woman, the domestic sphere, and woman's work were critical to all three.

The reading I offer here of Dickens's *David Copperfield* is not an interpretation that a nineteenth-century audience would have been likely to devise – not least because the definitions and functions of 'interpretation' have undergone such changes in the last one hundred years. Instead of attempting to reproduce whatever *meaning* the text might have held for its first readers, I am describing a set of structural patterns and transformations that are written into the novel as the very conditions of its intelligibility. I am arguing, in other words, that in so far as these substitutions and transformations constitute the terms of the novel's narrative development, they define the operations by which the text produces meanings; in so far as these operations organise the reading of *David Copperfield*, they construct the reader as a particular kind of subject – a psychologised, classed, developmental individual – even if the reader is not conscious of this pattern and even if the reader interprets the meaning of the novel differently from other readers or not at all. Because the kind of subject the novel constructs and describes enjoys as one of its definitive characteristics the illusion of universality, the twentieth-century reader seems simply to replicate the Victorian reader. One of the things I argue in this chapter is that, even though the kind of subject we see being constructed here *is* the modern subject and therefore seems 'like us', this subject is *not* universal but historically specific. Our apparent likeness to this subject is, in fact, the effect of the very ideological operations I describe here, and this appearance of likeness has helped keep this subject's internal contradictions invisible. I also argue, however, that the contradictions inherent in this subject constitute the basis for the distance readers *can* achieve from it and for the post-structuralist interpretive techniques by which the historicity of this subject is becoming visible to an increasing number of readers.[3]

I

The kind of subject described and reproduced by *David Copperfield* is individualised, psychologised, and ahistorical; it is also gendered. In fact, (masculine) gender is the constitutive feature of this subject; identity here takes the form of a physical and emotional development in which the male subject tempers his sexual and emotional desires by the possibilities of the social world. This conceptualisation of the subject, then, also entails a specific model of desire. This desire is insatiable and potentially transgressive; it begins in the home as the condition of the individual's individuation and growth; it motivates his quest for self-realisation; and, ideally, it is stabilised and its transgressive potential neutralised in the safe harbour of marriage.[4]

Structurally, this model of desire depends on difference being a constitutive part of the self, for without some difference within the individual, there would be no impetus for movement and no basis for change. I have previously argued that this internal difference was the basis for both the 'free' exchange of labour and goods and the alienation contemporaries associated with the market economy. Here I extend that argument by suggesting that, by the mid-nineteenth century, the economic and political components of this internal difference – and, indeed, of this entire model of desire – had been masked by a vocabulary of emotional needs and sexual drives. Whereas in one vocabulary, the insatiable nature of this desire might be said to fuel the apparently limitless expandability of the market economy, in the other, the insatiable nature of desire might be said to motivate a search for the partner of one's dreams. And whereas in one vocabulary, transgression might be figured as class conflict, in the other it might take the form of falling in love with an inappropriate person.

By the end of this essay, I will have set out the traces of this displaced system of class and economic issues, but for now I focus on the terms the novel foregrounds – the terms of personal attachment, psychological development, and romantic love. The figure who is critical to David's development, in these terms, is David's mother, Clara Copperfield. Clara plays two, apparently contradictory, roles in David's quest to become the 'hero' of his own story. On the one hand, she incarnates what seems to the boy and, retrospectively, to the man to be perfect love. When, as narrator, David looks back 'into the blank of [his] infancy', Clara's image is there alongside David's first 'experience of [him] self'. The effect of this narration is to tie the boy's sense of himself inextricably to his sense of Clara so as to make the mother the ground of the boy's identity. 'We are playing in the winter twilight', writes David, as he re-creates his childhood self, 'dancing about the parlour. When my mother is out of breath and rests herself in an elbow-chair, I watch her winding her bright curls round her fingers, and straightening her waist, and nobody knows better than I do that she likes to look so well, and is proud of being so pretty.'[5]

On the other hand, Clara's prettiness and her vanity make her susceptible to the admiration of others beyond her young son. In so doing, Clara undermines David's vision of union and perfect love, for she soon brings home Mr Murdstone, the 'pa' who decisively ends David's childhood happiness. David's trip to the Peggottys' and his terms at Mr Creakle's school are therefore indirect effects of his mother's vanity, and when Clara dies and David is exiled to the bottling warehouse, the full significance of her self-absorption becomes clear. In Murdstones 'crazy old house', David is no longer a special child, valued for who he is, but just another cog in the labouring unit 'boys', the subordinate member of a crew in which everyone is simply an instance of the lowest common denominator, labour: 'All this work was my work', he writes of this 'degradation', 'and of the boys employed upon it I was one' (p. 143).

Clara Copperfield's contradictory roles are critical to the novel for two reasons. In the first place, the imaginary plenitude she seems to embody constitutes the ideal that David will strive to re-create throughout the novel, even though – or, rather, precisely because – it is the discrepancy between what Clara seems to offer and what she indirectly causes that provokes David to run away in search of the love and station he 'deserves'. Only the fact that Clara is not (just) what she seems to David to be, in other words, allows for his separation from her and for that gap within himself between the experiences and infatuations he suffers and the perfect love he imagines is 'evermore about to be'.[6] In the second place, that the union with Clara is so obviously a retrospective construction by the adult narrator points to the symbolic reworking necessary to transform woman into the idealised mother. If his mother is not (only) the ideal David imagines and desires, then she must be transformed into this figure – for only then can she orient and domesticate his desire, just as only separation from her can inaugurate it. Even though the difference within the woman constitutes the condition of possibility for the difference *of* and *in* David, this difference must be repressed for the idealised unity to exist at all. In *David Copperfield*, then, we see the construction of the ideal of unity at the site of the mother; this takes the form of a series of substitutions that exposes and punishes the mother's guilt without jeopardising the idealised woman she retrospectively becomes. That this structural and ideological rewriting of the mother is explicitly represented as the story of David's psychological maturation – his education in how to know his own heart and choose the proper partner – masks the extent to which his identity depends on the contradictions repressed by this symbolic work.

David's first adult attempt to re-create his relationship with his mother comes when he falls in love with Dora Spenlow. Dora is explicitly presented as another version of Clara Copperfield. Just as David's mother was a 'wax doll' who was proud of her prettiness (p. 3), so Dora is doll-like, 'diminutive' (p. 360), and harmlessly vain. Just as David's mother was a charming but inept housekeeper, so Dora's French education has given her grace but no practical knowledge or skill. The counterpart to these similarities is the likeness between David and his father. Like his father, David initially finds Dora's childlike aversion to life's practicalities attractive, and he imagines, as his father did, that he can teach his wife what she does not know. When David and Dora marry with nothing to support them but David's 'earnestness', however, David begins to see what neither he nor, presumably, his father recognised about Clara – that a childish woman imperils the domestic ideal she is supposed to incarnate and superintend. When the younger Copperfields fall prey to their servants' petty larceny and to the casual exploitation of tradesmen, it seems to be simply a manifestation of the emotional ruin David suffers. In such an environment, he must 'discipline' his desire so that his unhappiness will not trouble his pretty wife, just as he must squelch complaints about the servants, lest Dora realise how incompetent she is.

David may try to hide the emotional and financial cost of Dora's childishness from her, but he does not hide it from the reader. In fact, the way David masks his misery calls attention to other episodes in the novel that reveal what is really at risk in such domestic misdemeanours. The first two traces of this other story are the phrases that initially expose David's unhappiness. Annie Strong utters these phrases in chapter 45, which immediately follows the first depiction of David's domestic woes. Both phrases – 'the final mistaken impulse of an undisciplined heart' and 'unsuitability of mind and purpose' (pp. 611, 610) – refer explicitly to Annie's immature infatuation with Jack Maldon, from which she was 'saved' by Dr Strong's proposal of marriage. These phrases are also metonymically linked to earlier references to the Strongs, which, when read in relation to David's history, disclose an uncanny similarity between the Strong's troubled marriage and the idealised union between David's parents. In the first place, the Strongs' December–May marriage reproduces David's parents' marriage in the sense that the partners are 'not equally matched' in terms of class or age. Also, both marriages are motivated by a man's infatuation with a woman who wants out of an unpleasant situation (Annie's 'situation' is her emotional entanglement with Maldon; Clara's is her class position, which is reflected in her employment as a nursery maid). In the second place, Dr Strong, as a 'sheep for the shearers' (p. 220) and an unworldly, 'unprotected' man, is very like David's father, the man who named a house the 'Rookery' simply because, despite all contrary evidence, 'he liked to think that there were rooks about it' (p. 5). Dr Strong is also like David's father in leaving his property to his wife 'unconditionally'. In the Doctor's case, this trust is eventually corroborated by the fidelity Annie reveals in this scene; the entire issue of fidelity, however, is shadowed by the outcome of that earlier trust: it was because Mr Copperfield injudiciously trusted his wife to marry wisely if she married again that he placed no restrictions on his bequest to her and therefore made no independent provision for his son.

These explicit connections between the Strongs and David's parents underscore the implicit link between Annie Strong and Clara Copperfield. The significance of this link emerges when David first glimpses what Mr Wickfield (and the narrator) have repeatedly insinuated – that Annie's affection for Jack Maldon might not be as innocent as it seems. Suddenly recalling the moment when Maldon left for India, David describes his awakening doubts.

> And now, I must confess, the recollection of what I had seen on that night when Mr Maldon went away, first began to return to me with a meaning it had never had, and to trouble me. … I cannot say what an impression this made upon me, or how impossible I found it, when I thought of [Annie] afterwards, to separate her from this look, and remember her face in its innocent loveliness again. It haunted me when I got home. I seemed to have left the Doctor's roof with a dark cloud lowering on it. The reverence that I had for his grey head, was mingled with commiseration for his faith in those who were treacherous to him, and with resentment against those who injured him. The impending shadow of a great affliction, and a disgrace that had no distinct form in it yet, fell like a stain upon the quiet place where I had worked and played as a boy; and did it a cruel wrong. … It was as if the tranquil sanctuary of my boyhood had been sacked before my face, and its peace and honour given to the winds.
>
> (p. 260)

The real victim of this 'stain' is David; the spectre of Annie's unworthiness makes it impossible for him to seek imaginative comfort in an unsullied 'sanctuary' of the past. But the phrases David uses to describe this past – 'the quiet place where I had worked and played as a boy', 'the tranquil sanctuary of my boyhood' – are phrases that refer not only to David's school days in Canterbury, but also to his childhood in Blunderstone. This image of a pretty young woman susceptible to the flattery of a dashing man (if not explicitly sexually aggressive) is a displaced version of the mother whose vanity betrayed both David's father's unworldly trust and the boy's unsuspecting love. Knowledge of the possibility that what seems like innocent prettiness and pride might actually signify (or be susceptible to) sexual desire is the 'stain' that David refers to here. That this 'stain' interrupts the story of David's first marriage suggests that it forms one of the repressed links between Clara and Dora, the two women whose domestic incompetence seems an innocent extension of their vanity and youth. Neither Clara nor Dora, however, is explicitly figured as a sexual woman, nor is their household mismanagement explicitly linked to sexual infidelity. Instead, the link between vanity, domestic misery, and sexual infidelity emerges in relation to another female character – David's childhood sweetheart, Little Emily.

When David (and, following him, almost every reader) refers Annie Strong's comment about 'the first mistaken impulse of [an] undisciplined heart' to his love for Dora, he obscures the other, and in some ways more obvious, emotion to which this phrase applies – his love for the fisherman's daughter, Little Emily. Dora may call herself David's 'child-wife', but Emily is as literally the 'child' of this compound phrase as Dora is the 'wife'. Of his youthful adoration of Emily, David comments: 'Of course I was in love with Little Em'ly. ... I am sure my fancy raised up something round that blue-eyed mite of a child, which etherealised, and made a very angel of her' (p. 34). It is this 'etherealisation' to which Rosa Dartle refers in the episode about Emily that appears in chapter 46. 'This devil whom you make an angel of', Rosa sneers, 'I mean this low girl whom he [Steerforth] picked out of the tide-mud ... may be alive, – for I believe some common things are hard to die' (p. 621). Whether men like David simply 'rais[e] up' 'devils' into 'angels' when they fall in love is exactly the point; for the problematic role Emily plays in David's maturation suggests that she – and through her, all the women in the novel – is as threatening as she is affirming to a man's adult identity.

David greets Rosa Dartle's 'vaunting cruelty' with a 'kind' wish that echoes another, similarly punitive fantasy. 'To wish [Emily] dead', he half-mocks Rosa, 'may be the kindest wish that one of her own sex could bestow upon her' (p. 616). In the episode to which this sentence alludes, the passage in chapter 3 where Emily is introduced, young David watches helplessly as Emily darts onto a 'jagged timber' that overhangs the sea. David's reaction to the girl's rashness explicitly belongs to the older narrator, not to the boy, and his comment develops the idea of the 'stain' to which I have already referred.

> The light, bold, fluttering little figure turned and came back safe to me, and I soon laughed at my fears. ... But there have been times since, in my manhood, many times there have been, when I have thought, is it possible, among the possibilities of hidden things, that in the sudden rashness of the child and her wild look so far off, there was any merciful attraction of her into danger, any tempting her towards him permitted on the part of her dead father, that her life might have a chance of ending that day. There has been a time since when I have wondered whether, if the life before her could have been revealed to me at a glance, and so revealed as that a child could fully comprehend it, and if her preservation could have depended on a motion of my hand, I ought to have held it up to save her. There has been a time since – I do not say it lasted long, but it has been – when I have asked myself the question, would it have been better for little Em'ly to have had the waters close above her head that morning in my sight; and when I have answered Yes, it would have been.
>
> (pp. 33–4)

The judgement implied by the phrase the 'merciful attraction of her into danger' is here projected by the adult narrator onto Emily's dead father; it will later be repeated by Ham Peggotty as well (p. 415). What crime does this 'blue-eyed mite' commit to merit such punitive 'mercy'? Emily's obvious fall, of course, is to Steerforth: in eloping with him she betrays not only her fiancé, Ham, but, perhaps more critically, her surrogate father, Peggotty. But I want to suggest that this transgression is really only the logical extension of other transgressions, crimes of which Emily is guilty even before Steerforth hurries her into his carriage. Only the persistence of these more recondite transgressions can account for the fact that the narrative's treatment of Emily is so much more punitive than is its treatment of the woman who presumably actually becomes a prostitute, Martha. Emily's punishment is multifaceted and extreme: she is almost completely exiled from the novel after her fall (unlike Martha, whose sexual error is the basis for her role in the novel); she is subjected to Rosa Dartle's vicious verbal scarification, of which both David and the reader are horrified observers (while Martha is forgiven and comforted first by Emily herself, then by Mr Peggotty and David); and she is denied marriage, even in Australia (as Martha is not). Such elaborate punishment suggests not only that her crimes exceed Martha's, but also that after her transgression her mere presence would contaminate the narrative of David's life.[7]

From one perspective, Emily's punishment follows from the position she occupies in David's maturation; from another, it can be seen as an inextricable part of Dickens's representation of sexuality. In David's history, Emily is the first substitute for David's mother, and she seems to offer the boy his best chance to recapture the imaginary plenitude he associates with his mother: 'What happiness', David thinks of his childhood courtship, 'if we were married, and were going away anywhere to live among the trees and in the fields, never growing older, never growing wiser, children ever' (p. 136). But Emily also stands at the threshold that irrevocably bars access to this innocence, for David's first enchanted visit to Emily makes him feel 'ungrateful' in forgetting his mother and his home. He returns to Blunderstone to find that his mother has been as unfaithful to him as he has been to her, that she is married and his no more.

That Emily is intimately connected both to David's fantasies of a childish 'marriage' and to his fears about his own and his mother's infidelity points to the way the novel implicates women in its complex and ambiguous representation of sexuality. Because Emily stands for both innocence and sexuality, she precipitates the contradictory effects of both. On the one hand, her initial innocence promises both pleasure and death: David's vision of his Edenic marriage to Emily ends with the two children 'laying down our heads on moss at night, in a sweet sleep of purity and peace, and buried by the birds when we were dead' (p. 136). On the other hand, the sexual response she provokes in David on his second visit to Yarmouth excites the boy but leaves him frustrated, confused, and angry as well. The more Emily 'captivate[s]' David, the more elusive she seems: 'she seemed to have got a great distance away from me', David comments ruefully, 'in little more than a year' (p. 133).

The way David's relationship with Emily is narrated – with the fact of sexuality a secret shared by the adult narrator and the reader

– effaces any connection between young David and sexual knowledge. Even though David's maturation is implicit in his responses to Emily, the narrative assigns to woman – in this case, Emily – responsibility for the 'stain' of sexual provocation, even though the extent to which Emily is conscious of her sexuality is left unclear. In *David Copperfield*, then, woman is the site at which sexuality becomes visible: not only does her provocation make men conscious of their own sexuality, but her vanity and wilfulness show that no man can be sure of securing her affections. In *David Copperfield*, as in the medical texts I have already examined, woman is made to bear the burden of sexuality and to be the site of sexual guilt because the problematic aspects of sexuality can be rhetorically (if not actually) mastered when they are externalised and figured in an other. In Dickens's novel, this mastery entails both the punitive exile whereby Emily's sexuality is 'cured' and the symbolic substitutions of less explicitly sexual women for ones who are more closely linked to sexuality.

Even though Emily's sexual transgression can be punished and 'cured', however, she also poses another, more indirect threat to the identity of the hero – a threat that will ultimately prove resistant even to such elaborate narrative treatment. Specifically, the possibility that David's childhood infatuation with Emily might mature into love introduces into the rhetoric of affection the spectre of class. Class difference exists as a threat in *David Copperfield* because 'innocence' in this novel entails not only sexual ignorance, but also the indifference to class distinctions that enables David to befriend and bring together 'chuckle-headed' Ham Peggotty and the well-born Steerforth. For reasons I discuss in the third section of this essay, such indifference to class is as crucial to David's heroism as is his boyish 'freshness', and one important sign of this is precisely David's affection for Emily, the fisherman's daughter. One promise of the liberal rhetoric of Victorian individualism was that every individual had the 'right' to follow the heart; according to this logic, class difference should not stand between David and Emily. And yet other incidents in the novel suggest that a sexual relationship between the two could only lead to harm: if he seduced but did not marry her, it would ruin David's honour; if he made Emily his wife, it would exclude David from the social position he 'deserves'. Both of these possibilities are made explicit in the representation of Steerforth, the character who takes over the infatuation from which David professes to have recovered. Steerforth brings dishonour on himself by seducing Emily, but, as his mother suggests, marriage might have been worse: 'Such a marriage', Mrs Steerforth informs Mr Peggotty, 'would irretrievably blight my son's career, and ruin his prospects' (p. 431). Steerforth's presence in the novel enables Dickens to levy this admonitory lesson without contaminating David's 'freshness' by an overly self-protective consciousness of class. Through Steerforth, Dickens has it both ways: on the one hand, in carrying out an infatuation initially associated with David, Steerforth acts out the complex of desire and punitive anger of which hostility toward sexuality is the cause and Emily the object; on the other hand, in actually doing what David will not do, Steerforth underscores David's honourable innocence.

As a nursery maid, of course, David's mother posed precisely the same threat to David's father that Emily does to David, just as David's father's indifference to class marked him as another 'fresh' and romantic young man. The 'blight' Clara Copperfield confers, however, falls not so much on her husband as on her son; as I have already argued, Clara Copperfield is indirectly to blame for David's being sent to the bottling warehouse, that degradation that momentarily threatens to 'blight [his] ... career, and ruin his prospects'. In *David Copperfield*, the 'stain' that seems to be a function simply of sexual knowledge is actually this 'blight': the possibility not just that innocence might grow into knowledge but that a desire conceptualised as sexual and irrational might be oblivious to class distinctions. In terms of the ideological operations of the novel, this possibility proves to be even more intractable than the 'simple' problem of sexuality, for too much attention to class rather than feeling smacks of callous self-interest just as too little threatens dishonour or ruin. To protect his hero from both of these disastrous fates, Dickens simply effaces this unresolvable dilemma: Ham and Steerforth intercede between David and Emily, and the problem of sexuality is transferred from the arena of class relations onto the figure of woman, where it can be symbolically addressed in the substitutions I have been describing. The symbolic 'solution' the novel offers to both the explicit problem of sexual knowledge and the implicit problem of the way in which desire can cross class lines is Agnes.

In repeating the 'angelic' qualities David associates with Clara Copperfield, Agnes preserves what is best about David's mother, but, because she is not vain, she 'cancels' the faults of the mother more completely than Emily, Annie Strong, or Dora can. Because

Agnes's love involves self-discipline rather than self-indulgence, she incarnates fidelity and is therefore proof against the kinds of temptation that drew poor Clara into that disastrous second marriage, Annie Strong to Jack Maldon, and Emily to Steerforth. David's turn to Agnes does not 'stain' him because he never has to see in her sexuality that exceeds or strays from her relation to him, and his love for her does not 'blight' his prospects because she brings to David the dowry of her middle-class virtue and efficient housekeeping skills. Transferring David's affection from his mother to Emily to Dora to Agnes thus works through the constellation of desire, anger, and anxiety structurally associated with but narratively distanced from the mother. By means of these substitutions, Dickens splits off and leaves behind the contradiction written into the mother that threatened to subvert the boy's happiness and to undermine the home. Emily and, to a lesser extent, Annie Strong and Dora carry the pernicious effects of female vanity with them as they disappear from the novel. In Dickens's final representations of Agnes she might as well be David's mother, so perfectly does she make him what he is. 'Clasped in my embrace', David exults to the reader, 'I held the source of every worthy aspiration I had ever had; the centre of myself, the circle of my life, my own, my wife.' 'What I am', David cries, 'you have made me, Agnes' (p. 802).

Because the process I have been describing is represented as a series of ever more judicious choices made by a maturing hero, the imaginative work carried out on the various incarnations of woman is subsumed by the effect it creates – that of (male) 'psychology' and development. That this effect is literally the work of the (male) novelist and not a mimetic description of either an emotional development or the power of a woman's influence is underscored by the fact that David Copperfield has become a professional writer by the time he chooses Agnes; even at the level of the novel's fictive world, the extraordinary image that inscribes Agnes as both the centre and circumference of David's identity is itself contained within the autobiographical narrative that Copperfield has written (which is, in turn, contained within Dickens's autobiographical novel). This narrative division of labour, whereby the (male) novelist's responsibility for his own self-creation is transferred to the woman he also creates but claims to describe, repeats the process by which contaminating sexuality is rhetorically controlled by being projected onto the woman. I return in a moment to the ramifications of this division. For now, I look briefly at the representation of writing that permits this work to remain almost invisible and therefore effective.

In marked contrast to his other representations of work in this novel, Dickens's references to David's writing are all euphemistic or nonchalant. Whereas David's work in the bottling warehouse was concretely detailed and his various jobs in Doctors' Commons, Dr Strong's study, and Parliament were metaphorically figured, the work involved in writing is explicitly effaced. When David becomes a writer, he advises the reader that he will not discuss his work. Expect only references to his 'earnestness', he tells the reader, not to 'the aspirations, the delights, anxieties, and triumphs of [his] art' (p. 783). The one time David's aunt asks about the labour involved in writing, David brushes the question aside: 'It's work enough to read sometimes. ... As to the writing, it has its own charms' (p. 797).

The closest equivalent to this representation of work is Agnes's description of teaching in her 'school': 'The labour is so pleasant', she explains, 'that it is scarcely grateful in me to call it by that name' (p. 779). Agnes's other work does not receive even this much narrative elaboration; despite numerous references to Agnes as her father's housekeeper, whatever domestic tasks she performs or oversees are signified only by her basket of keys. That these keys stand for actual labour is suggested only indirectly – by Dickens's comic rendition of Dora's domestic blunders. In both his representations of David's writing and Agnes's housekeeping, in other words, Dickens displaces the material details and the emotional strain of labour onto other episodes – thereby conveying the twin impressions that some kinds of work are less 'degrading' and less alienating than others and that some labourers are so selfless and skilled that to them work is simultaneously an expression of self and a gift to others.

The narrative transformation of Clara into Agnes functions not only to 'solve' the problem of sexuality and to cover over the problem of class, but also, and as an integral part of these effects, to construct the domestic sphere as an arena where work is performed as selflessly and effortlessly as love is given. This construction proceeds alongside of the other kind of labour that is effaced in the novel, the work of writing. The two images – of effortless housekeeping and effortless writing – are interdependent at every level: not only is the Copperfields' domestic security a function of David's material success as a writer, not only does his success as a writer (as he describes it) depend on the selflessness Agnes's example inspires, but the representation of the domestic sphere as immune to the alienation of work is produced by the very writing with which it is compared. To work through the causes and effects of this complex interdependence and to explain the relationship between these representations and David's psychological maturation, I turn for a moment to the mid-nineteenth-century discussion in which this novel participated – the discussion about what role a literary man might play in a society where most work was neither effortless nor hidden and the 'hero' was a figure everywhere under siege.

II

[At this point in her argument, Mary Poovey considers the ways in which writers around 1850 struggled to define their place in Britain's increasingly secular, capitalist society. Were they sages, with a unique contribution to make, or were they just the same as other workers, cogs in a commercial system, in this case the system of publishing? Serial publication of novels, for example, drew attention to the writer as 'labourer', who was required to produce 32 pages a month to order. The fuller implications of this are seen when Poovey suggests that writing was the site at which the broadest instabilities implicit in the capitalist system surfaced: 'Because it was conceptualised simultaneously as superior to the capitalist economy and as hopelessly embroiled within it, literary work was the work par excellence that denied *and* exemplified the alienation written into capitalist work.' The authors themselves, as we might expect, promoted authorship as an individualistic activity, resisting, for example, the impulse, common at the time (notably amongst medical men), to form a professional body. Yet the stress on competition, even free trade, in writing is misleading, for then 'as now, what counted as "publishable literature" was at least partly a function of class'. Indeed, what linked writers was how much they had in common, by virtue of belonging to the same class and being like the other men with whom they were free to compete. This leads to a central proposition in Poovey's argument about the structure of individualism in class society: this is the paradox 'whereby (class) difference is represented as (human) likeness, and this likeness becomes the ground of one's unique identity'.

As Poovey notes, what this means in effect is that Victorian writers were regarded as unique, yet were acclaimed for appealing to all readers – in other words, for being like everybody else. Dickens, in particular, was seen as establishing a 'common ground of humanity'. A further complication, however, is that this 'humanity' was not actually 'common' but specifically English. The writer was a definer and celebrator of national identity, whose work was 'to make all Englishmen like each other – or, more precisely, like the literary man'. The process of exclusion involved here is relatively clear: the middle-class male was constructed as the norm, the values and behaviour of other classes and women were aberrant (and must be aberrant because they failed to conform to the sense the writer had established of national identity, of English character traits). The Victorian period fostered an idea of opportunities for all, but this rhetoric of individualism depended upon not just a sense of middle-class male norms but also the denial of any tenable alternative class or gender values. The woman's role was thus simply defined as a supporting one; she was the faithful partner upholding the patriarchal identity of the family, and providing a domestic, and sexual, anchor for her husband (without curtailing his economic ambition). Such fidelity was necessary to enable other institutions to work. As we approach the end of *David Copperfield* it is, therefore, entirely fitting that David's assumption of the role of professional writer should be accompanied by his finding a faithful partner in Agnes.

At this point, having established a sense of the ideological implications of Victorian individualism, Poovey turns from her examination of what was being established as normative to look at the ways in which the novel also exposes the troubling ramifications of the individualist rhetoric of the period; in particular, as we see in the following pages, she looks at the class issue, specifically as articulated in the character of Uriah Heep. Ed.]

III

Despite both the extensive narrative work performed upon the representation of woman in *David Copperfield* and the less prominent but no less essential rewriting of David's work, Dickens's novel does not completely efface the contradictions these representations repress. For reasons I now explore, the site at which the traces of class issues return is Uriah Heep – or, more specifically, Heep's proximity to the novel's exemplary heroine and hero, Agnes and David Copperfield.

Heep's proximity to Agnes and to David is, in the first instance at least, physical. As her father's articled clerk, Uriah Heep spends most of his time in Agnes's house, and from this association grow both Heep's designs on Agnes and his entanglement in her father's business affairs. David's first introduction to Heep is marked by an even more startling physical image, the handshake that both 'attract[s]' David to the red-eyed clerk and leaves him trying to rub Heep from his skin. But despite the fact that Heep's desire to marry Agnes yokes a particularly revolting image to the picture of Heep's clammy hands and writhing body, the physical chill that Heep's bony fingers exude metonymically stands for a much more degrading contamination: the moral corruption Heep's manipulations insinuate – first into Wickfield's financial dealings, then into Mr Micawber's honesty and self-respect. Through their complicity with Heep, even these good characters lose their moral integrity; once in Heep's power, the good man betrays another's 'trust' (as Wickfield does), for he feels (as does Micawber) that he harbours an enemy within. 'My heart is no longer in the right place', Micawber mourns as he sinks into complicity with Heep. 'The canker is in the flower' (p. 648).

Uriah Heep, again to quote Micawber, is an 'interminable cheat, and liar', a 'transcendent and immortal hypocrite and perjurer' (p. 658). He is, in short, duplicitous: he shows one false, obsequious smile and hides his snivelling smirk of ambition, hatred, and greed. Not until Micawber explodes Heep's nefarious plot does the reader know what Heep's machinations and motivations have been, even though their effects have reverberated throughout the actions we see. In this, as in almost every other sense, Heep seems to stand as David Copperfield's opposite: whereas Heep's schemes are hidden, David's actions and self-commentary are always present to the reader; whereas Heep is false, David is true both to himself and to the reader. The sign of David's truthfulness is the honesty with which he discloses even the embarrassments of his youth – his drunkenness, his boyish love, and the galling memory of his disappointment with Dora.

Yet the contamination of that first touch lingers, and its corrosive effect becomes visible when David strikes Heep to punish him for his pretensions to Agnes. This blow draws David into odious complicity with Heep, both because Heep's revelation makes David the guardian of his trust and because Heep's pretensions are no more audacious than David's own. This blow is the mark of David's

likeness to Heep: not only do the two characters share some relatively superficial traits – intense filial attachment, for example, and
some experience of being dependent on others' charity – but they
also have in common the more sinister tendency to manipulate
others for their own self-serving ends. Here, in fact, their relative
positions in relation to honesty seem reversed, for whereas Heep's
connivances are eventually clearly revealed, David's manipulations
remain obscure. Only when the reader reads against the narrator's
disarming claims do certain actions appear as what they are: self-
aggrandising attempts to better himself at someone else's expense.
When David exposes Mr Mell's old mother at Mr Creakle's school,
for example, and when he introduces Emily to Steerforth, David is
using other people to win respect for himself.

At least once, David acknowledges his 'unconscious part' in what
comes of Steerforth's acquaintance with Emily (even calling it 'the
desolation I had caused', p. 418). But for the most part, David's
role in such plots is revealed to the reader not by David but by
Uriah Heep. It is David's 'unconscious part', for example, that
Heep fingers when he accuses him of having been 'the first to kindle
the sparks of ambition in [Heep's] umble breast' by suggesting that
Heep might someday be a partner in Mr Wickfield's business
(pp. 348, 216). Heep exposes this 'part' again when he tells the
Doctor that David harbours suspicions about Annie Strong, thereby
shaking the old man's confidence in his wife and his own innocent
trust. This, then, constitutes Heep's real threat in the moral scheme
of the novel – not that he is fundamentally different from David
Copperfield, but that he is, in some important respects, the same.
To the extent that he is the same, Heep speaks for Copperfield;
Heep is David's 'unconscious part'. In this sense, the homoeroti-
cism mobilised by the physical contacts between Heep and
Copperfield further blurs the boundary between them. Just as
Heep's machinations conflate sexual and economic motives in his
ambition to cross class boundaries, so the uncertainty of his sexuality exposes in David a responsiveness he cannot control – a responsiveness not only to another man's touch, but also to his ambition
and moral ambiguity.

Despite these similarities, however, the crucial – and apparently
morally decisive – difference between David's self-serving acts and
Heep's manipulations is that the former are unconscious. Whereas
Heep sets out to use and hurt others, David's transgressions are,
for the most part, unwitting indiscretions. David is immune even to

the moral blight that contaminates Wickfield and Micawber because David does not know what he is doing or even what he has done. In emphasising this distinction between Heep and Copperfield, the novel symbolically reverses the paradox of individualism, whereby likeness covers over difference. In his representation of Heep and Copperfield, Dickens invokes the self-evident fact that people *are* (psychologically) different; some individuals *are* mean and self-serving, while others are generous and good. But in the world of the novel, this difference proves unstable. The sign that there is some difficulty with difference is the contradiction inherent in the narrative device necessary to create its effect – the autobiographical narration.

Given the autobiographical narrative of *David Copperfield*, the effect of a difference between Heep and Copperfield depends on there being a difference between the narrator-David and the character-David. The narrator must know Heep's evil as he retrospectively narrates David's life, even though the young David remains innocent of this knowledge. But while this effect merely capitalises on the paradigm of development and change, the narration of David's self-serving actions as something other than what they can retrospectively be read to be depends on even the adult narrator not fully knowing what he says or being responsible for what he has done; it depends, in other words, on the narrator and the character being in some fundamental sense the same, even if their obvious difference hides this. Structurally, in fact, the young David Copperfield and the narrator are simultaneously the same and different – just as, in another sense, Copperfield and Heep are both alike and different. And it is the internal complexity in the first pair that transforms the unstable combination Heep–Copperfield into an apparently stable binary opposition.

Yet this complexity seems ominously like duplicity when we come to the matter of David's role in Annie Strong's exposure or Little Emily's fall. The duplicity is masked (and exposed) by the narrator's attempts to distract the reader's attention from young David's actions through misrepresentations so harmless or slight that they almost pass unnoticed. Immediately after David begins to suspect Annie Strong (p. 260), for example, he insists that he feels 'dreadfully young' (p. 262), that he is 'painfully conscious of [his] youth' (p. 262), that he feels 'younger than [he] could have wished' (p. 267; see also pp. 276, 277, 283). The actual occasion of this embarrassment is simply David's first attempt to assert himself as an adult, a difficulty exacerbated by David's reunion with the older and more sophisticated Steerforth. But the fact that these statements occur when they do has the additional effect of distancing from the character the knowledge with which David has just been 'stained' and therefore of reinforcing the innocence that contributes to make David's part in Emily's fate 'unconscious'. In other words, having acknowledged enough imaginative familiarity with illicit sexual desire to feel it as a 'stain', the character downplays that familiarity and therefore the responsibility that might be assumed to follow from it.

In a sense, here as elsewhere, David is protecting himself with silence, just as Miss Mowcher protects herself by silently colluding with her customers. But this 'self-protection' is possible only because the 'hero' of the novel is split into two parts. The narrative persona protects that part of his 'self' that is figured as the character by shielding him from both contaminating knowledge and the judgement of irony. The effects of this division are to split agency from knowledge in such a way as to detach responsibility from action, to deny intention, and to defer responsibility so that self-serving means never show themselves as what they are. By the end of the nineteenth century, this division would be reified and the 'other' of the self dignified as the unconscious; in Dickens's novel, however, the rudimentary notion of some 'unconscious part' cannot account for or accommodate the difference within David. In fact, these differences do not even remain within David but reappear outside him – as if the entire landscape of the novel were a series of mirrors, each of which reflects some 'unconscious part' of David Copperfield. Thus Heep is David's selfishness, Steerforth his feckless sexuality, and Micawber his foolishness.

What we have in *David Copperfield*, then, is a novel in which the identity of the 'hero' is never completely stabilised or fully individuated because the main character is split and distributed among so many other characters and parts. Given Dickens's presentation of sexuality, and Little Emily in particular, this split may *seem* to be a function of sexual knowledge and of female sexuality in particular. But as I have already argued, this representation of sexuality is itself an *effect*, not a cause, of something else – specifically, it is an effect of the deployment and denial of the structure of the individual in class society. The irrepressible cause of this character's fragmentation, as the issues that Heep brings into the novel reveal, is the difference built into the individual in this society – a difference that readily becomes hypocrisy when it is engaged in the hierarchy of class. This effect of class society is revealed by the duplicitous Uriah Heep, the character who emerges, fittingly, as the novel's conscience, the figure whose effects the narrator cannot contain.

When Micawber and Traddles 'explode' Uriah Heep, the snivelling clerk retaliates with a vicious attack on his assailants. David describes this outburst as cowardice, but Heep's words cut uncomfortably close to the collective bone. To David's bland platitude – 'there never were greed and cunning in the world yet, that did not do too much, and overreach themselves. It is as certain as death' – Heep responds,

> Or as certain as they used to teach at school (the same school where I picked up so much umbleness), from nine o'clock to eleven, that labour was a curse; and from eleven o'clock to one, that it was a blessing and a cheerfulness, and a dignity, and I don't know what all, eh?. ... You preach, about as consistent as they did. Won't umbleness go down? I shouldn't have got round my gentleman fellow-partner without it, I think.
>
> (p. 704)

In this passage, Heep reveals the two lessons the narrative otherwise conceals. The first is that hypocrisy is built into the individualist rhetoric of class society. The second is that David is complicitous with this society in the very morality he espouses and the success he enjoys. The same society that dispenses guilt to contain (working-class) ambition goads all men to work by calling it 'a dignity' and 'a blessing'. But Heep's rhetorical 'I don't know what all' points to the carrot that the stick of guilt holds out – the promise, unspoken here but everywhere evident in the novel, that material success will reward labour, that one will receive one's 'blessing' on earth. The same society that offers this blessing to everyone, however, sets limits to the achievements of all but a few. The same society that rewards the self-made David Copperfield punishes the self-made Uriah Heep. The same society that proclaims the likeness of all humans institutes class difference and calls it moral character.

That Heep's hypocrisy simply reproduces the duplicity that is built into class society is driven home to the reader by David's visit to Mr Creakle's Middlesex prison. In the prison (as was not true in Mr Creakle's school), everything reveals itself simultaneously as what it is and what it pretends to be. Individualism is perfected in the form of solitary confinement, which is represented as equality and justice. Heep's hypocrisy serves his own interests, even though it is lauded as wisdom. In the prison Heep is the 'Model Prisoner'; as such, he can tell the visiting 'gentlemen' the truth that David did not want to hear. Heep's words smack of rank hypocrisy, but they simply reproduce the hypocrisy society both produces and rewards. 'I should wish', Heep piously declares, in a revealing parody of filial concern, 'I should wish mother to be got into my state. I never should have been got into my present state if I hadn't come here. I wish mother had come here. It would be better for everybody, if they got took up, and was brought here' (p. 792).

Even though David Copperfield dismisses Heep's 'profession' as a 'rotten, hollow, painfully suggestive piece of business', neither he nor the reader can so easily leave behind the system that inculcates and rewards hypocrisy. Or, more precisely, the reader cannot leave this system behind because its duplicity is inscribed in the very narrative device that attempts to deny it – the splitting of the protagonist into an innocent hero, who does not know such deceitfulness because he is too young and good, and a worldly narrator, who knows but will not tell. When *David Copperfield* simply relegates the prison episode to the marginal position of 'social commentary', the novel perpetuates the hypocrisy it seems to deny. The operative difference among the characters – the difference of class – is repressed (but not erased) by the vocabulary of emotion and development that subordinates class difference to the individual's upbringing and his personal, moral growth.

The possibility of David's not knowing – even provisionally – the extent to which class difference is institutionalised alongside – and as part of – alienation and psychological complexity as the very conditions of the individual in the society Dickens describes depends on there being some alternative to the deceit, self-interest, and hypocrisy that otherwise seem the very stuff of society itself. The possibility that David's innocence, the difference between Copperfield and Heep, and the happy ending of the novel will be believable, in other words, depends on Dickens constructing as part of his representation of this society his vision of Agnes's home. Only if class difference is first psychologised as an inherent difference in moral character and then projected outward as the difference (of sexuality) among or within women can it be (symbolically) 'treated' and 'cured' in the process I have described. Only if woman can be so 'cured' can a sphere exist that is outside and different from the sphere of market relations. Only then will there be a place in which the (male) individual's desire can be produced as an acquisitive drive and then domesticated as its economic aggression is rewritten as love.

If Agnes and the home implicitly collude in covering over the hypocrisy and alienation that pervade class society, then so does the literary man. In fact, the literary man derives the terms of his ideological work from the idealised vision of domestic labour epitomised in Agnes. Like a good housekeeper, the good writer works invisibly, quietly, without calling attention to his labour; both master dirt and misery by putting things in their proper places; both create a sphere to which one can retreat – a literal or imaginative hearth where anxiety and competition subside, where one's motives do not appear as something other than what they are because self-interest and self-denial really are the same. But even though they seem to provide an alternative to the alienation endemic to class society, the creation and maintenance of the domestic sphere and the work of the literary man actually reproduce the very society from which they seem to offer escape: in creating the illusion of equality on which the false promises of capitalism depend, both contribute to (and depend on) a rhetoric of individualism and likeness that hides the facts of class difference and alienated labour. Indeed, both produce the illusion that class society *could* end and alienation *could* be overcome through their efforts to make others like themselves and work a selfless act. Because of the middle-class woman's influence, the working-class servant could be encouraged to aspire to bourgeois virtues; by the writer's pen, the English 'national character' could be presented as what it should be – domestic and middle class; by the exemplary exception of literary labour, all workers could imagine that some kinds of work lay outside the inexorable logic of market relations, even if they were not so lucky in their own work-a-day lives.

That this ideological work was performed at midcentury upon the two sites of the woman and the literary man points to the critical – and highly problematic – position these two figures occupied in Victorian society. On the one hand, representations of the woman and the literary man could disguise the inequities and hypocrisies of class society because these figures carried the symbolic authority of moral superiority in a society everywhere else visibly permeated by self-interest and exploitation. On the other hand, the extent of symbolic work necessary to deploy these figures as markers of morality revealed that they were not really outside of the market economy or class society. The effort necessary to construct and maintain the separate spheres of the home and literary labour reveals itself in its failure: the reappearance elsewhere of what has had to be displaced – the 'stain' of sexuality, the 'blight' of class, the 'degradation' of work.

IV

I conclude this essay by addressing specifically but briefly two ramifications of the argument I have been presenting. The first concerns the place of 'imaginative' texts like *David Copperfield* in the production and reproduction of ideology. For literary critics, this is a particularly vexed and volatile issue, because one source of the 'value' of our work has been held to be literature's unique immunity to ideology, politics, and power. Even many critics who have not argued that literature articulates universal values have maintained that literature can expose the operations of power in or even to a society otherwise mystified or blind, that literature tells truths other discourses can or do not. I have two responses to this position. One is to argue that this formulation of the position and effect of literature is itself both historically specific and ideological. To maintain that literature resists ideology is to cover over its participation in and dependence on the kinds of commercial relations I have been discussing here, not to mention its coercive reproduction of likeness (a 'national character', 'universal' values, shared kinds and degrees of access to print) and its obliteration of (class and gender) differences. 'Literature' cannot exist outside a system of social and institutional relations, and in a society characterised by systemic class and gender inequality, literature reproduces the system that makes it what it is. In resurrecting some of the issues raised in the debates about the social role of literary men at midcentury I have tried to remind readers that *David Copperfield* reproduced the rhetoric and representations of class and gender that covered over the writer's problematic place in the market economy and the proprietary form of the subject. By restoring to visibility the material conditions that these debates simultaneously addressed and displaced, I have tried to suggest how these debates were themselves complicitous in the universal instrumentalisation that works of 'genius' like *David Copperfield* seem to transcend.

My second response, however, to the argument that literature can expose the operations of ideology within class society is to agree. Because imaginative texts do not wield the same kinds of social authority or produce the same kinds of social effects that some other discourses (like law or medicine, for example) do, they occupy a different social position and perform their ideological work in a slightly different way. Because literary texts mobilise fantasies without legislating action, they provide the site at which shared anxieties and tensions can surface as well as be symbolically addressed. In fact, if one of the functions of literary work is, as I have argued, to work through material or ideological contradictions so as to produce such symbolic resolutions, then one component or stage of this working through will necessarily involve exposing to view the very contradictions the text manages or resolves. This is not to say that the literary man is necessarily more free, moral, or wise than his contemporaries or that he can read in his own works what subsequent readers read. But it is to say that the slippage produced by the double narration of *David Copperfield* is a property of all texts and that literary texts in particular often exploit such inconsistencies as part of their double duty of voicing and silencing ideological contradictions.

The second issue this discussion of *David Copperfield* raises is the fallout from the term I have repeatedly used – 'literary men'. By the middle of the nineteenth century, it was patently not true that all writers *were* 'literary men'. So numerous were literary *women*, in fact, that one (male) commentator was led to complain in 1866 that 'of late . . . the women have been having it all their own way in the realm of fiction'.[8] To another (female) writer this fact was cause for celebration, not complaint. 'Literature', Jessie Boucherette remarked in the *English Woman's Journal*, 'is followed, as a profession, by women, to an extent far greater than our readers are at the moment aware of. Magazines of the day are filled by them; one of the oldest and best of our weekly periodicals owes two-thirds of its content to their pens.'[9] Whether either of these assessments was accurate is less important than the fact that such opinions were widely held. Indeed, the perception and the fact were dialectically related, for the perception that literature *was* a profession open to women encouraged women to write and publish in increasingly large numbers.

I have been arguing that to enhance the social status of the literary man, Dickens constructed and appropriated a representation of work that rested on and derived its terms from the ideological separation of spheres and from the representation of women's domestic labour as non-alienated labour. In this sense, Dickens may be said to have participated in what Nancy Armstrong has called 'the rise of feminine authority in the novel' – that process by which literary discourse became a 'feminised' discourse by the mid-nineteenth century.[10] But even if literary discourse did acquire its moral authority by its (putative) distance from the 'masculine' sphere of alienation and market relations, what effect did this 'feminisation' have on actual women who did or wanted to write? The answer to this question is obviously complex, and it is not my aim to enter now into those discussions feminists have already undertaken in order to address it.[11] I simply want to point out that the same process that helped clear the way for women to write and publish also erected barriers against all but limited access to such 'self-expression'. If the feminisation of authorship derived its authority from an idealised representation of woman and the domestic sphere, then for a woman to depart from that idealisation by engaging in the commercial business of writing was to collapse the boundary between the spheres of alienated and non-alienated labour. A woman who wrote for publication threatened to collapse the ideal from which her authority was derived and to which her fidelity was necessary for so many other social institutions to work.

From Mary Poovey, *Uneven Developments: The Ideological Work of Gender in Mid-Victorian England* (London, 1989), pp. 89–101 and 116–25.

NOTES

[The first essay in this collection, by Chris R. Vanden Bossche, looks at the issue of class in *David Copperfield*. The second essay, by Simon Edwards, looks at the construction of the self in Victorian society. Mary Poovey's essay (it is, in fact, a chapter from a book) could be said to combine these two approaches as she examines the importance of the 'psychological narrative of individual development, which both provided individual readers with an imaginative image of what identity was and created a subject position that reproduced this kind of identity in the individual reader'. What is central in Poovey's essay is an extended discussion of the complex relationship between a new type of historically specific, modern subject and broader social and economic issues of the capitalist market and class relations. In the first section of the essay she looks at the issue of sexual desire and David's complex relationships with his mother, Dora and Emily. As

Poovey explains, it is the woman who is seen as the site of sexual guilt, 'because the problematic aspects of sexuality can be rhetorically ... mastered when they are externalised and figured in another'. By the end of this first section, we have arrived at a sense of a whole cluster of tangled issues that are contained within the novel's apparently straightforward story of a maturing individual who, with Agnes, eventually arrives in a safe harbour of marriage. The essay, then, however, takes things further as it turns to the issue of work, specifically the role of the writer, someone who engages in a form of work that, as presented in the novel, seems effortless. In a substantial section that has, for reasons of space, unfortunately had to be cut, Poovey discusses the image of the writer in the nineteenth century and how, in the widely-held view of the writer as a uniquely gifted individual, we can detect both the deep contradictions and the lineaments of the power structure within Victorian society. To some extent these issues have already been explored by Vanden Bossche and Edwards, but Poovey offers a more elaborate impression of the ideological implications of the nineteenth-century's establishment of a new kind of male norm. In particular, she looks at the ways in which the process of defining a new sense of 'self' demanded the mobilising and stabilising of a certain image of women. The essay provides a particularly clear illustration of the common ground between New Historicist and feminist criticism, both of which look at the ideological work of a text (especially its representations of class and gender), and both of which read the past in the light of what interests, and is of political relevance to, the twentieth-century reader. Ed.]

1. Raymond Williams discusses the history of 'literature' in *Keywords: A Vocabulary of Culture and Society* (New York, 1976), pp. 15–54. See also Patrick Parrinder, *Authors and Authority: A Study of English Literary Criticism and Its Relations to Culture, 1750–1900* (London, 1977), esp. pp. 20–1, 104; and Nancy Armstrong, *Desire and Domestic Fiction: A Political History of the Novel* (New York, 1987), ch. 3.

2. On the importance of the public press, see David Musselwhite, 'The Trial of Warren Hastings', in Francis Barker, Peter Hulme, Margaret Iversen and Diana Loxley (eds), *Literature, Politics and Theory: Papers from the Essex Conference, 1976–84* (London, 1986), p. 92. See also Etienne Balibar and Pierre Macherey, 'On Literature as an Ideological Form', in Robert Young (ed.), *Untying the Text: A Post-Structuralist Reader* (Boston, 1981), pp. 79–99.

3. Critics who have begun to investigate the historicity of subjectivity include Armstrong, *Desire and Domestic Fiction*; Clifford H. Siskin, *The History of Romantic Discourse* (New York, 1988); Walter Benn Michaels, *The Gold Standard and the Logic of Naturalism* (Berkeley, 1987); and Catherine Belsey, 'The Romantic Construction of the Unconscious', in Barker et al., *Literature, Politics and Theory*, pp. 57–76.

4. For a relevant discussion of this paradigm, see Armstrong, *Desire and Domestic Fiction*, Introduction and ch. 1.

5. Charles Dickens, *David Copperfield*, Bantam Books edition (New York, 1981), pp. 12, 14–15. All subsequent references to this edition will be cited by page number in the text. For a critical essay that complements my discussion of *David Copperfield*, see John O. Jordan, 'The Social Sub-Text of *David Copperfield*', *Dickens Studies Annual*, 14 (1985), 61–92.

6. I quote Wordsworth because this is the paradigm of individual growth that the English Romantic poets celebrated. See Siskin, *History*, ch. 4. This paradigm becomes the basis for the Freudian model of subjectivity, which was articulated in the late nineteenth century.

7. Mr Peggotty explicitly and repeatedly forgives Emily, but even his love becomes part of her punishment because it exacerbates her guilt.

8. E. S. Dallas, *The Gay Science* (London, 1866), 2, 295.

9. 'The Profession of the Teacher', *English Woman's Journal*, 1 (March 1858), 8. In 'What Should We Do with Our Old Maids?' Frances Power Cobbe summarised the situation as follows: 'whether doctoresses are to be permitted or not, may be a question; but authoresses are already a guild, which, instead of opposition, has met the kindliest welcome. It is now a real profession to women as to men, to be writers' (*Fraser's Magazine*, 66 [1862], 609).

10. Armstrong, *Desire and Domestic Fiction*, ch. 1 and passim.

11. See Elaine Showalter, *A Literature of Their Own: British Women Novelists from Brontë to Lessing* (Princeton, 1977); Sandra M. Gilbert and Susan Gubar, *The Madwoman in the Attic: The Woman Writer and the Nineteenth-Century Literary Imagination* (New Haven, 1979); and Margaret Homans, *Bearing the Word: Language and the Female Experience in Nineteenth-Century Women's Writing* (Chicago, 1986).

4

The Lost Self: Gender in *David Copperfield*

MARGARET MYERS

Whether *David Copperfield* is read as a *bildungsroman*, a novel of individual growth to artistic and moral maturity, or as an Oedipal drama in which David quests for an idealised version of the lost mother, it remains quintessentially a novel about the search for self.[1] Indeed both the Freudian interpretation of the novel and the more conventional literary exegesis share ground in so far as the autobiographical narrative voice articulates – and therefore imposes – a coherence upon his own experience. While criticism has amply expanded upon the moral, artistic and sexual content of David's narrative, it has at best only obliquely recognised the sequence of gender role-playing that vitally informs his journey to self-discovery. For the adult David Copperfield must re-discover and re-integrate into a coherent sense of self those aspects of his male selfhood culturally designated as feminine. It is a task finally too radical in its espousal of an achieved state of androgyny to be affirmed at the novel's end, but until then *David Copperfield* clearly indicts the cultural extremes of masculinity and femininity. All that is best in David – his artistic and moral impulses – is identified as feminine, and this he loses in early adulthood when he adopts the culturally approved and strictly masculine persona. His rebirth in the Swiss Alps and his marriage to Agnes appear to reclaim the feminine aspects of that androgynous selfhood. Through David's development, his loss and recovery of selfhood, the key figures of Agnes Wickfield and Tommy Traddles act as harbingers of what should be and what may be. Moral barometers, both, they also offer the promise of reconciling the feminine with the masculine, the moral and the imaginative with the social, the private and the public.[2]

The novel itself, of course, structures the literal journey of self-discovery in David's symbolic rebirth during his Wordsworthian encounter with the grandeur of the Swiss Alps following Dora's death.[3] David's prolonged stay in Europe enables him to recover that which he had lost. The novel focuses that loss on Agnes as the appropriate wife for David, though many critics now argue that Agnes more significantly represents a selfhood which David also needs to discover and recover. J. Hillis Miller is one who sees Agnes as the creator of David's selfhood 'without whom he would be nothing'.[4] In the religious analogy which Miller uses, 'David has that relationship to Agnes which a devout Christian has to God'. Alexander Welsh goes on to refine Miller's thesis by noting that the definition of self 'becomes crucial at death, after which he [the hero] will be nothing unless the heroine can save him'.[5] Finally, Stanley Friedman in his subsequent discussion of the novel picks up Welsh's delineation of Agnes as the familiar of death and argues that she offers the necessary consolation to the older narrator as he confronts his own death, and that in such consolation the narrator is able to reconcile with a Providence over which he has no control.[6] All this criticism correctly follows Dickens's lead in designating Agnes the 'heroine' of the novel.[7] She functions in the novel as the agent of male destiny rather than as the creator of her own, although Friedman concludes his discussion by quoting Milton, arguing that since, like Adam and Eve, 'their state cannot be sever'd', both David and Agnes 'serve together as the hero of David's life'.[8]

This line of criticism invites further refinement. *David Copperfield* is structured around the ironic juxtaposition of simultaneous loss and achievement. At one crucial point in his life David acquires a conventionally masculine demeanour, but he does so at the unrecognised expense of a selfhood which at a later stage in his life is only recovered by his wife's death. That lost selfhood is feminine-identified in so far as the moral, the emotional and the artistic are culturally associated with the feminine, an association which the novel itself confirms. Finally the novel seeks to reconcile that feminine selfhood with a masculine identity, not simply in individuals and their private relationships, but also by implication in the larger social context. The last chapter overtly attempts to expound a social optimism based on such a reconciliation. The attempt proves futile. The story of conventional success, and even triumph, is permeated with a sense of irrevocable loss so that even at its end the novel holds true to the ironic pattern of its basic structure. While it attempts at a covert narrative level to deny the pattern by which achievement is inevitably alloyed with loss, a haunting sadness permeates the novel's end. In part that sadness derives from the recognition in the final chapter of the proximity and permanence of death, but death's closeness is a recognition that has informed the novel from its beginning (and David's caul): in *David Copperfield* birth always has death in attendance. There is, I think, a further source for the subdued atmosphere of the final chapter, and that can be found in the novel's inability to achieve an effective and convincing optimism for life while it is lived. Whatever the promise of an androgynous reconciliation, the masculine-identified world of *David Copperfield* cannot finally admit the feminine-identified into the prevailing social and economic structures. Psychological truth must give way finally to cultural convention.

Modern criticism has marvelled at the psychological insight of the novel, and there is no need here to recapitulate David's loss of Eden with the intrusion of the sexually potent adult male, Murdstone. David's consequent expulsion to Salem House moves him into a 'homosocial' world, an exclusively male company which in common with all such societies still divides experience into masculine and feminine domains. The emotional, the moral, and the artistic are all feminine-identified, and it is here as schoolboys that both Tommy Traddles and David Copperfield are most overtly identified with the feminine. In this enclosed environment, James Steerforth enacts the masculine role and here, as in later life and in the larger social world, he comes to represent the worst aspects of indulged cultural manhood. Socially successful, revered by his male peers, he is sensual, amoral, and self-absorbed. The moral and the emotional Tommy Traddles suffers much in this exclusively masculine community, and in Salem House his moral sensibility and his emotional sensitivity are contemptuously identified with the feminine. After Steerforth's public mistreatment of Mr Mell, an incident in which Mell is not only humiliated but is also dismissed from his only means of livelihood, David feels 'self-reproach' and 'contrition', though he does not reveal his feeling for fear of Steerforth's contempt. Traddles, unlike David, is afraid neither to weep in sorrow for Mr Mell nor to upbraid Steerforth for his cruel mistreatment of the impoverished teacher. Steerforth's response to Traddles is to call him 'a girl', and 'Miss Traddles', and all the other boys, on hearing that Steerforth plans to compensate Mr Mell with money (the masculine substitute for feeling), are 'extremely glad to see Traddles so put down' (ch. VII).[9]

David's inability to act upon his best moral instincts, a weakness crucial to his subsequent life, does not deny that at Salem House, he too is feminine-identified. No sooner has he arrived at the school than the handsome Steerforth asks David if he has a sister:

> 'You haven't got a sister, have you?' said Steerforth, yawning.
> 'No,' I answered.
> 'That's a pity,' said Steerforth. 'If you had had one, I should imagine she would have been a pretty, timid, little, bright-eyed sort of a girl. I should have liked to know her. Good night, young Copperfield.'
>
> (ch. VII)

Not for the only time in his life, David is identified with a mythic sister (although clearly Steerforth could just as well be describing David's surrogate sibling, Little Em'ly). Steerforth, from their first meeting, identifies a feminine in David which is central to the nature and development of their friendship. Moreover, this exchange takes place late at night in the bedroom David shares with several other boys, including Steerforth, and it follows the feast of cakes and wine which David's pocket-money has purchased under the magisterial supervision of Steerforth. The experience of secrecy and sensuality is very much in keeping with subsequent revelations of Steerforth's character, particularly in his treatment of Little Em'ly. Such secret sensuality is further associated with David's imagination and artistic abilities. While at Salem House, David is the 'plaything' of his dormitory because of his night-time story-telling.

> Whatever I had within me that was romantic and dreamy, was encouraged by so much story-telling in the dark; and in that respect the pursuit may not have been very profitable to me.
>
> (ch. VII)

The evaluative disassociation of the narrative voice from his 'romantic and dreamy' youthful self seems curious given the nature of the adult's professional success as a writer – such earlier practice has indeed 'proved profitable'. It is a clue that the narrator is anxious about the feminine identification. Uncertain and ambivalent about both sensuality and artistic ability, the adult male artist distances himself from those 'feminine' characteristics on which, ironically, his art and worldly success are founded. By the time David reaches cultural manhood, feminine art will have been transformed into masculine enterprise. The suspect will have been made culturally safe.

Meantime, David's boyhood continues to engage in gender role-playing. The enactment of male and female roles survives through the shared experience of Salem House to the renewal of David and Steerforth's friendship in London. The intervening years have been spent by David in a household where sexual role-playing does not conform to traditional precepts. Davey, the son of David and Dora, is transformed into Trotwood Copperfield, the adopted child of Mr Dick and Betsey Trotwood. The emotional and artistic Mr Dick, florid, full of childish delight, without a strong rational sensibility, is in marked antithesis to the Victorian paterfamilias. Betsey Trotwood, on the other hand, is explicitly masculine-identified. When David first meets her in Dover, he describes her as 'handsome', her dress is severe and neat with 'linen at her throat not unlike a shirt-collar, and things at her wrists like little shirt-wristbands' (ch. XIII). She wears a man's watch, with chain and seals, and when, much later, she visits Dora's aunts Lavinia and Clarissa, she is regarded as 'an eccentric lady, and somewhat masculine with a strong understanding' (ch. XL). In such an environment, David is not identified as exclusively masculine. Constantly encouraged to think and act as would his imaginary sister, Betsey Trotwood Copperfield, he is also confirmed in an identification with both natural parents, for he 'would be as like his father as it's possible to be, if he was not like his mother, too' (ch. XIII). Even his new name, Trotwood, defines gender identity.

Names play a telling role in David's life. Significantly it is not until they meet again as young men that Steerforth coins the nickname 'Daisy' for David Copperfield. In an act of sensitive generosity Betsey Trotwood has given the eighteen-year-old David the freedom and the money to spend a month as he wishes while travelling to visit Yarmouth. Stopping in London for his first night, intimidated by waiters, abashed by the palpable fact that he has no need of the hot shaving water the maid leaves outside his door in the morning, David runs into Steerforth, now an Oxford undergraduate. The dynamics of their boyhood friendship continue into adulthood. Steerforth is masterful and knowledgeable while David is full of romantic enthusiasm, 'as fresh as a daisy at sunrise' (ch. XIX), ready to be tutored and eager to be liked by the older man. They visit Steerforth's mother and spend a week 'in a most delightful manner' with Steerforth giving lessons in the manly arts of riding, boxing and fencing:

> The week passed rapidly, as may be supposed, to one entranced as I was; and yet it gave me so many occasions for knowing Steerforth better, and admiring him more in a thousand respects, that at its close I seemed to have been with him for a much longer time. A dashing way he had of treating me like a plaything, was more agreeable to me than any behaviour he could have adopted.
>
> (ch. XXI)

Steerforth, of course, then joins David in his visit to Yarmouth, thereby initiating the sequence of events which leads to the seduction of Little Em'ly, Steerforth's new 'plaything', and all the betrayals of family and friends attendant upon their elopement.

Until that disillusionment, the friendship of David and Steerforth continues in the pattern of their childhood. Steerforth is the dominant, experienced, condescending superior in a relationship comfortable in its operating assumption of inequality. Their relationship has only the subtlest of moral content, and the nature of that content explicitly lies within the power of the superior Steerforth. Though founded on genuine love, the friendship of David and Steerforth hints at the corruption of innocence in its best moral impulses. Thus David represses his sympathy for Mr Mell; thus Steerforth allows the inexperienced David to spend a drunken night on the town. As Agnes warns David, Steerforth is his 'bad angel', a charge which at the time David vehemently denies. In so doing, David is covertly defending that aspect of self which is most akin to Steerforth: the social male self. Throughout their early relationship, David is morally superior to Steerforth only in the innocence of his instinct, never in an actual choice in terms of action or behaviour.

The loss of Steerforth marks David's movement from androgynous boyhood to masculine adulthood. It is a loss which coincides with two other markers in this rite of passage. The first is his love for Dora. The second is David's initiation into cultural manhood when, with the news of his aunt's financial ruin, he shoulders the traditional male burden of economic responsibility for his family. For David, social and cultural maturity means the adoption of a rigorously masculine role, a role which relies for its definition on the clear separation of the feminine from the masculine. David becomes earnest, rational and hardworking. He masculinises his own selfhood. The art of writing is turned into the enterprise of Parliamentary reporting so that he can make a living. Simultaneously, David looks for his domestic and personal happiness to a woman who matches the extremity of his own cultural role-playing. Conforming to stereotype, their differences come to represent the separation of the instinctive from the rational; neither is able, however, to make moral or emotional coherence out of the polarity. As such their relationship develops into an indictment of extreme sexual roles, an indictment confirmed by the parallels which exist between their marriage and the friendship of David with Steerforth. While Doady is never Dora's 'bad angel', their relationship, in its content, the dynamic of its development and even, in some measure, the nature of its eventual outcome, echoes the earlier and older friendship. In giving priority to a social male self, David diminishes his emotional sensitivity and blunts his moral sensibility. In so doing he hurts Dora, he betrays the child of nature, the 'young innocence' whom experience cannot teach.

The audience of *David Copperfield* is warned from the outset of the inherent moral ambivalence of David's masculine role-playing. The famous incident of the beggar in the street calling 'Blind! Blind! Blind' refers to the matrix of experience in which it occurs, not solely to David's choice of Dora over Agnes. Part of that matrix is his espousal of the work ethic, which happens simultaneously, and from which the narrator deliberately and ironically distances himself. Chapter XXXVI, 'Enthusiasm', follows immediately upon the beggar's call of 'Blind! Blind! Blind!' and opens:

> What I had to do, was, to turn the painful discipline of my younger days to account, by going to work with a resolute and steady heart. What I had to do, was, to take my woodman's axe in my hand, and clear my own way through the forest of difficulty, by cutting down the trees until I came to Dora. And I went on at a mighty rate, as if it could be done by walking.

The single most important source of David's manifold 'blindness' is his capacity for uncritical and exuberant enthusiasm. Agnes, who like the narrator is also a major source of moral comment in the novel, tempers David's youthfully passionate response to life, though she always does so with a gentle humour as when, for example, she teases him by 'threatening to keep a little register of

[his] attachments with the dates, duration, and termination of each
... ' (ch. XXV) when David confesses that he is half in love with
Rosa Dartle. Unlike either his relationships with Agnes or Tommy
Traddles, David's relationships with both Steerforth and Dora are
characterised by an early passionate enthusiasm which blinds him
to the moral implications of personality and behaviour, both in
himself and in those he loves. So it is with work.

Meanwhile, the loss of Steerforth intensifies David's passionate
love for Dora, though, as with Walter Gay's devotion to Florence
Dombey, his early love is centred on an ideal rather than an
actuality:

> All this time, I had gone on loving Dora, harder than ever. Her *idea*
> [italics mine] was my refuge in disappointment and distress, and
> made some amends to me, even for the loss of my friend. The more I
> pitied myself, or pitied others, the more I sought for consolation in
> the image of Dora. The greater the accumulation of deceit and
> trouble in the world, the brighter and purer shone the star of Dora
> high above the world. I don't think I had any definite idea where
> Dora came from, or in what degree she was related to a higher order
> of beings; but I am quite sure I would have scouted the notion of her
> being simply human, like any other young lady, with indignation and
> contempt.
>
> (ch. XXXIII)

It reads almost as purely as Ruskin and hence the parody. But the
humour does not disguise the serious consequences of this culturally-condoned view of women. It is David's inability to comprehend
the reality of Dora which causes his failure to mediate between her
perceptions of life and his excessive enthusiasm, a failure compounded by his disastrous attempt at playing the teacher and
mentor in Dora's life, which Steerforth has played in his.

David alone fails to understand Dora's essential nature, and, as
becomes the pattern, their relationship is in fact mediated through
other women: Julia Mills, Betsey Trotwood and Agnes Wickfield.
David and Dora are thus trapped in the contradictions of their own
culture. David has enthusiastically espoused the ideals of masculinity
and femininity: he will work earnestly toward an inevitable worldly
success while relying on a 'Cottage of Content' for his domestic happiness. He has fallen in love with an ideal of decorative womanhood,
a woman who is childish, without intellectual depth or strong understanding, but one who delights and pleases him, and who, by every

implication, excites him physically. He is superior, she is inferior: he will teach her, she is his 'plaything'. It is one of the further ironies, of course, that David is attempting to amalgamate the divided maternal image of the two Claras. He wants Dora to acquire the domestic skills of Peggotty. The undoubted, if narratively unacknowledged, sensuality of David and Dora's relationship connects significantly with the secrecy of their engagement: it is a constellation of moral ambivalence which marks all the disastrous relationships in the novel, and one which is most clearly identified with Steerforth. In upbraiding David for this deceit towards Dora's aunts, Agnes serves to remind the audience of David's moral fallibility; it undercuts any claim David might make to moral superiority in his relationship with Dora.

The pleasures of courtship prove to be the dilemmas of marriage, and so David pursues the painful pedagogical course of attempting 'to form Dora's mind'. The profound unhappiness he causes her rests on David's conviction of the superiority of the rational, a conviction which operates in defiance of the 'natural' realities of Dora's personality and capabilities. David, for all his sense of the superiority of the masculine-identified attribute, that of rationality, is the very last to comprehend the fixed nature of his marital relationship. Agnes, Betsey Trotwood, even Dora herself, all understand and warn David about the nature of his choice in marriage. The 'instinctively' feminine has a moral sensitivity denied to the intellectually based. Thus Betsey Trotwood who, like David, regains a feminine selfhood which she had denied in the bitterness of experience, refuses to repeat the pattern of the past. She declines to interfere in the marriage by advising Dora on practical matters, as David had requested, and instead accepts 'Little Blossom' as she is without criticism. It is Dora herself who asks to be called 'child-wife'; she too comprehends that she can never be what David wants her to be. He, however, does not take the warning seriously, and so he sets about making Dora 'reasonable', with the only palpable results being his own loneliness and her unhappiness. Finally deciding it had been a wrongheaded scheme, David brings home gifts and a good mood to reconcile himself to his wife. Their conversation works around the key polarities of the rational and the instinctive:

> I sat down by my wife on the sofa, and put the ear-rings in her ears; and then I told her that I feared we had not been quite as good company lately, as we used to be, and that the fault was mine. Which I sincerely felt, and which indeed it was.

'The truth is, Dora, my life,' I said; 'I have been trying to be wise.'

'And to make me wise too,' said Dora, timidly, 'Haven't you, Doady?'

I nodded assent to the pretty inquiry of the raised eyebrows, and kissed the parted lips.

'It's not a bit of use,' said Dora, shaking her head, until the ear-rings rang again. 'You know what a little thing I am, and what I wanted you to call me from the first. If you can't do so, I am afraid you'll never like me. Are you sure you don't think, sometimes, it would have been better to have—'

'Done what, my dear?' For she made no effort to proceed.

'Nothing!' said Dora.

'Nothing?' I repeated.

She put her arms around my neck, and laughed, and called herself by her favourite name of a goose, and hid her face on my shoulder in such a profusion of curls that it was quite a task to clear them away and see it.

'Don't I think it would have been better to have done nothing than to have tried to form my little wife's mind?' said I, laughing at myself. 'Is that the question? Yes, indeed, I do.'

'Is that what you have been trying?' cried Dora. 'Oh what a shocking boy!'

'But I shall never try any more,' said I. 'For I love her dearly as she is.'

'Without a story – really?' inquired Dora, creeping closer to me.

'Why should I seek to change,' said I, 'what has been so precious to me for so long! You can never show better than as your own natural self, my sweet Dora; and we'll try no conceited experiments, but go back to our old way, and be happy.'

'And be happy!' returned Dora. 'Yes! All day! And you won't mind things going a tiny morsel wrong, sometimes?'

'No, no,' said I. 'We must do the best we can.'

'And you won't tell me, any more, that we make other people bad,' coaxed Dora; 'will you! Because you know it's so dreadfully cross!'

'No, no,' said I.

'It's better for me to be stupid than uncomfortable, isn't it?' said Dora.

'Better to be naturally Dora than anything else in the world.'

'In the world! Ah, Doady, it's a large place.'

She shook her head, turned her delighted bright eyes up to mine, kissed me, broke into a merry laugh and sprang away to put on Jip's new collar.

(ch. LIII)

David, of course, is remarkably obtuse as to the hidden content of this conversation, which is founded on Dora's accurate perception that he regrets the marriage. The failure of David's 'wisdom', of his male-identified rationality, to engage successfully with Dora's naturalness, represents the failure of the culturally-endorsed concepts of masculinity and femininity. There is appeasement, but there can be no reconciliation between such fixed extremes: David and Dora's marriage is a thorough-going indictment of the 'Cottage of Content'. It is only after the loss of such sexual extremes that a structure of possible reconciliation can be discovered when David regains those feminine aspects of selfhood which he has repressed or denied.

The deaths of Dora and Steerforth are narratively fortuitous. They relieve David of a life-long commitment to erroneous youthful choice, an instance of authorial generosity common in mid-Victorian novels. Their deaths, moreover, take on further significance if the characters do indeed represent the culturally-approved concepts of masculinity and femininity. Steerforth, readily admired, forever associated with money and easy social success, is without moral instinct, a lack he himself recognises, and for which he blames his mother.[10] Dora, on the other hand, pretty and foolish, enjoys a moral innocence, a native inability for conscious malice, one which qualifies (if it never actually compensates for) her complete lack of intellectual comprehension.[11] David, potentially androgynous, has loved them both and loses them both. Neither Daisy, the feminised male, nor Doady, the corrupted male, survives: it is Trotwood Copperfield who returns, renewed, from Europe. As Trotwood (the name which Agnes uses), David is able to make a living as an artist, he is able to weep openly (when he was married to Dora, David would weep only in secret), and perhaps most important of all, he is able to acknowledge his love for the 'right' woman, Agnes. At the same time, David loses none of the quality of masculine enterprise; he retains his capacity for earnest hard work, an earnestness 'thorough-going, ardent, and sincere' which David claims he owes all to Agnes (ch. XLII).

Agnes is central to the significance of David's rediscovery of selfhood while in Switzerland, but the sequence by which David reaches Dover after his return to England is equally telling. Apart from Mr Chillip, as much in attendance at this spiritual birth as he was at David's natural birth, the only people David visits in London en route to Agnes are Tommy Traddles and Sophy, 'the dearest girl', whom Tommy has married. Tommy Traddles plays an extremely important role in *David Copperfield*, not least of which is his apparent representation of a social no less than personal reconciliation between the masculine and the feminine. In his selfhood, Tommy is posited as an ideal: emotional and intensely moral, Tommy is nonetheless capable of the hard work and intellectual endeavour necessary for eminence in the public domain. Thus he appears to reconcile internally the masculine with the feminine, the rational with the moral and the emotional, but even more significantly he appears to reconcile the private with the public. Married to the woman he loves, together they serve with maternal self-sacrifice the whole impoverished Crewler family. The image of Tommy Traddles in the dusty chambers of the Inns of Court surrounded by laughing women, all enjoying the best of communal and familial times, attempts a genuine optimism. Hidden away, at the very heart of the very driest male institution, an institution which deliberately excludes the emotional and the moral from the structure on which it rests, is a group of happy women chatting around a fire while a contented and busy man makes tea for everyone. The scene is as overtly optimistic as is Traddles's eventual success in law. The assumption, at the novel's end, of his appointment to the Bench represents the most positive view of the law in Dickens's novels. With Traddles a judge, there would be an active moral agent at the highest levels of a major social institution. Moreover, that agent is identified as possessing the feminine qualities of sensibility and domesticity. The difficulty of the final chapter which embodies this social optimism, derives in part from its failure to make this optimism convincing. It is a failure which operates in conjunction with the portrayal of Agnes, a character who has always provoked critical unease.

It is cliché of literary criticism that nothing is more difficult than to portray sympathetically and convincingly a positive idea of good. As with all clichés, it has a strong measure of truth to it. Certainly one of the difficulties surrounding Agnes Wickfield is that she is supposed to represent an ideal of womanhood, an ideal which has mercifully lost favour with the passing years. The ideal is of a woman who is domestically competent yet who has the 'softened beauty of a stained-glass window'; a woman who embodies the best moral impulses, impulses which are instinctively structured on selflessness, yet one who simultaneously enjoys a calm and serious intelligence. Whatever the problems of this cultural ideal of womanhood, there are certain specific elements in the portrayal of Agnes which are essential to an understanding of the novel's final failure to carry through on its promise of espousing an unconventional sexual and social ideology.

Agnes Wickfield is the great lost character of *David Copperfield*. Although Dickens gives little real narrative substance to her extraordinary life, he was fascinated as an author with the nexus of family character and experience which constitute the main details of her biography. As with almost every other major Dickens character (and thus the exceptions become significant[12]), Agnes is motherless. Her mother, having married socially beneath her family and against its wishes, dies shortly after Agnes' birth. Throughout her childhood and early adulthood, Agnes has thereby provided the sole rationale for her alcoholic father's obsessive and criminally unethical behaviour, much as Little Nell is her grandfather's own excuse for his compulsive gambling. The male burden of economically supporting women (and this seems especially so when the women are explicitly identified as 'good angels') often takes a neurotic, and finally criminal cast in Dickens's novels. Simultaneously Agnes plays housekeeper to her widowed father, another key and recurrent relationship in Dickens's writings. Moreover, in love from childhood, Agnes must bear the additional burdens, not only of unrequited love, but of loving a man too blind to comprehend the nature of her feelings, and one who marries a woman thoroughly and entirely different from herself. In this sea of troubles other dangers lurk: she is desired by the morally odious and physically repulsive Uriah Heep, her father causes the bankruptcy of their dearest friends, and she must over a period of several years run a school to support herself and her father following the public revelation of his dubious work habits. Yet despite a life so ripe for artistic exploration and revelation, Agnes as an autonomous character remains hidden from the audience. We know nothing of her emotional or intellectual responses to these traumatic events; we never even discover what she feels about Uriah Heep and his courtship of her, or of her father's public disgrace. Agnes is presented entirely from David's point of view, a view which is always egocentric and often unperceptive.

In part the difficulty of revealing Agnes may derive from the nature of autobiographical technique. It is a technique which, as used by Dickens, inherently subordinates all other characters, limiting the audience's access to them to the agency of the first-person persona. David, unlike Nick Carraway, for example, is never offstage; events and characters are all revealed through his presence, if not his consciousness. But the limitations of first-person narration cannot be blamed entirely for the unavailability of Agnes as an autonomous character. Dickens demonstrates, for example, an easy capability of using the possibilities of retrospective in the revelations of Steerforth: the superior knowledge of the narrator constantly qualifies the limited awareness and understanding of the character of David Copperfield at the various stages of the narrative. No such technique is ever used to generate a complexity of characterisation for Agnes; not once does the narrator reflect or concede an enhanced understanding of Agnes as a character who has suffered great pain and humiliation: retrospective experience merely confirms the stereotype. Moreover, other characters are demonstrated to have experiences and feelings unknown to David Copperfield, and for the audience to be aware of the depth and significance of that unknown life, if ignorant of the details. Betsey Trotwood has enjoyed a complex and profound range of experience and emotions in her marriage to, separation from, and blackmail by a man she has loved passionately. It is as apparent to David as to the audience that her fear of fire is a symptom of this hidden life, that it reveals the presence, but not the nature, of deep feelings held under severe control. With the exception of her love for David, and then only at the very end when David himself is suffering the pangs of unrequited love, Agnes is never implicitly granted an autonomous moral or emotional life. Finally, it is a perverse comment on the significance which Agnes has in the novel that she must remain hidden from the audience, hidden, that is, except as David perceives her. If she were revealed as a character, Agnes Wickfield would threaten to displace David from the centre of his own narrative, a displacement which would run counter to the egocentric nature of the novel's theme and structure.

Agnes, then, exists only as an idea in the mind of the narrator. What the idea of Dora is to the young David Copperfield, Agnes is to the older narrative persona: as the heroine of his life she exists only in relationship to him. Agnes, moreover, is not simply the heroine of the narrator's life; she is also, as Alexander Welsh has argued, the prefiguration of his death.[13] The last chapter of *David Copperfield* is haunted by a preoccupation with the inevitability of the narrator's own death, at whose dying and at whose wake Agnes will stand guard, harbinger and protector both. The fear of the feminine resides in part in the anxiety inspired by death and its human guardians. Even the feminine-identified Tommy Traddles doodles constantly the skeletal image of human morality. But the problem posed by the final chapter of *David Copperfield* resides not only (and perhaps not even primarily) in the fear of the feminine identification with death; that fear is significantly compounded by the male anxiety of feminisation, an anxiety which helps create a conventionality at the novel's end which defies its own sexual radicalism. The portrayal of the Copperfield household in the last chapter is socially and sexually safe: he and Agnes (a soundly conventional couple) are blessed with healthy children, those they love are enjoying a golden old age, and David's writing, his 'feminine' art, is acknowledged only in terms of successful worldly enterprise. The narrator has retreated from the true heroism of David Copperfield, the individual recognition of the complexity of sexual identity and the necessity of incorporating the feminine into that which is masculine identified. The intensity of Romantic experience, the self lost and found again in defiance of social convention and definition, is enbourgeoised: *David Copperfield* retreats from the radical into a safe domestic harbour, a Victorian middle-class home.

From *Gender Studies: New Directions in Feminist Criticism*, ed. Judith Spector (Bowling Green, 1986), pp. 120–32.

NOTES

[Margaret Myers's essay, a distinctive example of contemporary feminist criticism, shares a degree of common ground with Mary Poovey's (see the previous essay in this collection). Both critics are concerned with the ways in which the Victorians constructed gender: how they developed a sense of men and women as radically different beings inhabiting separate spheres. As in Poovey's essay, the issue of the Victorian individual is again at the centre, but what Myers focuses on is what happens to feminine characteristics in the men of the period. Her argument is that David acquires a conventionally masculine demeanour, but this is at the expense of feminine-identified ideas of selfhood. A Victorian concern with the 'manly self' is an idea that appears in several of the essays in this volume, but the particular emphasis here is on 'male anxiety of feminisation, an anxiety which helps create a conventionality at the novel's end which defies its own sexual radicalism'. David, through his marriage to Agnes, becomes part of a household that is socially and sexually safe, but at many points along the way, Myers argues, Dickens recognises the complexity of sexual identity, and the limitations of the assertively masculine frame of mind that developed in the nineteenth century. A possible criticism of Myers's approach is that it could be argued that she tends to work with essentialist notions of what is masculine-identified and what is feminine-identified (Poovey, by contrast, sees gender characteristics as more exclusively a social construction), but any slight reservations about Myers's stance are more than outweighed by the overall sharpness of her argument and analysis, and the essay's alertness to the essentially political nature of both sexual relations and gender representation in fiction. Ed.]

1. For an excellent reconciliation of the 'intentionalist' and psychoanalytic readings of the novel, see Gordon D. Hirsch, *Victorian Newsletter*, 58 (1980), 1–5.

2. Throughout this discussion of *David Copperfield*, I use the term 'feminine' much as Marilyn French characterises the 'inlaw' (i.e. culturally approved) characteristics designated as feminine in 'The Garden Principles', *Shakespeare's Division of Experience* (New York, 1980).

3. *The Prelude* was of course published in the same year as *David Copperfield*. John Lucas argues that Dickens may well have read the poem (which appeared in July 1850) before beginning work on the number which includes Dora's death (*The Melancholy Man: A Study of Dickens' Novels* [London, 1970], pp. 169–70).

4. J. Hillis Miller, *Charles Dickens: The World of His Novels* (Bloomington, 1969), p. 157.

5. Alexander Welsh, *The City of Dickens* (Oxford, 1971), p. 181.

6. Stanley Friedman, 'Dickens's Mid-Victorian Theodicy', *Dickens Studies Annual*, 7 (1978), 128–50.

7. John Butt and Kathleen Tillotson, *Dickens at Work* (London, 1957), pp. 128–30.

8. Friedman, 'Dickens's Mid-Victorian Theodicy', 150.

9. As Bert G. Hornback has noted, Dickens took some care over the choice of these epithets: Dickens changed the text in manuscript from 'stupid' to 'you girl', and the phrase 'Miss Traddles' is an interlinear addition (*'The Hero of My Life': Essays on Dickens* [Athens, 1981], p. 82). The text used in this essay is from *The Oxford Illustrated Dickens* (London, 1948). All subsequent references are by the chapter, and are included in parentheses in the text.

10. Blaming the mother for a moral failure in self is not simply an abdication of individual responsibility. It also represents an additional burden women bear in a culture which deems them the moral standard-bearers.

11. The incident of the page finally transported after repeated revelations of theft from the Copperfield household is one small demonstration of the central differences between a rationally-based and an instinctively-

held morality. David attempts to explain the moral 'contagion' of their domestic incompetence (that it leads their servants into theft and other nefarious activities); Dora emotionally understands the accusation (that *she* is being blamed and compared to a transported page), but is incapable of understanding the intellectual concept of responsibility by default (ch. 47).

12. Arthur Clenman is the single most important exception to the general Dickens rule of motherless central characters.

13. Welsh, *The City of Dickens*, pp. 180–3.

5

In Search of *Beein'*: *Nom/Non Du Père* in *David Copperfield*

VIRGINIA CARMICHAEL

Victorian novels are remarkable for missing parents who, in most cases, are not missed. Their absence usually functions as a fictive device allowing the hero or heroine maximum freedom in the task of constituting himself or herself as subject in society. The main characters are spared the experience of the loss of the parents, and they proceed directly to the task of establishing themselves as vocationally, socially and maritally defined subjects. Becky Thatcher, Dorothea Brooke, Emma Woodhouse, and Jane Eyre have to establish themselves in the world without maternal or parental support, and their actions, even though sometimes wrong-minded or compensatory for parental absence, are also explicit responses to present reality and future plans. Dickens's protagonists however, and especially David Copperfield, are often preoccupied with 'that old unhappy loss', and appear to be as involved with attempting some sort of recovery from their pasts as with achieving an identity in the present.[1] As David struggles toward maturity, he re-enacts precisely the backward-looking and repetitive struggle of a child-becoming-adult whose original family triangle was insufficient. This working-through occurs in his fragmented, flawed, or partial identification with surrogate father and mother figures and alter egos; his repeated involvement with men who are unsuccessfully attempting to find themselves vocationally; and his selective memory for and repetitive participation in triangular structures of sexual competition.

Leonard F. Manheim gives us a multi-faceted classical Freudian reading of *David Copperfield*, also noting similarities between David's life and the mythological pattern of the hero as analysed by Otto Rank; J. Hillis Miller points out that this is the first of Dickens's novels 'to organise itself around the complexities of romantic love'; and Dianne Sadoff analyses the Oedipal work of the text.[2] The Oedipal material is certainly there, but there are also elements of the text that suggest a reading that is culturally and critically more inclusive in its complexity than a psychological or mythological interpretation. In Lacan's understanding of the individual's development, the third term that interrupts the dual and immediate relationship between mother and child is language, or the Symbolic Order, represented by the 'name of the father', and the pun in French, *le nom du père*, also comprehends the 'no of the father', *le non du père*, by which the child's desire of the mother is prohibited by the father. The symbolic father, through his naming/claiming authority in a patriarchal linguistic order, both institutes and denies the child's desire as he propels him or her out of infancy into the social order of language. *David Copperfield* is a novel of search for *beein'*, Yarmouth dialect for 'home', and this pun nicely resonates with Lacan's by suggesting David's search for both social vocation and sexual bonding. His two tasks of expressing himself through mature work and love are enormously complicated by the violence with which the name and no of his particular father are uttered. What is universally an agonising transition from the pre-linguistic Imaginary Order to the Symbolic Order of language becomes for David the repetitive struggle of his recorded life.[3]

It is possible to read the plot and character development in the traditional psychological terms of an individual's search for identity, but the language, the narrative structure and structures, and the sustained imagery all suggest a reading that considers David's development in terms of his desire to experience and express the Imaginary in a Symbolic Order of differential value. Such a reading also makes possible a consideration of the reciprocal relation between the particular individual and his or her society. As Fredric Jameson suggests, if we can convincingly establish identity between the image content and the Lacanian Imaginary, then we can analyse the interaction between the Imaginary and the Symbolic, thus adding another critical dimension to our interpretation.[4] We can discover whether the writing necessarily works to transform the Imaginary, or whether the Imaginary opens a momentary space for itself through its expression in the Symbolic. Such an analysis of *David Copperfield* suggests the extent to which David is being mastered as he writes, and the extent to which his writing itself bespeaks a problematic accession to the Symbolic realm, not only for David, but also for Charles Dickens as he wrote David writing.

Even the more successful half of David's search – for vocation – is characterised by puzzling encounters with language, beginning with the multiple and confusing names he is given by surrogate parents and friends (Copperfield, Murdstone, Daisy, Trotwood, Doady) and continuing into associations with people whose relationships to language are troubled by a prevailing need to deal with the past. With the exception of Mr Peggotty and Ham, every man with whom David feels friendship or hostility or identity is someone explicitly practising a particular relationship to language in an attempt to master his world. Their pathologies of expression reveal an attitude toward present reality skewed by long-held illusions or by past preoccupations with issues of dominance and sexuality. Micawber's bombastic language and unnecessary letters (Aunt Betsey thinks he dreams in letters) are, as R. L. Patten notes, his 'real medium of being'.[5] Mr Dick's compulsive writing of the King Charles Memorial is his way of managing intrusive desires and failures from the past; Dr Strong's life's work is a continual delimiting of meaning in the Dictionary he is compiling; Mr Wickfield has spent his life rationally reducing his experience and emotions to sole motives with his 'one inch rule' (p. 909); Uriah Heep strives for dominance – with his mother's help – by perverting meaning, as his father taught him, through a practice of manipulative hypocrisy and dishonesty; Steerforth utterly corrupts all meaning and relationships in an amoral and socially destructive way; and only 'plodding' Traddles moves along in his present world, limited in his achievements as a writer by what he recognises as a failure of imagination. David, who is trying to discover by writing his life whether he is its hero or not, manages through discipline, earnestness, patience, and imagination to develop a felicitous and fruitful relationship to language. His laborious learning of shorthand, which he undertakes in order to find work, becomes also a means of defining in a fairly sophisticated way his relationship to the arbitrary and powerful system of meaning in which he resides. He ultimately matures into a level of competence as a successful writer that satisfies him vocationally.[6]

We don't have to take David's word for his success; we have the book we are reading as evidence of his, and Dickens's, imaginative mastery of the symbolic realm of language. But if we take his words – instead of his word – and the images, configurations, and story he remembers and constructs with those words, we discover something more troubled in the other half of his search, toward sexual bonding. This struggle is instituted by the no of the father and characterised by a triangulation of desire that occurs and collapses repetitively in David's life and the lives of his friends. David's selective memories are of course motivated by his particular entry into life as a 'posthumous child' (p. 50). Since he begins life in a triangle collapsed by the death of his father, he is able to continue for a while in an exclusive relationship with his child-like mother; his birth is marked by a sign (a caul) of this extended connection with his mother. Even as a child he already vaguely understands the effect of the missing father, for he has nightmares that his father might rise again, Lazarus-like, and interrupt his dual relationship with his mother. He tells Emily that 'my mother and I had always lived by ourselves in the happiest state imaginable, and lived so then, and always meant to live so; and how my father's grave was in the churchyard' (pp. 84–5). When he returns from this first trip to Yarmouth to be told, 'You have got a Pa', he responds, 'Something – I don't know what, or how – connected with the grave in the churchyard, and the raising of the dead, seemed to strike me like an unwholesome wind' (p. 92). Mr Murdstone's entry into the family establishes the first familial triangle for David, and his hostility toward this intruder is natural. But because of the inadequacy of Clara and Mr Murdstone as maternal and paternal participants in this structure, David is not to be allowed or enabled to work his way through and out of the triangle into maturity. Neither Clara nor Mr Murdstone can tolerate the presence of the third person. Clara now embraces David 'hurriedly and secretly, as if it were wrong', and must let go of David's hand before she can take her husband's arm (p. 97). Murdstone's no to David's desire of his mother is a totally excluding one; he will not tolerate *any* show of affection for her son on Clara's part. And furthermore, by refusing David the word of 'welcome home' by which, as David says, '[I] might have been made another creature, perhaps for life' (p. 96), that is, by withholding the naming/claiming of the father, Murdstone effectively shuts David out of the mediation of the family process.

From the time of Murdstone's arrival, David experiences himself as 'a somebody too many' (p. 174), betrayed by his mother and rejected by his father. His biting of Murdstone's hand results in his physical expulsion from home, and he begins his journey of self-definition without benefit of parents. But, as he notes later in his writing, 'the things that never happen are often as much realities to us, in their effects, as those that are accomplished' (p. 891). He has been rejected by the father who has denied him a mother, and because of the nature of Murdstone's no, denying not only the sexual but even the nurturing mother, the desire instituted by that no is radically divided, leaving David attempting to recover split images of the Imaginary mother of immediate relationship. He carries with him the compelling imaginative presence of the nurturing mother on whose shoulder he had rested his head with 'her beautiful hair drooping over me – like an angel's wing' (p. 165), a spatial image that recurs in various configurations in his future relationships with women. But he will also remember her 'from that instant, only as the young mother of my earliest impressions, who had been used to wind her bright curls round and round her finger, and to dance with me at twilight in the parlour' (p. 186), that is, as the sexual mother of prohibited desire. And so we see David beginning a dance of his own as he attempts to recover what he has lost, led on by this split image from the past, unwittingly replicating in various configurations the particularly violent triangulation that instituted his loss. In what he notices in his world, and in the imaginatively projected or real forms through which he relates to the people of his world, David encounters and experiences different versions of triangulated desire, always attempting to achieve some sort of mastery over this structural obstacle to the recovery of the desired mother.

The Murdstone triangle was not David's only experience with competitive triangles by the time of his mother's death and his departure from home. He has noticed the rivalry that exists because Clara Copperfield perceives Peggotty as a threat to her love for David; Peggotty is, in Clara's words, 'my most inveterate enemy' (p. 94). Miss Murdstone, with her 'hard steel purse' (p. 97) and her appropriation of the keys, inserts herself as a third rival for control into the relationship between Peggotty and David, between Clara and David, and between Murdstone and Clara. In fact, one reason David is a somebody too many is that there is already a closed triangle between Miss Murdstone, Mr Murdstone, and Clara, with Clara as the exploited child. By the time of his mother's death, David has also begun his attraction to and identity with alternative figures who can in some way substitute and compensate for his loss and feelings of deprivation. While Clara is his child-like mother of desire, Peggotty gradually becomes his substitute mother of nurture, giving him food, money, acknowledgement, and affection. Mr Peggotty's household provides him with an ideal father figure and a young lover, Emily. And when he is sent away to Salem House and falls under the sway of Steerforth's 'protective' and powerful personality, he tells us, without noting the connection, that Steerforth is the only student who can stand up to Mr Creakle, who has turned out his own son for protesting the father's abuse of the mother. Steerforth becomes a compensatory alter ego and hero for David by virtue of his ability to stand up to the abusing father, a task David found himself inadequate to perform except at the cost of exclusion and loss.

After his mother's death, when he is home again anticipating nothing but abuse and neglect, he realises that in some sense he is at a crossroads: he sees that he can grow up as 'a shabby moody man, lounging an idle life away, about the village', or he can 'go ... away somewhere, like the hero in a story, to seek my fortune' (p. 188) – like the heroes David has heard about in his 'only and ... constant comfort' (p. 106), his books. So by the time David is subjected to what he perceives as the degradation of working at Murdstone and Grinby, he has already discovered the creative potential of surrogates and substitutes, alternative identities, and the imaginative authorship of one's life. After his brief and not untroubled, but somehow happy, stay with the Micawber family, he has made his choice: he will begin his quest as hero of his own life, and he will begin by 'tell[ing] my story to my aunt, Miss Betsey'. He chooses Aunt Betsey because, even though he thinks of her as a 'dread and awful personage',

> there was one little trait in her behaviour which I liked to dwell on, and which gave me some faint shadow of encouragement. I could not forget how my mother had thought that she felt her touch her pretty hair with no ungentle hand; and though it might have been altogether my mother's fancy ... I made a little picture out of it. ... It is very possible that it had been in my mind a long time, and had gradually engendered my determination.
>
> (p. 232)

It is this little picture that guides David through the nightmare journey he makes on foot, deprived of food, shelter and clothing, to her house, and he doesn't know whether he dreams or wakes when be believes that in putting him to bed the night he arrives, Aunt Betsey bends over him, puts his hair away from his face, and lays his head more comfortably.

David's choice of Betsey is felicitous, for he finds a substitute mother both nurturing and disciplining, a 'somewhat masculine lady, with a strong understanding' (p. 668), without the complications of sexuality. Betsey has removed the possibility of sexual triangulation by putting 'the tender passion – all that sort of sentiment [David's euphemism for sexual desire], once and forever, in a grave, and fill[ing] it up, and flatten[ing] it down' (p. 757). She lives in a nonsexual companionship with Mr Dick, another figure with whom David is able to identify. From this point on, with Aunt Betsey's guidance, support, and wisdom, and his own earnestness, David is able to progress steadily, Aunt Betsey's financial failure notwithstanding, in his search for vocational and even social identity. But it is precisely in the realm of his identity with Mr Dick that he is left to his own painful, repetitive and divided search: the realm of sexual desire. As Sadoff notes, Mr Dick is suffering from 'the prohibitions visited upon a desiring boy'[7]. His obsession with King Charles's beheading is the product of his own guilty desire for his sister and felt impotence in protecting her from an abusing husband. Mr Dick, like David, was rejected from a triangle in which he as a child was unable to protect the desired other from a threatening rival. As Betsey tells David, the King Charles story is Mr Dick's 'allegorical way of expressing it. He connects his illness with great disturbance and agitation, naturally, and that's the figure, or the simile, or whatever it's called, which he chooses to use' (p. 261). David's way of expressing 'it', or coming to terms with 'it', is by means of the various triangles – dynamic, or collapsed and static – he keeps working through, either as an intensely interested observer, or as a constituting participant. This 'it' Betsey uses without a clear antecedent David defines repeatedly during his search for romantic, sexual bonding as that 'old unhappy loss or want of something' (p. 713), 'something that had been a dream of my youthful fancy, that was incapable of realisation' (p. 765): 'it' is desire of the irrecoverable mother.

With the exception of the three familial structures in which David participates as an included and valued member – those of Peggotty and Barkis, Aunt Betsey and Mr Dick, and the Micawbers – he experiences a proliferation of flawed, corrupted, or imagined triangles, all of which have been engendered by an original collapsed triangle, and which are characterised by displaced Oedipal relationships. Steerforth, who laments the absence of 'a steadfast and judicious father' (p. 381), has a mother whose claim upon her son is total and exclusionary:

> My son, who has been the object of my life, to whom its every thought has been devoted, whom I have gratified from a child in every wish, from whom I have had no separate existence since his birth – to take up in a moment with a miserable girl, and avoid me!
>
> (p. 531)

If David is trying to become the hero of his own life, he has indeed found a dark double in Steerforth; it is because of his problematic attraction to and identity with him that so much destruction is wrought on the people David loves and admires. Steerforth's seduction of Emily disrupts and triangulates the bondings of David and Emily, David and Steerforth, Ham and Emily, Peggotty and Emily, Peggotty and Steerforth, Rosa and Steerforth, and Steerforth and his mother. Uriah Heep, who has also lost his father, lives in a collapsed triangle with his mother – 'We are much attached to one another' (p. 292) – and together they practise their destructive version of 'umbleness' as a means of acquiring a position and a wife for Uriah. He is the only person who is able to disrupt the Micawber relationship, not in a sexual triangulation, but in one having to do with power, money, and authority. He imagines David as his rival in his plans for Mr Wickfield as well as for Agnes, and he intrudes himself into the Strong marriage to proclaim the existence of another imagined triangle, to the grief of both Dr Strong and Annie. Annie comes to Dr Strong from the collapsed triangle brought about by her beloved father's death, but she comes under the cloud of her mother's exploitative and corrupt 'love' for her daughter. The Strong marriage has in fact been arranged by Mrs Markleham, who 'pretended, in consulting her own inclinations, to be devoting herself to her child' (p. 716). She betrays her real intentions, however, after Annie has innocently agreed to the marriage, by explaining:

> Dr Strong will not only be your husband, but he will represent your late father: he will represent the head of our family, he will represent the wisdom and station, and I may say the means, of our family; and will be, in short, a Boon to it.
>
> (p. 298)

Mrs Markleham thinks she has sold her daughter for profit into this marriage, and the way she perceives the relationship enables the destructive speculations about Annie and Jack Maldon. It is Mr Dick who becomes for the Strongs 'what no one else could be – a link between them' (p. 689), resolving the destructive imagined triangle into the loving and secure relationship that exists between Annie and her 'husband and father' (p. 724).

Though these three characters – Steerforth, Heep and Mrs Markleham – embody David's experience with moral corruption, Annie, Mrs Micawber, Mrs Wickfield, Mr Wickfield, Agnes, Traddles, Sophy, and Dora are also the products of collapsed triangles. Mrs Micawber always knew her father to be 'too partial' (p. 842) to her, resulting in his rejection of her when she married Mr Micawber. Mr Wickfield's wife, who marries against her father's wishes, and is renounced by him, dies from grief over that triangulation, and Wickfield's response, just like that of Mrs Steerforth, is to attach all his affection and life's energy to his daughter:

> My natural grief for my child's mother turned to disease; my natural love for my child turned to disease. I have infected everything I touched. ... I thought it possible that I could truly love one creature in the world, and not love the rest; I thought it possible that I could truly mourn for one creature gone out of the world, and not have some part in the grief of all who mourned.
>
> (p. 642)

He understands that his love for Agnes 'was a diseased love' (p. 915), another mutually damaging misapprehension of the 'economy of love'.[8] Traddles is the disinherited nephew of a guardian-uncle who turned against him and married his housekeeper, and Sophy is the victim of another exploiting mother who, unable to assume her own familial responsibilities, tries to restrain Sophy from marrying Traddles. From this group only Traddles and Sophy, perhaps because of their ability to deal with present reality, are able to move from limiting and even destructive familial relationships into what we perceive through David's eyes as realised domestic and sexual harmony.

For David, however, the journey to this state is neither so direct nor so successful. He is still searching in the present for the dancing mother with the bright curls, and the moment he first sees Dora Spenlow he recognises her:

> All was over in a moment. I had fulfilled my destiny. I was a captive and a slave. I loved Dora Spenlow to distraction! She was more than human to me. She was a Fairy, a Sylph. ... I was swallowed up in an abyss of love in an instant. There was no pausing on the brink; no looking down, or looking back; I was gone, headlong, before I had sense to say a word to her.
>
> (p. 450)

In David's description of his transports of romantic love throughout the next several hundred pages, he indicates no awareness of the ways in which he reveals this love as an illusory attempt to recover his lost mother. He is swallowed in the 'abyss' of this love; he could 'drown' in it (p. 535); it is an 'insubstantial, happy, foolish time' (p. 550); the 'idea' – not the real experience – of Dora is his 'refuge in disappointment and distress'; and her 'image' is his 'consolation' (p. 534). Their courtship is filled with elements of a fairy tale: Mr Spenlow is the dragon of Wantley, who devours children, and David feels as though he were wandering in a 'garden of Eden' with Dora (p. 452). Not only does Miss Murdstone magically reappear as Dora's companion and 'protector', as she had been Clara Copperfield's, but Dora herself shakes her curls, dances, and is a child, just like his mother: 'Her childish way was the most delicious way in the world to me' (p. 603). The only qualification to David's rapture is a feeling that comes over him when Aunt Betsey asks him if Dora is silly or light-headed: 'Without knowing why, I felt a vague unhappy loss or want of something overshadow me like a cloud' (p. 565), and that night he dreams a series of dreams of deprivation and distress, followed by one of Dora dancing incessantly, 'without taking the least notice of me' (p. 566). His inability to understand the connection between the feeling of loss and deprivation from his mother and his present experience with the childish Dora allows him to believe that in his courtship and marriage with Dora he will recover the relationship represented by the image, that he will achieve Imaginary immediacy in his present world. And not surprisingly, since his original desire of the mother was interrupted and punished by an intruding third figure, David's courtship is an ongoing proliferation or even paroxysm of imagined triangles.

The David–Dora–Mr Spenlow and David–Dora–Miss Murdstone triangles are real; both Mr Spenlow and Miss Murdstone want Dora to themselves and David out of the figure. But he is unable to experience any other person except as a rival; only the asexual Miss Mills, who suffers the permanent scarring of a 'misplaced affection'

(p. 544), escapes his jealousy. 'What a state of mind I was in! I was jealous of everybody' (p. 452): the old grey-headed great-grandfather with whom Dora is speaking when David meets her ('I was madly jealous of him' [p. 451]); 'Red Whiskers' at Dora's birthday picnic; the little dog Jip, who 'was mortally jealous of me' (p. 455), and 'who barked madly all the time' (p. 549) during David's declaration of his idolising 'worship' of Dora. (It was a new fierce dog in the kennel at Blunderstone Rookery barking madly at David that marked Murdstone's intrusion into David and Clara's relationship.) During his courtship David perceives – with humour, but also with terror – what he construes as rivalry for him between Peggotty and the dread Mrs Crupp, and also between Aunt Betsey and Mrs Crupp. But most telling, and most reminiscent of his youthful desire to have his mother all to himself, is David's response to Mr Spenlow's death:

> What I cannot describe is, how, in the innermost recesses of my own heart, I had a lurking jealousy even of Death. How I felt as if its might would push me from my ground in Dora's thoughts. How I was, in a grudging way I have no words for, envious of her grief. How it made me restless to think of her weeping to others, or being consoled by others. How I had a grasping, avaricious wish to shut out everybody from her but myself, and to be all in all to her, at that unseasonable time of all times.
>
> (p. 621)

David is not talking about a relationship between himself and another person; he is rather revealing the Imaginary dimensions of his desire to recover an original and irrecoverable unmediated relationship, a dual relationship that was once 'all in all'.

David's feeling about his marriage to Dora, however, is not one of 'all in all', but instead is characterised by a sense of insufficiency, of something lost. So in an inversion of the triangle with a rival that threatens his attachment, he introduces Agnes as the third person in an attempt to compensate for the insufficiency of his attachment. As soon as he and Dora had become secretly engaged, David wrote a letter marked by its tone of denial:

> I entreated Agnes not to regard this as a thoughtless passion which could ever yield to any other, or had the least resemblance to the boyish fancies that we used to joke about. I assured her that its profundity was quite unfathomable, and expressed my belief that nothing like it had ever been known.
>
> (p. 551)

While he is writing this letter, his memory of Agnes 'soothe[s] [him] into tears'; in all the 'agitation' in which he has been living, he experiences Agnes as one of the 'elements of [his] natural home', the place where his heart finds 'its refuge and best friend' (p. 552). Since David first met Agnes and associated her with the stained-glass window, she has provided an external completion for David's lack of self-reliance; she has been 'an influence for all good' (p. 288). He keeps insisting that he does not love her, 'no, not at all in that way' (p. 289) – sexually that is – but that all that is good and moral in him is attributable to her: 'I seem to want some faculty of mind that I ought to have. You were so much in the habit of thinking for me ... and I came so naturally to you for counsel and support, that I really think I have missed acquiring it' (pp. 630–1). Although he insists that Agnes is his beloved sister, she is also the other half of the desired mother, the nurturing mother, the approving, sustaining mother whom both David and Dora draw into their child-like relationship to form a stable triangular familial structure following Mr Spenlow's death: as he tells Agnes after Dora's death, 'when I loved her – even then, my love would have been incomplete, without your sympathy' (p. 936). Aunt Betsey wisely refuses to be drawn into any such parental role, insisting instead that David and Dora establish their marriage as two adults. But self-sacrificing Agnes, who has been in love with David since meeting him, is quite willing to provide the soothing comfort and approval he and Dora so desperately need throughout their predictably troubled marriage. During this marriage, however, which is 'the realisation of my boyish day-dreams', in which 'nothing is real' (pp. 694, 695), while he is patiently but futilely struggling to enlist Dora's help in their life together, David begins to be troubled by the recurrent feeling of 'the old unhappy loss or want of something' (pp. 713, 722, 734, 765, 885). This much-repeated phrase expresses the futility of David's attempting to recover the image, rather than searching for a viable metonymic substitute for the irrevocably lost mother.

David's narrative has been 'proceed[ing] to Agnes, with a thankful love' (p. 672), since he became engaged to Dora, and when his child-wife 'falls asleep' – dies – on Agnes's 'bosom, with a smile', he first awakes

> to a consciousness of her [Agnes's] compassionate tears, her words of hope and peace, her gentle face bending down, as from a purer region nearer Heaven, over my undisciplined heart, and softening its pain.
> (p. 840)

David has lost the dancing mother of desire, but he awakens from this loss to find another mother – the comforting one – bending over him in the same spatial relationship as that of the image he has carried with him all his life, of little David and Clara, with his head on her shoulder and her hair 'drooping over [him] like an angel's wing' (p. 165). With his 'good Angel' Agnes's encouragement, he goes away for an extended period of time during which he '[is] left alone with my undisciplined heart ... [with] no conception of the wound with which it had to strive'. Healing and wisdom come 'but little by little, and grain by grain' (p. 885). During this time David grieves for 'all that had been shattered – my first trust, my first affection, the whole airy castle of my life' (p. 886). But most critical for his ability to begin a marriage with Agnes upon his return to England, he mourns 'for the wandering remnants of the simple home, where I had heard the night-wind blowing, when I was a child' (p. 886), the remnants that had powerfully lived on in his mind as memories and images, pulling him always toward the recovery of a child-like state instead of toward a more present reality.

The transcendentally ideal marriage David finally appears to achieve with St Agnes is, however, a problematic resolution of David's search for sexual bonding. In his relationships with women he has been attempting to recover the split image of his desire, instituted and divided by the no given and the name withheld by Murdstone. David's passion for Dora was sexual, and he explicitly insists that his feelings for Agnes are not; Agnes is like a sister to him, and she evokes for him again and again his specific image of the nurturing mother. We can see in this splitting a reflection of the Victorian tendency toward idealisation of the non-sexual woman and degradation of the sexual one, and that cultural dichotomisation was undoubtedly also at work in Murdstone's and Clara's inability to deal with a desiring child. They had their own individually and socially instituted prohibitions and desires regarding sexuality and the politics of possession and dominance. Once the splitting of desire was so effectively accomplished in David by his particular initiation into the Symbolic realm, he found ample reinforcements and expressions of this division and repression in his larger world. And although at the end of his writing of his life he asserts complete contentment at last with Agnes, the imagery and the triangulated structures of the narrative, as well as the transcendental language, betray this ending's tone of resolution, showing David still firmly imprisoned in the illusions of the Imaginary realm.

But at what costs? What fragmentation has been exercised on the Imaginary by David's inevitable but unnecessarily violent emergence into the Symbolic Order? At this point we need to consider Charles Dickens writing David's writing and recognise the fictive resolution he was attempting on David's behalf as a compensation for a felt insufficiency in his own life. Dickens wrote this novel when he was 37, married, with eight children. 'Why is it', he exclaimed in later life, 'that as with poor David, a sense always comes crushing upon me now, when I fall into low spirits, as of one happiness I have missed in life, and one friend and companion I have never made?'[9] In killing off the insufficient Dora, and in providing David with that 'one friend and companion' which he himself had never found, he, like David, attempts to give fictive expression to the recovery of the Imaginary; instead both have produced a narrative text in which the Imaginary is radically bifurcated and transformed by the telling. The image of sexual love is first split into mutually exclusive images of sexuality and love, and then the image of sexuality is transmuted into death, and the image of love, deprived of its body, is abstracted into virtual transcendence. Through the work of this text, devoid of irony, and with no dimensions of the tragic, the desire for sexual love ends in death and abstraction. The questions I leave open are to what extent were Dickens and David writing as they had been written, perpetrating in the telling the very denial and division of desire they were attempting to reverse and reconcile, and secondly, to what extent is Dickens through his literary work uncritically rein-stituting and passing on the name and the no of the father?

From *English Literary History*, 54 (1987), 653–67.

NOTES

[It is inevitable that a novel concentrating as much on the 'self' as *David Copperfield* does should have attracted psychoanalytic readings, but traditionally such responses tended to be rather unfocused or to dwell too much on attempting to psychoanalyse Dickens himself. The ideas of Jacques Lacan, reinforced by other poststructuralist thinking, have, though, given a fresh impetus, and sense of purpose and direction, to psychoanalytic criticism. Lacanian thinking can, however, prove rather intractable, not to say baffling, when some critics apply it to individual texts. One of the many noteworthy qualities of this essay by Virginia Carmichael, therefore, is the ease with which she presents a Lacanian framework of ideas and makes use of this frame in her reading of *David Copperfield*. Working from relatively simple basic premises – the splitting of desire on entering the Symbolic realm (where the law of the father holds sway), and the lifelong attempt to recover the Imaginary – Carmichael quickly establishes the foundations for a reading of *David Copperfield* that sees David coming to terms with, indeed eagerly absorbing the discourse of, the middle-class world (i.e. becoming a fully-fledged member of the Symbolic Order). At a psychosexual level, however, David is always pursuing an image of his mother, until the very end at least, when he marries the eminently sensible Agnes. The clarity of Carmichael's account is in part due to her clear awareness of the correspondence between the psychosexual issues in the text and the broader political issues of the day; for example, she emphasises how David's very different feelings for Dora and Agnes reflect 'the Victorian tendency towards idealisation of the non-sexual woman and degradation of the sexual one', and at the end of her essay, she draws attention to how Dickens, through his literary work, might be uncritically 'reinstating and passing on the name and no of the father'. Carmichael touches only briefly on such issues, but the reader should be able to see how the psychological analysis in her essay both gels with and provides another dimension to the arguments in the previous essays about male authority, gender and class relations, the vulnerable self, and the rhetoric of the middle-class world. Ed.]

1. *David Copperfield*, ed. Trevor Blount (Harmondsworth, 1966), p. 713. All citations are from this edition.

2. Leonard F. Manheim, 'The Personal History of David Copperfield: A Study in Psychoanalytic Criticism', *The American Imago*, 9 (1952); J. Hillis Miller, *Charles Dickens: The World of His Novels* (Cambridge, 1959), p. 150; Dianne F. Sadoff, *Monsters of Affection: Dickens, Eliot and Brontë on Fatherhood* (Baltimore, 1982).

3. In Lacan's topology the Symbolic Order is primary, since it is the only means of 'thinking' the other two orders. The Imaginary stands for the pre-linguistic experience of unmediated dual relationship with the (m)other, and the Real, according to one of Lacan's formulations, is 'what resists symbolisation absolutely' (quoted in Jameson, 384). The Individual's accession to the Symbolic Order of language gives him/her a capacity for mediation and articulation of the other two realms, as well as the experience of being a subject separate from others. These terms represent not so much a progression of discrete states as the revisionist Lacanian dialectic that is the movement of 'the subject in his reality' (*Ecrits*, p. 196), an extension through displacement that can only asymptomatically approach the Real. Individual development makes it possible, however, to speak of relatively successful or failed acquisitions of the Symbolic; a person unable to construct subjectivity in his or her experience of the language of the other may tend to deal with the Real in terms of the Imaginary, as in the imaged fantasies of neurosis. See Jacques Lacan, *Ecrits: A Selection*, tr. Alan Sheridan (New York and London, 1977); Anthony Wilden, *Jacques Lacan: Speech and Language*

in Psychoanalysis (Baltimore and London, 1968); Anika Lemaire, *Jacques Lacan* (Brussels, 1977); and Fredric Jameson, 'Imaginary and Symbolic in Lacan: Marxism, Psychoanalytic Criticism, and the Problem of the Subject', *Yale French Studies*, 55/56 (1977), 338–95.

4. Jameson, 376.

5. R. L. Patten, 'Autobiography into Autobiography: The Evolution of *David Copperfield*', *Approaches to Victorian Autobiography*, ed. George P. Landow (Athens, 1979), p. 276.

6. I am indebted in part for this analysis to Manheim, 'Personal History of David Copperfield', 21–43, and to Sadoff, *Monsters of Affection*, pp. 10–64.

7. Sadoff, *Monsters of Affection*, p. 46.

8. Manheim, 'Personal History of David Copperfield', 29.

9. Edgar Johnson, *Charles Dickens: His Tragedy and Triumph*, revised and abridged (New York, 1952), p. 415.

6

Self-conflict in *David Copperfield*

JOHN KUCICH

Early in his career, Dickens tended to identify his protagonists exclusively with either passion or repression, usually along predictable male/female lines. As a result, these early characters do not in themselves seem to evoke the synthetic paradoxicalness of Dickensian desire. Early and relatively homogeneous characters like Little Nell or Smike veer too far toward the extreme of repressive self-negation, whereas characters like Nicholas Nickleby or Kit seem too conservatively bounded by the focus of their passions on middle-class happiness. Conversely, many of Dickens's early villains – Quilp, Bill Sikes – are too passionately self-destructive, whereas the benevolent and virtuous self-effacements of minor good characters like the Garlands or Cheerybles are far too modest to seem anything other than paternalistic and protective. The problem is simply that single states of passion or of repression, no matter what the general potential of either, can always seem to be either subjectively bounded or subjectively unbounded when they are expressed as the dominant impulses of individuals. By combining already ambiguous states of passion and repression within the same characters, however, Dickens is able to complicate interiority to the extent that a paradoxical state of desire might, indeed, seem to be a reality within an individual psyche.

David Copperfield is one of the more obvious examples of this kind of complexity, the first to be achieved so scrupulously, for the doubleness of both passion and repression is expressed in the special nature of David's love life. David's uniqueness consists in his doing successfully what others in the novel are systematically punished for – taking a second sexual partner. The significance of this dispensation cannot be taken lightly, given the extreme punishments meted out to those who cannot discipline their hearts to one partner – from Mrs Copperfield, whose remarriage literally kills her, to Little Em'ly, whose betrayal of Ham leads to her ruin – and given the host of characters who proclaim their celibacy or monogamy, or some combination of both: Annie Strong, Peggotty, Betsey Trotwood, Mrs Micawber. A suspicion about sexual faithlessness is, in fact, announced with David Copperfield's first reported concern in life: 'But if you marry a person, and the person dies, why then you may marry another person, mayn't you?'[1] wonders the young Copperfield, eliciting Peggotty's ominous response: 'That's a matter of opinion'. Of course, David's second marriage enables him to unite the novel's thematic polarities of change and changelessness, loss and recovery. But it is more than just a fortunate union of metaphysical opposites. In this novel, and in others written during these years, Dickens is clearly working out his own troubled attitudes toward marriage, divorce, and adultery, and exploring the circumstances that may or may not permit the enlarging of one's sexual experience. Yet it is not simply wish fulfilment, either, that allows Dickens to kill off Dora and unite David with his true love and childhood friend. For the legitimation of David's triangular love life depends on his having achieved a contradictory emotional balance, and the problem of his sexual transition can even be seen as a device for representing this kind of harmonious self-contradiction. In David's special love life, passion and repression work together to keep open the doubleness within each impulse.

David's love for Agnes is presented as a careful mediation between the self-destructive extremes represented by Steerforth and Little Em'ly's elopement, or Annie and Jack Maldon's temptation, and a more conservative economy of domestic happiness. In a purely symbolic sense, David's passionate nature is linked to transgression, and to the sense of criminal self-abandon adultery always carries in Dickens – in this novel, through the compulsive braving of death by drowning that we see in both Stererforth and Little Em'ly, or in the loss of control we see in Annie's swoon when Jack Maldon leaves for India, and in Maldon's reckless and indiscreet behaviour. This connection of David's love to illicit and self-destructive passion is suggested by the suspicions of Dora and others that if David doesn't love Agnes while he is still married to Dora, then he certainly ought to. It is further strengthened by David's characteristic fickleness, for which Agnes herself reproves him, and by David's own self-conscious association of his resistance to Agnes with his general need to 'discipline' his heart – as well as by more subliminal connections like his intense and shameful encounter with Agnes in the theatre on the night of his 'first dissipation' (ch. 24); or the excessiveness of his grief at Dora's death, which has sometimes been interpreted as a sign of his unconscious wishes; or his 'arrangement' of Em'ly's seduction, in which Steerforth seems to serve David as a kind of proxy.[2] But David's love for Agnes is also a clear choice for the self-conservation represented by domestic happiness over the radical self-negation of celibacy. The marriage represents more than just domestic peace, for it also means the recovery of David's lost past – as do all the marriages to child-brides and childhood loves in this novel. It restores to David the coherence of his identity over time. David's exchange of sexual partners thus makes possible a state of passionate feeling that is obscurely connected to the novel's self-destructive and self-preserving extremes at the same time.

The important point here is that this paradoxicalness in David's desire would have been greatly diminished – his second marriage would have been simply a compromise between desires – if the double potential of his love of Agnes had not been balanced by the double potential of his initial repression of love, which stalls and helps to distinguish the oppositional pressures within his passion. That is to say, David's repression of passion is, on the one hand, a conservative curb on self-negation – a refusal that reveals the self-destructive potential inherent in David's love (his affinities with Steerforth or his father; his own irresponsible side), and the need for self-sufficiency and emotional stability instead. David refers to his celibacy as 'gaining a victory over myself' (ch. 60), and celibacy is clearly an extension of the control over his tendency to wild infatuation that he first achieved through his patient faithfulness to Dora. But on the other hand, David's repression is a form of ascetic self-annihilation that counters the lure of safe, domestic happiness promised by a conventional marriage to Agnes, and that proves his commitment to higher spiritual goals. Marriage to Dora had initiated David into a cloying world of domestic obligations that had trivialised his capacities for feeling and imagination – 'all the romance of our engagement put away upon a shelf, to rust' (ch. 44). Though Agnes is, presumably, a better housekeeper and less of a drain on his energies than Dora was, nevertheless, the many marriages in the novel reinforce the central lesson of David and Dora's marriage. As Betsey Trotwood lectures David, marriage is above all a 'duty' in which, whenever certain expectations are unfulfilled, 'you must just accustom yourself to do without 'em'. David's resolution to resist marriage to Agnes, therefore, clarifies his release from the limited, domestic concerns of ordinary individuals, and the emotional prison represented by marriage generally in this and other Dickens novels. Each aspect of David's refusal of Agnes thus counters one of the dangers of desire by stressing an opposite desire – conservative, moralistic repression instead of passionate expense (David's 'undisciplined heart'); but radically ascetic repression instead of conservative marital love (as in David's marriage to Dora). A doubled repression thus keeps the dual potential of passion (both transgressive and domestic, self-negating and self-conserving) in play. Without this reciprocal, internal doubleness – if David had simply turned to Agnes as soon as custom would permit – Dickens could not have made the doubleness of David's love apparent, or at all significant. The death of Dora would then have appeared to be merely convenient, and the narrative would not have been sensitised to the two extreme potentials inherent in David's passion.

This symmetrical counterpointing can be seen at work from the perspective of David's passion as well. For the presence of David's passion also distinguishes the doubleness within his repression.[3] On the one hand, David's repression must be differentiated from the purely utilitarian repressions of characters like Uriah Heep, Lattimer, and the Murdstones. Unlike these characters, who squelch all appearance of passion in themselves solely for the sake of profit or prestige, David does, indeed, feel passion for what he renounces. This difference makes it clear that his repression is an act of extreme self-sacrifice, and that it outweighs any conceivable personal return he might take from it. David must truly love Agnes for his repression to seem an act of extreme disinterest, rather than a form of cowardice, or scrupulosity, or pride. On the other hand, though, Dickens needs to distinguish between David's renunciation and the completely self-annihilating repressions that have characterised Peggotty, Mr Dick, Ham, or even Annie Strong, whose nunlike marriage seems to carry the narrative's approval but not its interest. However admirable such characters might be, they are diminished by the absoluteness of their asceticism and rendered emotionally simple. David, however, effaces himself incompletely, in the sense that his refusal to act on his love actually sustains that love and keeps it from being destroyed. It is precisely because David wants to retain his ambiguous relationship to Agnes that he hesitates, refusing to jeopardise his enigmatic feelings for her: 'It was all that I had left myself, and it was a treasure. If I once shook the foundations of the sacred confidence and usage, in virtue of which it was given to me, it was lost, and could never be recovered' (ch. 60). Later, he reveals that restraint in the present will permit a more rapturous love in imagination, and in a heavenly future: 'in the mystery to come, I might yet love her with a love unknown on earth, and tell her what the strife had been within me when I loved her here.' In this way, David's stalled relationship to Agnes can be seen not simply as a stalemate between the needs of self and the needs of an elaborate and overly nice morality but as a complexly balanced paradox of intense self-abandon and personal circumspection, in which both passion and repression sustain this tension in each other. David's attitude toward Agnes remains complexly multiple, rather than simply oppositional, and he spends a good part of the end of the novel articulating what he calls the 'shifting quicksands of my mind' (ch. 58).

It may sound much too neat to describe the symmetry of David Copperfield's feelings in this kind of synopsis, for his impulses are never felt as entirely equal ones, but as constantly shifting pressures. And the novel does, in fact, incline us to favour David's eventual avowal of his love. Nevertheless, the delicate tension created here produces self-conflict within self-agreement, in which passion and repression contradict but complement each other at the same time. The resultant enlargement of subjectivity prepares an ambient emotional state of paradoxical desire that can be transferred wholesale to whichever result, marriage or celibacy, finally prevails – as later Dickens novels will show more clearly – since both love and asceticism have been doubled against themselves. This conception of emotional doubleness severely qualifies the notion of mature self-completion that most critics have identified as the goal of the narrative,[4] for David's 'maturity' is of a luxuriously self-divided, unstable variety.[5]

The special status of David's self-division is reinforced in the novel by the presence of other characters who are distinguished by their

inward contrariness. Self-conflict comes to seem the general, privileged sign of maturity in this novel about emotional development.
Betsey Trotwood is the most striking example, divided as she is
between her conflicting instincts for tyranny and for tenderness; her
passionate, sometimes warlike character and her surprising passive-
ness and vulnerability to the claims of her husband; her generosity
toward David and Mr Dick and her inflexible retreat from the
world. Agnes, too, turns out to mirror the romantic conflict within
David. At the end of the novel, we find that she has long lived with a
similar internal war, a passion that is disturbing but vitalising and a
renunciation that is both practical and angelic. The presence of this
kind of self-division only increases David's love for Agnes, for he
often exalts her emotional struggle as an image of her beauty.
Hearing her story, David observes that in his childhood 'I knew,
almost as if I had known this story, that there was something inex-
plicably gentle and softened, surrounding you; something that might
have been sorrowful in some one else (as I can now understand it
was), but not so in you' (ch. 60). He goes on – without yet recognising that she loves him – to identify that romantic appeal in Agnes's
sorrow with a perfect description of what the reader suspects to be
Agnes's divided feelings for David: 'I felt, even then, that you could
be faithfully affectionate against all discouragement, and never cease
to be so, until you ceased to live.' Agnes is not just a paragon of
ethics; she is an image of perfected internal conflict. Although self-
conflict is never as elaborately developed in Agnes or in Betsey
Trotwood as it is in David (this imbalance will be discussed more
fully later in this essay), and although Dickens always seems more
interested in men as passionate lovers of women than the other way
around,[6] self-conflict in these female characters is always also based
on a shifting relation between passion and repression as contrary
but complementary forms of Dickensian desire. ...

As we have seen, Dickens's focus on internal tensions tends to
promote self-conflict for its own sake, and to increase the value of
the self-conflicted character. Like Brontë and Eliot, Dickens equates
personal development with the heightening of emotional tension,
and an important consequence of this trend is that self-conflict must
always be internally initiated by Dickens's characters, rather than
being a response to external pressures. That is, rarely do the protagonists of the novels simply assume a responsibility imposed on them
from without, or develop their sense of the options available to
desire through dialogue with others. When they do – as in the case

of Amy Dorrit's allegiance to her father, or Pip's to Magwitch, or Arthur's to Dora – such responsibility is not rejected outright, but it is circumvented by the plot in one way or another, usually by providential death. The more narratively approved self-sacrifices in the novels occur when characters voluntarily repress themselves, often by constructing imaginative, byzantine rationales for their renunciations, which seem puzzling or incomprehensible to other characters.[7] Such is the case with David Copperfield's meditations while in exile. Without any apparent external necessity, David decides the terms of his emotional stalemate. It puzzles Betsey Trotwood later that David cannot see what she herself – as well as the reader – sees so plainly: that circumstances do not compel any such renunciation. The same is true of Arthur Clennam's bizarre decision to publish in newspapers his assumed guilt for ruining Doyce's business. Arthur's meditations while in prison are exemplary in this regard, for his thoughts continually return to Amy, as if newly discovering her importance to him; and yet this return always produces a gratuitous conviction that he is too late. This kind of self-immolation requires a great deal of obtuseness on Arthur's part (the narrative must assist this solipsism through the strange absence and non-interference of Doyce during Arthur's imprisonment). These mistaken perceptions are more than just tricks of the plot – flimsy rationales for a cycle of suffering and relief calculated to augment our sympathies. For excessive and inwardly initiated self-sacrifice seems to be an important capability of these characters.

The extravagance of these solitary initiations gives the repressions of such characters the force of a voluntary, internally compelled self-negation. When circumstances alone do enforce a final separation of lovers, as with Blackpool or Carton, these characters nevertheless go far beyond their obvious responsibilities, and they initiate actions that seem to transcend any obligations or expectations from without. Carton's action is one that no one would dream of asking from him, and Blackpool makes promises to Rachael that he is in no way constrained to make – promises that even Rachael later regrets having bound him to. It is partly through their inward origin that such acts acquire their extravagance, for by not responding to concrete circumstances, the degree of renunciation in these characters comes to seem unlimited and self-destructive.

Another consequence of these inwardly initiated self-conflicts is that Dickens's later characters are often caught up in a tenuous cycle of secrecy and disclosure. Confession, the ability to speak oneself, is the conventional Victorian method of developing and controlling the truth of selfhood – as the spate of Victorian fictional and non-fictional autobiographies attests.[8] But Dickensian confessions must be faithful to the secret and exclusively inward origins of desire in order to maintain the purity of self-conflict, and to avoid any compromised cultivation of external regard. Freedom from the need for recognition from others is a sign of complete self-negation. At the same time, it is also a proof of the self's ability to conserve and protect itself over long periods without the need to fly to reckless self-exposure. The hermetic inward balance of secrecy and disclosure must be witnessed very carefully, then, and usually confession in Dickens is retrospective, to demonstrate the intensity achieved in private emotional states that have been successfully protected over time from outside intrusion. In *David Copperfield*, characters live for years with secrets, then confess their secrets in highly charged scenes that, strangely enough, do not alter relationships in any significant way. Betsey Trotwood's concealed history of marital trouble is such a secret, confessed abruptly and arbitrarily later in the novel without any larger effect than to make us aware of her divided capacities both for self-negation and for survival. Annie Strong's secret – her quiet, mental faithfulness to her husband – is also kept for years and then dramatically unveiled in the harshest public light, but without significantly changing her relationship to Dr Strong, who had long ago made his peace with their relationship on his own secret terms. These mutual revelations are, indeed, the strangest in the novel, for the reciprocally self-contained love of both Annie and Dr Strong is presented as superior to this misunderstanding, even though the rectification of the misunderstanding is made to seem important as a moment of mutual self-articulation. Before Annie's confession, Dr Strong affirms that 'there is no change in my affection, admiration, and respect' (ch. 45), and that he has no suspicions about his wife. Similarly, Annie's confession affirms only her unwavering love. The isolation of these two characters from the rest of the novel's action (and, in particular, the self-involved irrelevance of the lesson that David draws about 'disparity in marriage', a phrase Annie applies to her 'adulterous' relationship to Maldon rather than to her own marriage) is partly a result of the radical autonomy of their emotional lives, an autonomy that is not significantly changed by knowledge of the truth. And of course, the novel itself, which David 'never meant to be Published on any Account', is another confessed secret.[9] In all these cases, secrets point to the divided needs of the self, but only in retrospect, in order to insist on the protraction and the proud resistance of the self to any needs for recognition or interaction with others.

This emphasis on secrecy in the novels also points to the extreme fragility of inward states, and the intense force of reserved personalities. By the same token, characters who presume any easy confidence, or who use secrets against others – like Steerforth or Uriah Heep – are exposed as violators of a cardinal Dickensian rule: reverence for the privacy of others. That the world can so distort and misinterpret the secret life of Mr Mell or that Uriah can take advantage of what David tells him in confidence suggests Dickens's paranoia about disclosure, and his extreme sense of the self's vulnerability to scrutiny.[10] In Dickens's own life and private writings, the dread of exposure is a constant theme,[11] and it results in the continual tension between confidence and concealment that his biographers have often noted. Edger Johnson, speaking of Dickens as a young man, summarises the problem:

> Already deeply grained in Dickens was a quality whose existence he himself did not come to realise clearly until long after, when he referred it to the wound Maria Beadnell had given his heart. But even before that, so far as all his deeper emotions were concerned, he had become intensely reserved. ... Mere acquaintances of later years were apt to believe that Dickens was all spontaneity and warm-hearted intimacy; and his friendliness was entirely sincere, of course, in its way. But it did not involve taking people really into his confidence. He did that with very few and the appearance of intimacy with all the others was imaginative and dramatic exuberance.[12]

On his first American tour, beset by invasive crowds, Dickens wrote: 'I never knew less of myself in all my life, or had less time for those confidential interviews with myself whereby I earn my bread'.[13] 'In the [respect] of not being left alone', he complained more than once, I have suffered considerably'.[14] Similarly, Dickens seems to have been uncomfortable with portraits or biographical sketches of himself. On a portrait done by Ary Scheffer, for example, Dickens told Forster: 'As a work of art I see in it spirit combined with perfect ease, and yet I don't see myself. So I come to the conclusion that I never do see myself'.[15]

But the most important consequence of Dickens's emphasis on inward, self-conflictual tension is the absolutely idiosyncratic nature of the resolutions his characters achieve. Although readers have long ago agreed that Dickens leaves us with predictable and formulaic ethical messages at the ends of his novels, these novels actually give us set a of byzantine, unrepeatable resolutions, in which the successful fulfilment of desire seems to depend on highly implausible circumstances and personal adjustments, rather than on widely available formulae for behaviour. The synthesis of self-negation and self-conservation seems to take place only in special individuals, who are played off against a large number of rejected alternatives, and who come to seem enigmatic in the uniqueness and complexity of their redemption.[16] The necessity of these idiosyncratic personal and circumstantial resolutions follows plainly from the strained symmetry that Dickens maintains in his protagonists. But this symmetry seems an enigmatic, even a privileged distinction when it is placed beside the many roads not taken, and the ease with which other characters fall short of the mark.

In *David Copperfield*, the conflict between passion and repression is confusedly dispersed across sets of characters who parallel David in many different, partial ways. This dispersal highlights the complexity of David's emotional life by reducing the lives of other characters to single aspects of it: Em'ly and Steerforth abandon their child-lovers (as David seems to have abandoned Agnes); Mr Copperfield and Dr Strong do marry child-brides (as David marries Dora); Steerforth and Heep defy authority (as David defies Mr Spenlow); Traddles and Betsey Trotwood submit to unreasonable authority (as David does, temporarily, with the Murdstones); Peggotty and Agnes honour authority (as David does Betsey); Peggotty, Annie, and, in her way, Mrs Micawber are sexually faithful (as David is to Dora); Em'ly is unfaithful (as David is, indirectly, to Dora). All the important stages in David's emotional life are embodied and extended in isolated ways by other characters, but only David synthesises these experiences. David crosses boundaries established by the contrasts between other characters, and he exploits various emotional potentials without contradiction, whereas other characters seem to be defined in more limited ways by fragmented actions. Gillman and Patten comment that Dickens uses doubling techniques like this to convolute systematically the identities of his protagonists, and that in these novels 'identity therefore becomes more mixed, and even mixed up'.[17] David's ability to assimilate the often contradictory characteristics that have been defined by various more limited individuals becomes the condition for his paradoxical emotional potential.[18] Yet the circumstances that make this complex assimilation possible – his double adoption, his double marriage, the death of Mr Spenlow – are so singular as to make his experience seem radically unique. By being so elaborately contrived, David's situation comes to seem intensely personal, and not an arrangement of circumstances that is widely available to others, even if its emotional appeal is formulaically recognisable.

All of Dickens's later novels feature resolutions that are similarly idiosyncratic, and that seem to make the complexity of inwardness available only through specialised, unrepeatable opportunities for special individuals. Though the libidinal configuration of doubleness is repeatable enough in the abstract – and it certainly is repeated for the central characters in novel after novel – the situations and actions that bring it about seem to be so highly complex and fragile that they do not result in clear-cut patterns of behaviour, but rather in mysterious and often fortuitous exceptions to the general rules. That is to say, we recognise internal states in Dickens, and not the social circumstances that might produce them. Such a pattern seems surprising in a novelist celebrated for his social principles and his populist leanings. Instead of promoting widely accessible patterns of action, Dickens seems to construct inwardness as a fragile, mysterious, and often inexplicable or uncontrollable resolution. Ultimately, desire becomes subjectivised, not socialised.

From John Kucich, *Repression in Victorian Fiction: Charlotte Brontë, George Eliot and Charles Dickens* (Berkeley, Cal., 1987), pp. 228–35 and 244–51.

NOTES

[This essay is extracted from John Kucich's book *Repression in Victorian Fiction* in which he reconsiders the complexity of inward states in the Victorian novel, specifically in novels that have been ahistorically tied to fear, guilt or avoidance. His book offers a more positive view of the patterns of behaviour encountered in certain novels. The term 'repression' preserves the sense of a self-conflictual, self-divided interiority that withdraws from the spheres of action and speech, but Kucich suggests that this in fact amounts to a nineteenth-century exaltation of interiority. His book explores this 'self' that Victorian repression produced, a self that 'was more responsive libidinally, more self-sufficient, and – oddly enough – more antisocial than we have yet understood'. The area of concern is, then, as it is in the other essays on *David Copperfield* in this volume, an interest in the historical construction of the subject, Kucich's particular emphasis falling on the ways in which the Victorians made intense feeling (particularly sexual feeling) matters of secrecy and self-reflexiveness. The major theoretical influence on Kucich is Michel Foucault who, in *The History of Sexuality* (London, 1979), considered repression as the very means of producing nineteenth-century subjectivity. Another influence is the work of Georges Bataille, particularly his 1962 book *Death and Sexuality: A Study of Eroticism and the Taboo*, with its emphasis on destabilisation and abolishing the trivial, unified self. One aspect of this, as explored in Kucich's book as a whole, is the way in which the Victorians, in turning to the self, rejected the collective or communal; *David Copperfield*, for example, may be said to 'introvert the middle-class vitality and optimism that, at an earlier stage of Dickens's career, had produced large, open Pickwickian groups'. We are confronted instead by an isolated subjectivity, for when Dickens, Eliot or Brontë speak in a way that appears to give community its due, their choice of repression as a means by which individuals are supposedly integrated into groups works, in fact, to insulate emotional life. In its ambitious attempt to make sense of such large cultural and historical issues, Kucich's essay, like the other essays on *David Copperfield* in this volume, provides a striking example of the way in which many critics today proceed on the basis of thinking through problems in psychology, social theory and philosophy in relation to literary texts. Ed.]

1. *David Copperfield*, Penguin edition (Harmondsworth, 1966), ch. 2. All subsequent references are to this edition.

2. See, for example, Carl Bandelin, 'David Copperfield: A Third Interesting Penitent', *Studies in English Literature*, 16 (1976), 601–11, for a discussion of these last two points.

3. Since Gwendolyn B. Needham's essay 'The Undisciplined Heart of David Copperfield', *Nineteenth-Century Fiction*, 9 (1954), 81–107, almost all critics writing on this novel have acknowledged the centrality of self-discipline. But few have recognised Dickens's ambiguous attiude toward the 'disciplined heart'. An interesting exception is James R. Kincaid's discussion in *Dickens and the Rhetoric of Laughter* (Oxford, 1971), pp. 162–91. Kincaid argues that, on the whole, discipline is made an ambiguous or even a distasteful quality by the novel.

4. Writers have commented on David's self-conflict at great length, but mainly to show that he 'masters' these conflicts. Even a more modern reading, like Gordon D. Hirsch's psychoanalytic interpretation, 'A Psychoanalytic Rereading of *David Copperfield*', *Victorian Newsletter*, 58 (1980), 1–5, poses unity of the self as an unachieved but necessary goal.

5. The role of memory in the novel can also be seen to contribute to this self-division. David's memory often gives him a doubled sense of himself as it constantly juxtaposes childhood purity to adult guilt, or

former self-indulgences to present circumspection. William T. Lankford,
' "The Deep of Time": Narrative Order in *David Copperfield'*, *English
Literary History*, 46 (1979), 452–67, argues that David's memory continually disrupts and destabilises his sense of himself: 'Time itself thus
becomes both threat and redemption, and the force of the novel as an
account of experience in time is deeply divided' (456). This divisive-
ness, Lankford points out, accounts for David's feelings of insubstan-
tiality when he dwells on the past.

6. Michael Slater, *Dickens and Women* (London, 1983), p. 275, identifies
   this imbalance with the middle novels, though I think it can easily be
   located in the later novels, as this chapter will show.

7. Psychoanalytic interpretations often comment on the 'projective'
   quality of reality in general for Dickens's characters. In the context of
   David Copperfield, see, for example Mark Spilka, '*David Copperfield*
   as Psychological Fiction', *Critical Quarterly*, 1 (1959), 292–301 ; or
   Leonard F. Manheim, 'The Personal History of David Copperfield: A
   study in Psychoanalytic Criticism', *American Imago*, 9 (1952), 21–43.

8. See Barry Westburg, *The Confessional Fictions of Charles Dickens*
   (Dekalb, Ga., 1977). Westburg is happily convinced that confessional
   fictions reveal a 'system of truth, where events acquire significance by
   relation to one another and to the constellation of events forming the
   whole of a life' and that 'Dickens was evidently more interested in this
   kind of personal truth than in inherited cultural truths' (p. xiii).

9. The phrase is included in the full original title of the novel.

10. Alexander Welsh's essay 'Blackmail Studies in *Martin Chuzzlewit* and
    Bleak House', *Dickens Studies Annual*, 11 (1983), 25–35, describes the
    general dread of exposure in Dickens's novels, as reflected in the 'crimi-
    nalisation of blackmail' (26) in the nineteenth century.

11. See, for example, Edgar Johnson, *Charles Dickens: His Tragedy and
    Triumph*, 2 vols (New York, 1952), vol. 1 p. 383, on Dickens's despair
    over intrusions.

12. Johnson, *Charles Dickens*, vol. 1, p. 132.

13. Letter to Thomas Beard, 1 May 1842, *Letters*, vol. 1, p. 447. See also
    J. Hillis Miller's fascinating essay 'The Sources of Dickens's Comic Art:
    From *American Notes* to *Martin Chuzzlewit'*, *Nineteenth-Century
    Fiction*, 24 (1970), 467–76, which traces Dickens's dread of exposure
    to a feared loss of self.

14. Letter to William Macready, 22 March 1842, *Letters*, vol. 1, p. 414.

15. Letter to John Forster, March 1856, *Letters*, II, p. 754.

16. Since Julian Moynahan's essay, the existence of multiple parallels for
    Dickens's heroes has often been noted, though usually either as a

means by which protagonists reject negative examples, as in Barbara Hardy, 'The Change of Heart in Dickens' Novels', *Victorian Studies*, 5 (1961), esp. 67; or as a way to stigmatise their desires. In David Copperfield's case, this has led to accusations of irresponsibility, as in Lankford, 'The Deep of Time', 464, or in Ross H. Dabney, *Love and Property in the Novels of Dickens* (Berkeley, Cal., 1967), esp. p. 72.

17. Susan K. Gillman and Robert L. Patten, 'Dickens: Doubles: Twain: Twins', *Nineteenth-Century Fiction*, 39 (1985), 445.

18. As noted by Edwin M. Eigner, *The Metaphysical Novel in England and America: Dickens, Bulwer, Melville, and Hawthorne* (Berkeley, Cal., 1978), p. 74, these parallels are derived from German Romantic fiction, and are related to the *doppelgänger* in their ability to embody contrary psychic potentials, though Eigner argues that these complex potentials are never meant to divide characters against themselves in *David Copperfield*, or in other works that he terms 'metaphysical'.

7

Deconstructing Dickens: *Hard Times*

STEVEN CONNOR

Bleak House is, in obvious ways, an eminently 'deconstructable' novel. Because of its very size, range and complexity, the issue of unity is a crucial one for the reader precisely because it is so difficult to achieve. The novel, we might say, is about the effort to make sense out of a mass of troublesome, diverse particulars which all the time frustrate neat and conclusive imaginative structures. Until now, literary criticism, including structuralist criticism, has concentrated on the ostensible structures of meaning in texts and has largely ignored all the hesitations, indecisions and contradictions which make up most texts and most readings of them. It is these that deconstructive criticism in part aims to restore.

But why? Why pay such obsessive attention to incoherence rather than coherence? Why not see incoherence as just an unimportant sort of interference in a text, like the crackle round a radio signal which distracts but does not prevent the signal coming through? After all, despite all this fancy talk about the text's differences from itself, don't we all mean more or less the same thing when we talk about *Bleak House*?

I think I would agree that there are dangers in allowing privileges to any kind of incoherence at the expense of any kind of coherence, for this can become just a new sort of orthodoxy. (There are signs that this is happening in some varieties of deconstructive criticism.) But it is honestly difficult to maintain that texts have the sort of coherence and intelligibility that literary criticism has been concerned to find in them. If we do know more or less what we mean when we talk about *Bleak House* then that is not a function of the text itself but of the contexts, linguistic, ideological and institutional, in which we read it, all of which combine to confirm us in our recognition of *Bleak House* as a certain sort of novel. But, just as no readership can ever be wholly homogeneous – perhaps especially not the contemporary readership of 1851 – so any text is likely to be divided and inconsistent with itself in important ways. If meaning is dependent upon differences in language, then those differences are likely to split and differentiate meaning itself.

All this doesn't mean, however, a licence to mash any text up into a dog's breakfast, about which anyone can say more or less what they like. On the contrary, deconstructive criticism sets out to try to show the particular ways in which the conflict between presence and difference is established in texts, and in which the awareness of that conflict is then repressed. One of the clearest formulations of this I know is Barbara Johnson's:

> *Deconstruction* is not synonymous with *destruction* ... The deconstruction of a text does not proceed by random doubt or arbitrary subversion, but by the careful teasing out of warring forces of signification within the text itself. If anything is destroyed in a deconstructive reading, it is not the text, but the claim to unequivocal domination of one mode of signifying over another. A deconstructive reading is a reading that analyses the specificity of a text's critical difference from itself.[1]

It is because of this that Dickens's later novels seem to offer themselves for deconstructive criticism, even, in a sense, to deconstruct themselves from within; as the novels project increasingly complex and contradictory fictional worlds, the desire to enclose and control those worlds grows in proportion to the intensity of the internal arguments that the novels conduct with themselves.

There is, however, one novel of this period in which, most critics are agreed, there is not quite the same conflict between coherence and incoherence. The novel is *Hard Times*. Many readers of the novel have been disappointed by the way that the issues with which it deals seem to have been conclusively sewn up from the start. The insistence with which it seems to present its rigid binary opposition between 'system' and 'fact', exemplified in Gradgrind's school and Bounderby's mill, and 'life' and 'fancy', exemplified in Sleary's circus, has seemed to many readers to make *Hard Times* seem more like a diagram or fable than a proper novel, pulsating with complex human life. John Lucas articulates this view when he writes that 'Hard Times is in the grip of an idea' and this view seems to be shared by different critics employing different methodologies.[2]

This would seem to make *Hard Times* a good test case for a deconstructive analysis like the one I have just described. What can deconstruction do with such a simple and reductive text, one that seems to have done so complete a job of silencing all internal dissension?

One way to approach this would be to look at the ways in which the principal thematic issues are represented in linguistic terms in the text, in order to examine the way in which the text's own form and language represent its content. As with *Bleak House*, metaphor and metonymy provide a good starting-point.

From the first pages of the novel it is clear that Gradgrindery is to be characterised by an excess of metaphor, shown in the desire for absolute interchangeability between signifiers and signifieds. The definition of a horse that Bitzer offers relies upon the implicit claim that language can account absolutely for the things it names, so that, having heard the definition, Sissy is expected immediately to 'know what a horse is' (I:II, 5). In Gradgrindery, the assumption is that, because signs can substitute absolutely for things, they are indistinguishable from them – therefore, since horses do not walk up and down walls in reality, you should not paper walls with representations of horses, and, since you don't walk over flowers in reality (an odd assumption, this, for Gradgrind), you shouldn't put representations of flowers in a carpet (I:II, 7). Gradgrind's rage for substitution means that he can conceive easily of perfect translations of one sign into another – '"What is called Taste, is only another name for Fact"' (I:II, 6).

Sissy Jupe, however, has a different view of representation, recognising that the difference between the reality and the representation means that you can't hurt a picture of a flower (I:II, 7). For Gradgrind, no such distinction between signifier and signified exits, and especially not in speaking of himself, where his words correspond exactly with his image of what he is:

> In such terms Mr Gradgrind always mentally introduced himself, whether to his private circle of acquaintance, of to the public in general. In such terms, no doubt, substituting the words 'boys and girls', for 'Sir', Thomas Gradgrind now presented Thomas Gradgrind to the little pitchers before him who were to be filled so full of facts.
>
> (I:II, 3)

The image which recurs throughout the book to designate this perfect equivalence is the mathematical calculation; Gradgrind sees himself as 'a man who proceeds upon the principle that two and two are four, and nothing over, and who is not to be talked into allowing for anything over' (I:II, 3). This mode of exact substitution is characteristic not only of Gradgrind but of the other utilitarian characters in the book. Bounderby announces his linguistic creed in his wedding speech:

> 'as you all know me, and know what I am, and what my extraction was, you won't expect a speech from a man who, when he sees a Post, says, "that's a Post," and when he sees a Pump, says, "that's a Pump," and is not to be got to call Post a Pump, or a Pump a Post, or either of them a Toothpick.'
>
> (I:XVI, 108)

Bounderby is surrounded by objects in the material world which act as perfect signifiers for him; the correspondence between him and his front door is an absolute one:

> [Bounderby] lived, in a red house with black outside shutters, green inside blinds, a black street door, up two white steps, BOUNDERBY (in letters very like himself) upon a brazen plate, and a round brazen door-handle underneath it, like a brazen full-stop.
>
> (I:XII, 70)

Dickens's description here turns metonymy, the separate, contiguous details of Bounderby's house and front door, into metaphor, since every detail is merely repetition of the designation 'BOUNDERBY'. The figure is therefore that 'metaphoricised metonymy' which we have seen operating before [in an earlier discussion of *Dombey and Son*]. This kind of figurative exchange is found in descriptions of the Coketown workers, too:

> In the hardest working part of Coketown ... where the chimneys, for want of air to make a draught, were built in an immense variety of stunted and crooked shapes as though every house put out a sign of the kind of people who might be expected to be born in it; among the multitude of Coketown, generically called 'the Hands,' – a race who would have found more favour with some people, if Providence had seen fit to make them only hands, or, like the lower creatures of the seashore, only hands and stomachs – lived a certain Stephen Blackpool, forty years of age.
>
> (I:X, 63)

The 'stunted and crooked shapes' are here not metonymic details connoting variety and difference, but metaphoric signs, like Bounderby's front door, which signify only an identical poverty. The remarks about the 'hands' remind us that the narrowing of metonymy into metaphorical substitution (for all functional purposes, the men and women consist only of their hands), is an actual violence as well as a quirk of language.

As we might expect, the contrasting world of Fancy in the novel is characterised by a different attitude towards language and representation, and evoked in the text by different figurative means. Where Gradgrind's world is one of metaphorical substitution, the world of Fancy is characterised by metonymic accretion. This is brought out very well in the description of the sign outside the Pegasus's Arms:

> The name of the public house was the Pegasus's Arms. The Pegasus's legs might have been more to the purpose; but, underneath the winged horse upon the sign-board, The Pegasus's Arms was inscribed in Roman letters. Beneath that inscription again, in a flowing scroll, the painter had touched off the lines:
>
> > Good malt makes good beer,
> > Walk in, and they'll draw it here;
> > Good wine makes good brandy,
> > Give us a call and you'll find it handy.
>
> Framed and glazed upon the wall behind the dingy little bar, was another Pegasus – a theatrical one with real gauze let in for his wings, golden stars stuck on all over him, and his ethereal harness made of red silk.
>
> (I:VI, 28)

Obviously the sign of the bar does correspond metaphorically in some respects with Sleary's circus, in its fantastic improvisation of detail and its good-humoured dinginess. But what is more noticeable about the sign and the description of it is the way that this simple kind of reading of correspondence is deflected and postponed. The sign-board is, in fact, a series of metonymies, moving through the arms, legs and wings of Pegasus, the inscriptions beneath the picture, and into the details of the framed and glazed Pegasus inside the bar, with an energy that makes it difficult to see the bar sign as stable and self-contained. The discontinuity of signifier and signified is also brought about by the close attention to signifiers themselves, in their material shape and texture, the

'Roman letters' and 'flowing scroll' of the inscriptions and the gauze and silk of the framed Pegasus, as well as by the splitting of the sign-board into three signifiers – the painting of Pegasus, the inscription beneath which names it (and the bar, of course) and the verse beneath that inscription, each new signifier making a signified of the previous signifier. The sign therefore creatively exceeds what it signifies, in a way that contrasts very markedly with Bounderby's front door; the sign and the description of it produce a metonymic deferral rather than a metaphoric fixing of Sleary's circus.

This is reinforced by the inefficiency and indistinctness of language itself in Sleary's world. The circus people's manner of speaking, with its private slang (outlandish to Gradgrind's ears), seems to emphasise the resistant material quality of language, rather than the communication of specific meanings. Sleary's heavy, bronchial speech does the same thing and reminds the reader incidentally of the 'corpulent slow boy, with a wheezy manner of breathing' who mistakes Gradgrind's intentions in the classroom and offers free association instead of reasoning (I:I, 6).

The opposition of Fact and Fancy in *Hard Times* also results in a structural contrast between different kinds of and attitudes towards fiction. Where Gradgrind is suspicious of any fiction which exceeds verifiable fact, Fancy expresses itself indomitably in fictional forms which transgress the rules of realism or plausibility. It is for this reason that fairy-tale is so important in *Hard Times* (as in many other Dickens novels); fairy-tale is precisely that form of narrative which permits imaginative exceeding of the limits of the real world. It is appropriate that the story that Sissy remembers telling her father should be that of Scheherazade, in which a princess staves off her execution by telling a succession of stories; it is a narrative which is actually about the deferment of reality by an excess of narrative (I:IX, 59). But even realistic fiction, 'about men and women, more or less like themselves, and about children, more or less like their own' is regarded by the Coketown workers as a sort of relaxing addition to their lives, rather than an inert reflection of them, and Gradgrind is perplexed 'at this eccentric sum, and he never could make out how it yielded this unaccountable product' (I:VIII, 50).

So we can see that, as in *Bleak House*, the opposition between different kinds of language and different attitudes towards it is a way of sustaining important thematic oppositions in the book. As in *Bleak House*, the contrast seems to be between metaphor and metonymy, or language as presence and language as difference. We ought to pause here, however, to notice an interesting reversal. In *Bleak House*, we remember, it is the metaphorical world of Jarndyce and Esther which the narrative accredits against the endlessly multiplying, metonymic confusion of Chancery and the public world. But in *Hard Times* metaphor, or language as presence, stands condemned as characteristic of the life-denying world of Gradgrindery, while metonymy and difference are the guarantees of life, communication and 'amuthement'.

This is not to say that these distinctions are maintained absolutely. We saw how, in *Bleak House*, they were liable to be inverted in important ways, and the same seems to be true of *Hard Times*. Gradgrind's ruthless commitment to the public world of fact often manifests itself in a wasteful surplus of written material which is reminiscent of Chancery, as in the endless pamphlets that he produces on social questions – 'little rivers of tabular statements periodically flowed into the howling ocean of tabular statements, which no diver ever got to any depth in and came up sane' (I:VIII, 50). Opposed to this is the dignity and rugged earnestness of Stephen's speech (II:IV, 142) and the primarily oral culture of the millworkers – one of the principal grounds of objection to Slackbridge is the elaborately 'written' quality of his language, with its effacement of dialect and suspicious complexity of syntax.[3]

These inconsistencies indicate the arbitrariness of the contrasts which are set up in the novel and therefore in some ways threaten its thematic unity. Even more interesting and problematic is the way that Dickens's own language, produced as it necessarily is between the axes of the metaphorical and metonymic, is involved in this opposition and inversion of opposition.

The first thing to strike us ought to be the very high degree of metaphoric substitution in Dickens's own language. Much of this is evidently ironical, as in the description of Bounderby's front door or of the schoolroom in the opening paragraphs of the novel:

> The scene was a plain, bare, monotonous vault of a schoolroom, and the speaker's square forefinger emphasised his observations by underscoring every sentence with a line on the schoolmaster's sleeve. The emphasis was helped by the speaker's square wall of a forehead, which had his eyebrows for its base, while his eyes found commodious cellarage in two dark caves, overshadowed by the wall.
>
> (I:I, 1)

The speaker and the schoolmaster are here shrunk down to particular attributes, forefinger, sleeve, forehead, eyebrows and eyes, which then come to stand as complete images of them. This is again the metaphoricised metonymy found at the beginning of *Dombey and Son* and it gives something of the same sense of premature closure. But here there seems to be even less room for invention and free ranging over detail; even the metonymical relationship between the speaker and his surroundings is forced grimly into a relationship of metaphorical exchange, with the similarity between the 'plain, bare' schoolroom and the speaker's 'square wall of a forehead' and the connection between the 'monotonous vault' of the room and the 'two dark caves' of his eyes. In this passage, the text inflicts the same violent reduction on Gradgrind as he inflicts upon the world.

The irony is clear here. The very niggardliness of the narration marks it as an imitation of Gradgrind's putative style rather than the authentic voice of the narrator – if Gradgrind were writing a novel, it seems to say, this is the kind of parched and grudging stuff he would produce. The limitations of excessive reliance on metaphorical substitution are therefore asserted by implication and a longing for the liberating openness of metonymy established.

The interesting thing is that Dickens's narrative only rarely satisfies this longing. Metaphorical modes appear insistently throughout the narrative and often in much less ironic ways. In a sense, the whole purpose of the novel is to convince us of a number of equivalences, most particularly that between the educational philosophy of Gradgrind and the economic theory and practice of the new industrialism; and it is in metaphor that this association is established. The descriptions of Gradgrind and Bounderby in chapters I:I and I:IV establish a number of similarities between them which assist the metaphorical transposition of their roles and social positions: both men are more inanimate than animate, Gradgrind being like a wall, and Bounderby being 'brassy'; both have distorted shapes, though in different ways – Gradgrind is recurrently 'square' while Bounderby is round, 'puffed', 'swelled' and 'inflated' and both have bullying postures. One particular metaphor is applied to both of them in a way that seals the resemblance; Gradgrind's hair is described as 'a plantation of firs to keep the wind from its shining surface' (I:I, 1), while Bounderby's hair is 'all standing up in disorder ... in that condition from being constantly blown about by his windy boastfulness' (I:IV, 14). The equivalence between Gradgrind and Bounderby makes the interchangeability of industry and education upon which Dickens insists seem natural and solid (though also, of course, to be condemned).

It may seem rather odd that when, on one level, the novel is a condemnation of the metaphorical or substitutive frame of mind, Dickens should resort to metaphor to affirm the structural resemblances in his novel. Another example of the way that *Hard Times* connives in what it condemns is the account given of the predatory voyeurism of Mrs Sparsit as she spies on Louisa and Harthouse. Her fixation expresses itself in a metaphor:

> Now, Mrs Sparsit was not a poetical woman; but she took an idea in the nature of an allegorical fancy, into her head ... She erected in her mind a mighty Staircase, with a dark pit of shame and ruin at the bottom; and down those stairs, from day to day and hour to hour, she saw Louisa coming.
>
> (II:X, 201–2)

Mrs Sparsit's obsession with this metaphor is extreme and is clearly a mark of her jealous attempts to control and exploit people and events. The metaphor is of course a highly melodramatic one, and there is something satisfyingly appropriate about Mrs Sparsit's unconscious choice of this debased literary mode to embody her spite. But, although Dickens's narrative distances itself from the metaphor by means of its irony, it also begins to adopt it for itself and to extract profit from it. The Staircase becomes Dickens's leitmotiv as well as Mrs Sparsit's *idée fixe* – 'The figure descended the great stairs, steadily, steadily; always verging, like a weight in deep water, to the black gulf at the bottom ... Very near the bottom now. Upon the brink of the abyss ... She elopes! She falls from the lowermost stair, and is swallowed up in the gulf! (II:X, 206–13). The titles of the chapters, 'Lower and Lower' and 'Down' also emphasise the theft of the image, as does the culminating scene of book II, in which Louisa, having reached the bottom of the descent, falls in an insensible heap at her father's feet.

The unconscious complicity between Dickens's language and Mrs Sparsit's is a sign of a more deeply rooted association between the dominant metaphorical mode of signification in Dickens's text and the metaphorical mode of signification it condemns in Gradgrind and the party of Fact. Metaphor is repeatedly used to discredit metaphor as Dickens mounts a systematic assault on systematic thought.

All this is despite the fact that Dickens's own narrative tries repeatedly to associate itself with the fanciful openness of fairy-tale. Often fairy-tale images and references seem to offer an ironic kind of compensation for or revenge on the narrative and linguistic failure of the masters of Coketown, as, for example, when Gradgrind's room is compared to Bluebeard's chamber (I:XV, 96), or when Mrs Sparsit is described (absurdly) as the Bank Fairy and (more acceptably) as the Bank Dragon (II:I, 112). We've seen how fairy-tale is presented in *Hard Times* as a metonymic mode, typified by excess and casual association of ideas. Certainly, some of these authorial references to fairy-tale have this playfulness about them, as with the running joke about the mills being 'fairy palaces' with their 'melancholy-mad elephants'. But fairy-tale is often used in another way, to fix, caricature and punish – as, for example, in the repeated characterisation of Mrs Sparsit as a witch. The allusion to Ali Baba and the Forty Thieves which ends the second chapter does this, too; there is a show of whimsicality in the way that the details of the correspondence are improvised, but the concluding metaphor actually locks together the two halves of the equivalence in a way that narrows and fixes the reader's understanding rather than releasing it:

> He went to work in this preparatory lesson, not unlike Morgiana in the Forty Thieves: looking into all the vessels ranged before him, one after another, to see what they contained. Say, good M'Choakumchild ... When from thy boiling store, thou shalt fill each jar brim full by-and-by, dost thou think that thou wilt always kill outright the robber Fancy lurking within – or sometimes only maim him and distort him!
>
> (I:II, 8)

Dickens's narrative here takes possession of the idea of fairy-tale in a way that shows surprisingly how apt the simplification of character and situation of fairy-tale is to express the caricaturing outlook of Gradgrindery. This association is made even more firmly a couple of chapters later when a nursery rhyme is used to sum up the dismissive attitude of officialdom to the Coketown workers:

> There was an old woman, and what do you think?
> She lived upon nothing but victuals and drink;
> Victuals and drink were the whole of her diet,
> And yet this old woman would NEVER be quiet.
>
> (I:V, 24)

Clearly the use of the nursery rhyme is a deliberate insult to the dignity of Gradgrind and Bounderby, at the same time as it is a parody of their insulting attitude toward the Coketown workers and thus a device to focus the scorn of reader and author alike. But the status of the nursery rhyme is interestingly ambivalent here; does it stand as an example of liberating fancy, or as a characterisation of the brutalising simplications of the utilitarian outlook?

These examples of inconsistency in the use of metaphor and metonymy may not strike us in themselves as conclusive proof of the novel's self-deconstruction, but they do reflect an uncertainty about language, and particularly about the kind of language to be used in representing such strict binary oppositions as the one between Fact and Fancy. It comes down to a matter of authority. The text of *Hard Times* relies upon a notion of presence, upon its contract with its readers that it is speaking of real people and events, that its signifiers substitute for real signifieds, in order to give authority to its recommendation of the metonymic openness of Fancy. But if taken seriously the accreditation of metonymy and difference will tend to undo the firm opposition of Fact and Fancy essential to the book. The text is therefore recommending an openness of interpretation which it must itself resist in order that the recommendation may be made in the first place. Or, to put it another way, the text has to be strictly systematic in order to construct its condemnation of system.

This paradox produces some moments of uneasiness in the novel, not least in the rather odd relationship between seriousness and levity which it displays. The text recommends 'amuthement' against the dogged earnestness of Gradgrindery, but itself lacks the expansive and anarchic comedy, and particularly the comically self-conscious use of language which characterises other novels. The uncertainty about verbal comedy and its implication is made clear interestingly at the moment when Sissy makes a mistake in telling Louisa about her performance at school:

> 'Then Mr M'Choakumchild said he would try me once more. And he said, Here are the stutterings.'
> 'Statistics,' said Louisa.
> 'Yes, Miss Louisa – they always remind me of stutterings, and that's another of my mistakes.'
>
> (I:IX, 57)

There is a neat little joke here and it's a pity to be tedious about it, but I think it is worth spelling out what is going on. The joke involves, of course, the opposition between the ideas of efficiency and inefficiency in language. The word 'stutterings' is obviously in one sense mere noise, whose only meaning consists in representing Sissy's difficulty in pronouncing the word 'statistics'. This kind of inefficiency of language is not without its own significance in *Hard Times*, as we have seen, for it associates Sissy with the metonymic openness of the language of Sleary and the circus. Sissy's stuttering corresponds to Sleary's lisp, for both bring forward the materiality of signifiers, which delays or prevents the simple substitution of words for things. Indeed, Sissy's own name is involved in this. 'Cecilia' probably gives Sleary as much difficulty in pronunciation as 'statistics' gives Sissy, and, of course, as far as Gradgrind is concerned, 'Sissy' represents just the same objectionable metonymic slide away from distinctness as the use of 'stutterings' for 'statistics' (Sleary's own name seems to include a slide between 'slurring' and 'blearing').

But of course the joke consists in the happy accident that 'stutterings' is not just a meaningless mistake. The word that Sissy hits upon *does* have meaning, in that it is an implied judgement on the inefficiency of statistics themselves. Useless as they are for the measurement and understanding of the subtleties of human feeling, statistics really are just 'stutterings'. It is therefore crucial to the joke that 'stutterings' should be meaningless and meaningful at the same time – it would hardly work as well if Sissy thought of 'stilts' or 'stalactites'. But this brings about an inversion in the sign. The inefficient metonymy becomes an efficient, meaningful metaphor, while the metaphor ('statistics') becomes mere sound, as inefficient as we have taken Sissy's mistake to be.

This inversion involves other factors too. For one thing, it inverts the relationship between adult and child. The authoritative world is shown to be really only as playful and silly as the fanciful world of children. The joke plays as well on the opposition of speech and writing, for the authority of the written mode of statistics is undone by the oral mistake that Sissy makes. We could project some of the swapping of places which takes place in the joke into a diagram (the horizontal lines indicate the original associations, the diagonal lines the new associations established by the joke):

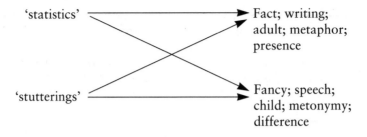

'statistics' ———→ Fact; writing; adult; metaphor; presence

'stutterings' ———→ Fancy; speech; child; metonymy; difference

But this brings about an instability or 'stutter' in Dickens's own narration and in the reader's reception of it. Sissy's innocent use of the word and the narrative's knowing use of it are incompatible with each other, though, because of the structure of the joke, they are also necessary to each other. The reader therefore flickers between the two readings, the adult and the childish, the meaningful and the meaningless, without being able to decide which has priority. The joke has a residue of internal difference which makes it difficult to decide on a serious or non-serious reading. Most importantly, it represents the deconstruction of the narrative's claim to authoritative language, because the joke reveals the structure of difference which constitutes authority of meaning.

Perhaps the most striking example of the dispersal of meaning is to be found in the language of Mrs Gradgrind. Though she is in many ways just a victim of the dominion of Fact, her scattered wits and language also associate her with the world of Fancy in the novel. For, in some senses, her feebleness with language is a strength; her vagueness about names, for example, and, in particular, her inability to use Bounderby's name after he marries Louisa (II:IX, 198), is a comic resistance to the rage for permanence of naming.

But there is also something very frightening about the tenuous grasp of language which Mrs Gradgrind has. Her subservience to a language which, instead of being her instrument, seems to speak uncontrollably through her, is like that of many characters in *Bleak House*; like the victims of Chancery, Mrs Gradgrind feels that she 'never hears the last of anything', because there is no end to language as difference. Personal identity is difficult to pin down once it is divided in this way by language, so that Mrs Gradgrind cannot even be sure that the pain she feels is her own (I:IX, 198). She ends up fixated upon an obscure and unnameable sense of lack:

> 'there is something – not an Ology at all – that your father has missed, or forgotten, Louisa. I don't know what it is. I have often sat with Sissy near me, and thought about it. I shall never get its name now. But your father may. It makes me restless. I want to write to him, to find out for God's sake, what it is. Give me a pen, give me a pen.
>
> (II:IX, 199)

Something strange has happened here; the metonymic diffusion of Fancy has come to seem like a symptom of the alienated language of Fact. It is as though the dominating structure of *Hard Times* had turned into that of *Bleak House*. The language of Mrs Gradgrind, both in her distracted speech, and in the 'figures of wonderful no-meaning' she traces with her imaginary pen (II:IX, 200), poses a challenge to the stability and coherence of *Hard Times*. She represents the largest of a number of blind spots in the novel where the dispersing play of language as difference is activated. The narrative officially celebrates but implicitly condemns and therefore represses this play of difference; but its very meaning is in a sense built upon it.

It is in the nature of these internal arguments within texts to be inconclusive. I have not been trying to build a case that, unknown to so many readers for so many years, *Hard Times* is really a gloriously fragmented modernist or post-modernist text which flaunts its incoherence and demands that its reader join in the vandalism of all meaning. What I do find interesting in the novel is the way that our firm convictions of the clarity of its structure actually require the suspension of awareness of certain rather important internal inconsistencies. These inconsistencies have a residual force though, working athwart the main narrative but also, in a peculiar way, sustaining it.

This is to say, then, that if our sense of the coherence and structural simplicity of *Hard Times* is an illusion, then it is a necessary illusion. Reading is a continually renewed struggle between the openness of text and the satisfying closure of interpretation. Each is related to the other indissolubly. Seen in this way, *Hard Times* may come to seem a little less naïve. Because the book is so committed to the projection of the stark opposites of Fact and Fancy, the risk is all the greater of discovering it to be haunted by internal difference, of the book being revealed as another text entirely from the one it represents itself to be. Nevertheless, this is the dangerous story that *Hard Times* begins to tell about itself.

This is not the last account that Dickens attempts to give of the conflict between 'humanity' and 'system'. In the next chapters [of *Charles Dickens*] I want to look at the different ways in which Dickens engages with this opposition in his last two completed novels. What will emerge is that the problematic shiftings between metaphor and metonymy, presence and difference, are more than just linguistic issues; they are related to fundamental questions about the nature and formation of identity in society and to specific questions of authority and power.

From Steven Connor, *Charles Dickens* (Oxford, 1985), pp. 89–106.

NOTES

[As Steven Connor points out, *Hard Times* makes a particularly good test case for a deconstructive approach. This is because so many critics have treated it as a didactic, thesis-dominated novel, in which Dickens argues the case for 'life' and 'fancy' as against 'fact' and 'system'. In Connor's words: 'What can deconstruction do with such a simple and reductive text, one that seems to have done so complete a job of silencing all internal dissension?' His approach is to look at the ways in which the principal thematic issues are represented in linguistic terms in the text. Part of the astuteness of Connor's argument is his recognition that his reading is not totally at odds with traditional views of the novel, for if the majority of readers have been struck by the coherence and structural simplicity of *Hard Times*, then this is more than an illusion, it is a necessary illusion, for *Hard Times* is a text that sets out to persuade the reader. But what Connor shows is that the didactic power of the text is achieved by Dickens dashing over internal inconsistencies in the argument. Critics have, in the past, attacked inconsistencies in the text as faults, but Connor accepts inconsistencies as inevitable, indeed as strengthening features, for they point to the genuine complexity of a text. The essay is a very clear illustration of a deconstructive approach to Dickens, but it is at the same time a rather difficult essay to follow because of the inherent philosophical difficulty of the deconstructionist's position. Connor starts from linguistics, in particular the distinction between metaphor and metonomy. Although both metaphor and metonomy are utilised in all texts, writers tend towards one axis or the other. Virginia Woolf, for example, leans towards metaphor, whereas a realistic novelist, such as Arnold Bennett, leans towards the use of metonomy. In Dickens's *Hard Times* the two tendencies are roughly equivalent to 'fancy' and 'fact'. As Connor shows, however, the text cannot sustain this

simple opposition in a straightforward way. At the most basic level of language, the text quickly becomes complicated, disrupting itself from the
inside. Texts might foster expectations of unity, significance and structure,
but at the same time they set up signifying processes which disperse, under-
cut and deconstruct these ideas. All references to *Hard Times* in this essay
are to the Oxford Illustrated Edition (London, 1955), and are by chapter
and book number in roman numerals, and by page number in arabic numerals. Readers wishing to find out more about the metaphor/metonomy
distinction in relation to fiction might like to consult David Lodge's *The
Modes of Modern Writing* (London, 1977). Ed.]

1. Barbara Johnson, *The Critical Difference: Essays in the Contemporary
   Rhetoric of Reading* (Baltimore and London, 1980), p. 5.

2. *The Melancholy Man: A Study of Dickens's Novels* (London, 1970),
   p. 254. Terry Eagleton finds the novel 'sealed and static ... a false and
   premature over-totalisation', *Criticism and Ideology: A Study of
   Marxist Literary Theory* (London, 1978), p. 130; and Fredric Jameson
   uses it to mount a specimen structuralist analysis, 'because, as Dickens's
   only didactic or "thesis" novel, it involves an idea content which has
   already been formulated for us in terms of a binary opposition', *The
   Prison-House of Language* (Princeton, 1972), p. 167. The notable dis-
   senter from this view is, of course, F. R. Leavis, who welcomes the 'insistent' moral intention, as a controlling influence on Dickens's
   tendency, in his creative exuberance, to spin out redundant detail; F. R.
   and Q. D. Leavis, *Dickens the Novelist* (London, 1973), p. 188.

3. Roger Fowler's 'Polyphony and Problematic in *Hard Times*', in
   R. Giddings (ed.), *The Changing World of Charles Dickens* (London,
   1983), pp. 91–108, examines interestingly the contrasts between different kinds of voices in the novel.

8

Family and Society in *Hard Times*

CATHERINE GALLAGHER

And yet, in my opinion, the world is but one great family. Originally it was so. What then is this narrow [family] selfishness that reigns in us, but relationship remembered against relationship forgot?

(Samuel Richardson, *Clarissa Harlowe*)

Never before did I hear of an Irish Widow reduced to 'prove her sisterhood by dying of typhus-fever and infecting seventeen persons,' – saying in such undeniable way, 'You *see*, I was your sister!' Sisterhood, brotherhood, was often forgotten; but not till the rise of these ultimate Mammon and Shotbelt Gospels did I ever see it so expressly denied.

(Thomas Carlyle, *Past and Present*)

By 1854 Chartism was moribund, but militant trade unionism lived on in the north of England, producing some of the most prolonged strikes and lockouts of the century. The strike and lockout at Preston in 1853–4, for example, lasted more than eight months,[1] convincing many observers that, although Chartism no longer flourished in factory towns, the classes there were still mightily and dangerously opposed. Charles Dickens and Elizabeth Gaskell were two such observers; in their respective novels, *Hard Times* (1854) and

North and South (1855), they attempted to describe industrial society and present solutions to the problems of class antagonism.

Like the magazine narratives of the time,[2] *Hard Times* and *North and South* ostensibly propose that social cohesion can be achieved by changing the relationship between family and society, by introducing cooperative behaviour, presumably preserved in private life, into the public realm. These two novels, moreover, use the same metaphoric and metonymic tropes the magazine stories employed to connect public and private realms. Like J. M. Rymer and G. W. M. Reynolds, Dickens uses the social paternalists' metaphor[3] and concomitant melodramatic conventions, whereas Gaskell explores the metonymic relationship between the family and society, incorporating elements from didactic domestic fiction into her novel.

Hard Times and *North and South* reveal, however, in a way that the magazine fiction does not, the contradictions latent in social paternalism and domestic ideology. Despite their attempts to make social relations personal, to advocate that the relations between classes become like the cooperative associations of family life, both novels ultimately propose the isolation of families from the larger society. Critics have complained that these novels finally retreat into the private, familial areas of the plot, apparently leaving their social concerns behind; the endings have, therefore, been seen as false solutions, and their falseness has been traced either to their authors' fears of working-class revolt or to some inherent incompatibility between the presentation of social problems and the novel form.[4]

We have seen, however, that the tendency to dissociate the family from society is prevalent in both social paternalism and domestic ideology. Both assume the separation of the public and private spheres they attempt to integrate. The novels, unlike the magazine stories, parallel the ideologies by initially establishing definite boundaries between their social and private plots. In the seamstress melodramas, as we saw, the metaphoric children of the aristocrats were also revealed to be their actual children; thus, the mere discovery of the seamstresses' identities integrated the social and familial plots. But in *Hard Times* the children are not actual workers; although family relations are compared to class relations, the two are not identical. In *North and South*, too, there is an initial disconnection between the family under consideration and the society needing reformation. Here the domestic heroine, the woman whose influence advances social progress, is the daughter of a clergyman, but unlike many heroines of didactic domestic tales, she is not a member of the working class, nor is she at the outset related to either of the classes involved in industrial conflict. In both novels, then, as in both ideologies, there is at first a distance that is never completely overcome between the public and private spheres, for although their ostensible purpose is to connect the two realms, both ideologies ultimately advocate the continued isolation of the family from society. Social paternalists argued that only through such isolation could the family be preserved as a model, benign hierarchy. The domestic ideologists, too, insisted that the family remain a separate sphere, one untouched by competition and strife, because the home would have no power to heal if it were itself contaminated by society's ills. The final retreats into personal, familial concerns that critics have noticed in the novels, therefore, have analogies in both social paternalism and domestic ideology. By advocating the integration of public and private life and then dissociating the two, the novels reproduce the paradox of the ideologies that inform them.

Unlike the magazine stories, moreover, *Hard Times* and *North and South* belong to a genre that mandates both the integration and the separation of public and personal themes. As we saw earlier, nineteenth-century English novels are characterised by a structural tension between impulses to associate and to dissociate public and private realms of experience. The tension, however, is unusually noticeable in these two industrial novels because they emphasise thematically the very thing they cannot achieve structurally: the integration of public and private life. A confluence of ideological and formal factors, therefore, caused the contradictions and reversals that critics of these novels have remarked.

The novels consequently not only lay bare the contradictions of two Victorian ideologies, but also magnify a paradox at the heart of the novel form. Just as the industrial novels of the 1840s exaggerated the novelistic tension between free will and determinism, the industrial novels of the 1850s highlight the novels' unstable relation between public and private realms. Like the earlier novels, the industrial novels of the 1850s focus attention on one of the genre's most problematic *données*. In *Hard Times* and *North and South*, therefore, Dickens and Gaskell explore the very foundations of their

art, exposing its structural inconsistencies. In fact, both of these realistic novels become, as we will see, reflections on their narrative
methods.

HARD TIMES: THE UNMAKING OF A METAPHOR

Of these two reflections, Dickens's is the more fractured and dis-
continuous, for in *Hard Times* the impulse to dissociate the family
and society is ultimately much stronger than the impulse to connect
the two. The strength of the dissociative tendency is partly due to
the fact that Dickens uses metaphor to connect his plots: metaphors
separate even as they interrelate the things they compare. But the
impulse towards separation is further strengthened by Dickens's
special use of the family–society metaphor, a use that, as we will
see, gives family reform priority over social reform and tries to substitute family solidarity for social cohesion. Finally, the novel questions the very enterprise of making metaphors in a world where
connections, when they are possible, are almost always destructive.

However, before we analyse the ways in which *Hard Times* subverts the family–society metaphor, we must outline the ways in
which the narrative first establishes its comparison between the
Gradgrind family and industrial society. The situation of the
Gradgrind children is both explicitly and implicitly likened to the
situation of the Coketown workers, and the relationship between
Louisa and her father is paralleled by the relationship between
Stephen Blackpool and his employer, Mr Bounderby. The first two
chapters of the novel, where the ideas of children and industrial
workers are merged in the figures of working-class children, lay the
groundwork for the family–society metaphor. In these chapters, we
observe the overpowering presence of Gradgrind and his philosophy, pacifying and repressing the school children. But in the third
and fourth chapters, the idea of oppressed children is split off from
the image of working-class children and embodied in the figures of
Tom and Louisa. This separation is so subtle that the reader is at
first only vaguely aware of the class difference between the little
Gradgrinds and the school children of the first chapter. In fact, in
our first view of Tom and Louisa, which is, significantly, through
Mr Gradgrind's eyes, they are indistinguishable from a group of
'young rabble from a model school'.[5] Moreover, once they are
clearly identified by their father and separated from the larger

group, they are taken home to an establishment so like the model school that class differences between the two groups of children still appear irrelevant to their oppression.

Chapter 5 introduces another victim of the Gradgrind philosophy: the adult working population of Coketown. At this point, working-class children all but disappear from the novel; Sissy and Bitzer become members of the Gradgrind and Bounderby establishments. Having separated children and the working class from one another, the narrative reconnects them through metaphor. Their original association in the composite figures of the opening chapters lingers, but the narrator now adopts a new mode of connection: explicit analogy. In one of those Carlylean questions that can only be answered affirmatively, the narrator asks, 'Is it possible, I wonder, that there was any analogy between the case of the Coketown population and the case of the little Gradgrinds?' (p. 19). The story that follows answers this question affirmatively and illustrates the proposed analogy in parallels between Louisa and Stephen Blackpool. Still, for the first half of the novel, Stephen's and Louisa's stories intersect only through their common inclusion of Mr Bounderby; otherwise the stories proceed on independent but parallel courses, the parallels constructed in such a way as to maintain the metaphoric connection between the middle-class family and the larger society: Stephen is to Mr Bounderby as Louisa is to her father.

The parallels are implicitly developed in the interviews between Stephen and Bounderby in chapter 11 and between Louisa and Gradgrind in chapter 15. In each interview, the topic is marriage; in each the 'father' is called on to give advice to the 'child', and in each the former fails to give the proper advice, leaving the latter with a diminished sense of life's possibilities. Both Gradgrind and Bounderby discount the emotional reality of marriage. Bounderby maintains that Stephen's miserable marriage is a fact that he must continue to live with: 'You didn't take your wife for fast and for loose; but for better for worse. If she has turned out worse – why all we have got to say is, she might have turned out better' (p. 58). In Bounderby's opinion, Stephen has taken a calculated risk – and lost. Mr Bounderby stands behind the divorce law that condemns Stephen to suffer perpetually for his wife's intemperance. The employer's dismissal of his workman's problem clearly represents Bounderby's failure, and the failure of others like him, to recognise the human needs of the working class. 'Show me the law to help me!' Stephen demands, and Bounderby's reply emphasises the class injustice built into English law: 'There *is* such a law ... But it's not for you at all. It costs money. It costs a mint of money' (pp. 57–8).[6]

Bounderby and the laws he upholds keep Stephen in his unhappy marriage, and Gradgrind, through a similar sort of blindness, leads Louisa into an equally miserable liaison, her loveless marriage to Bounderby. Like Bounderby, Gradgrind refuses to consider the emotional dimension of marriage. His advice to Louisa is significant in what it leaves out:

> I would advise you (since you ask me) to consider this question, as you have been accustomed to consider every other question, simply as one of tangible Fact. The ignorant and the giddy may embarrass such subjects with irrelevant fancies, and other absurdities that have no existence, properly viewed– ... you know better.
>
> (p. 75)

Louisa's requests for help are understated compared to Stephen's, but they are repeated and insistent, and Gradgrind's failure to answer them is glaring. Gradgrind refuses to recognise his daughter's emotional needs, just as Bounderby has refused to recognise Stephen's.

The two interviews have similar effects on Stephen and Louisa. The first reaction of each is despondency. Stephen's desperate ''Tis just a muddle a'toogether, an' the sooner I am dead, the better' echoes in Louisa's quieter reply, 'What does it matter?' Both Stephen and Louisa then embrace the consolation to be found in chaste and self-sacrificing attachments outside their marriages, but for both such love is also self-destructive. Because of Stephen's dedication to Rachael, he refuses to take part in the strike, and Louisa's love for Tom impels her to marry Mr Bounderby. Having been denied the paternal guidance they sought, the worker and the child find emotional transcendence in self-sacrifice. Stephen combines his loyalty to Rachael with his religious sentiments, seeing her as an angel and promising ' t' trust 't th' time, when thou and me at last shall walk together far awa', beyond the deep gulf, in th' country where thy little sister is [heaven]' (p. 69). Louisa's hope is secular, but it reveals a similar devaluation of her present life. She believes herself unfitted by her education to do those things that according to the popular ideas of femininity might have saved Tom: 'I don't know what other girls know. I can't play to you or sing to you. I can't talk to you so as to lighten your mind, for I never see any amusing sights or read any amusing books that it would be a pleasure or a relief to you to talk about, when you are tired' (p. 39). But because Tom has been her only love, she resolves to dedicate her otherwise useless life to his service by marrying Bounderby: 'While it [life] lasts, I would wish to do the little I can, and the little I am fit for' (p. 77).

Indeed, when Stephen and Louisa meet, they feel an immediate sympathy for one another. In his second interview at the Bounderby home, Stephen 'instinctively' addresses himself to Louisa, finding his 'natural refuge' in her face (p. 113), and Louisa rushes out to help Stephen as soon as she discovers he is fired. Later she will have an interview with her father that parallels Stephen's second conversation with Bounderby; in it she confronts her father with his failings, just as Stephen presents the grievances of the working class to his employer.

In the second half of the novel, however, where Dickens joins his plots together, the family–society metaphor disintegrates. The contact between Stephen and Louisa begins the process of disintegration. Because the point of a metaphor is to find likeness in difference, and because its terms normally replace one another, introducing the two terms literally into the same scene destroys the necessary distance between the metaphor's levels. The metaphoric connection is then attenuated by this literal proximity, for the differences between the terms become more evident than the similarities. Integrating Louisa's and Stephen's stories, therefore, gradually destroys their metaphoric link: the differences between Gradgrind's daughter and Bounderby's workman become clearer than the likenesses.

The differences between Stephen and Louisa were always, of course, one dimension of their metaphoric connection. While Dickens paralleled Louisa's and Stephen's stories, he kept them distinct. The principle of metaphoric integration, therefore, led to a separation of the plots. Conversely, the train of events set off by Louisa's and Tom's visit to Stephen's house destroys the point of the metaphor: the idea that middle-class children and workers share a common oppression and hence a community of interests. That is to say, the family–society metaphor breaks down because Louisa and Tom grow up and have their own roles to play in the larger society, roles that are, moreover, opposed to Stephen's well-being. Certainly, Tom's interests are more directly antagonistic to Stephen's than are Louisa's: indeed, part of the reason for comparing workers to daughters was that both were believed to be perpetual children who never develop completely separate interests. Nevertheless, to the extent that Louisa's primary loyalty is to Tom, she does grow up to have interests opposed to Stephen's. The metaphoric connection between the worker and child – the connection that depends on separation – might have been potentially healing, but their literal connection is destructive.

Indeed, most literal relationships in this novel are destructive: *Hard Times* uses the family–society metaphor in a way that exaggerates its tendency toward separation. In developing the idea of a common oppression for workers and children, Dickens initially uses the metaphor in the pessimistic way that G. W. M. Reynolds and Thomas Carlyle used it,[7] to describe an extreme state of social crisis. As do Reynolds and Carlyle, Dickens reverses the usual direction of the paternalist metaphor. Instead of presenting us with an ideal family on which society should model itself, he depicts a family that is itself no more than a mirror of an exploitative society. At the outset, the Gradgrind family does not represent potential relations of social harmony, but actual relations of domination, denial, and oppression. The Gradgrinds embody none of the positive values normally associated with the family; Coketown is remarkably homogeneous publicly and privately. In fact, the narrator, in his descriptions of Coketown and the Gradgrind establishment, emphasises the consistency of this oppression: the entire environment is 'severely workful' (p. 17). The workers and the children suffer not from simple neglect, not from a lack of connection with their employers and parents, but from actively destructive connections. The relationships in the novel are like the 'serpents of smoke' that coiled themselves around the town 'and never got uncoiled': they suffocate the inhabitants. Louisa's relationships to her father, to Tom, and to Bounderby, are too close. Stephen is also caught in a destructive relationship, the continuance of which is enforced by legal coils, laws that only hinder and never help him. All of Bounderby's relationships are seen to be exploitative as well: he ends his connections with his mother, Mrs Sparsit, Louisa and Stephen only when he can no longer profit from them.

Hard Times, therefore, does not present industrial society as disconnected, nor does it initially display the family as a model of cohesive, non-exploitative relationships. Dickens's inverted use of the family–society metaphor gives the first part of the novel a definite structural symmetry, but it also makes social reform the second item on the novel's agenda. In order for paternalist reform to proceed here, for society to be reorganised as a harmonious extended family, the family itself must first be reformed. However, the process of bringing about family reform, of making the Gradgrind family cooperative and nurturing, creates disconnections: it divorces the family from the rest of society, and it separates family members from one another.

The first of these disconnections, the divorce of the Gradgrind family from the rest of society, can be seen as a characteristic discontinuity within social paternalism, a discontinuity exaggerated by Dickens's pessimistic use of the family–society metaphor. In *Hard Times*, Dickens, like many social paternalists, seeks to connect the family and society through metaphor alone. An additional literal connection between the two not only destroys the distance necessary to the social paternalists' metaphor, but also makes the family vulnerable to society's corruptions. In this novel, where almost all literal connections are destructive, the only imaginable regeneration establishes a new kind of distance between the Gradgrind family and industrial society, the distance not of metaphoric difference but of actual antagonism.

The Gradgrind family becomes a model of harmony and security, a paradigm for proper social relations, only by undergoing internal change. Gradgrind taught his children to act on what they rationally determine to be their own best interests, but Tom's crime exposes the failure of an education based on this principle. Through Louisa's crises and through Sissy Jupe's subtle influence, Gradgrind comes to realise his love for his children and his responsibility to guide and protect them. He no longer views them as young automatons but as children in need of his emotional attention. Gradgrind's conversion to this new mode of fatherhood is proved by his conduct toward young Tom at the book's conclusion. In this episode, Gradgrind sacrifices his old principles of reason and self-interest to his new belief in family loyalty. The confrontation between Gradgrind and Bitzer, for example, is designed to emphasise the former's conversion from extreme utilitarianism to paternalism. The Gradgrind family manifests its new solidarity by conspiring with that other model of cohesion, the circus, to help young Tom escape. Thus, the Gradgrind family ostensibly comes to embody the virtues of loyalty and compassion, and thereby takes a necessary step toward becoming an appropriate model for society.

But what significance does this Gradgrind solidarity finally have for the larger society? How does the familial metaphor work itself out? Paradoxically, the new Gradgrind family cooperativeness accomplishes the final dismantling of the novel's metaphoric organisation. At the very moment Dickens restores the usual, optimistic direction of the paternalist metaphor – the ideal family as a model for society – the parallel between the Gradgrind children and the working class collapses. For the Gradgrinds become a model family only by symbolically betraying the working class and breaking society's laws: although young Tom is primarily responsible for Stephen's death, the Gradgrind family rallies to his defence. Later, Mr Gradgrind does clear Stephen's name of Tom's crime, but his first effort is to save his own son from justice. Moreover, as both Bitzer and Sleary point out, the act that proves the triumph of the cohesive forces of the novel compounds Tom's felony. For the Gradgrinds, therefore, becoming a model family means cutting themselves off from larger social considerations and retreating into the morality of clannishness.

Hard Times, then, ultimately exposes a dilemma inherent in the proposal that society be modelled on the family. The advocates of paternalist reform often idealised the family as a bastion of harmony and order, isolating it in their thought from the as yet unregenerated society in order to make it worthy of imitation. By advocating the isolation of the family, however, social paternalists reconstituted the very disjunction between the public and private spheres they set out to overcome. This dilemma, which inheres in *Hard Times*' structuring metaphor, partly accounts for the seeming reversal at the end of the book. By ending the novel with a depiction of the family as a protective dominion, Dickens is not turning away from his social ideology to meet some formal demand; he is, rather, drawing out to an absurd extreme the ideology's own paradoxical logic. The same social beliefs that have led Dickens to maintain the family–society analogy throughout the novel have led him to retreat into the purely private sphere at the story's end.

In *Hard Times*, however, the retreat into the family circle is fraught with ambiguities: a novel that advocates easier divorces, and one that in fact separates the heroine, Louisa, from her husband in order to achieve family solidarity, cannot be said to create unequivocal optimism about family relations. The establishment of truly cooperative family connections in *Hard Times* requires not only the reform of certain relationships but also the complete severance of others. Stephen might have had a happy family life with Rachael if he could have been divorced from his drunken wife. Louisa can find a father in Gradgrind and a sister in Sissy Jupe only if she leaves Bounderby.

The establishment of proper father–child relations between Gradgrind and his children, moreover, results in separations among the Gradgrinds themselves. Louisa's crisis, after all, does not immediately turn Gradgrind into a father capable of protecting and guiding her. Rather, it teaches him that he has already interfered too much in her life, and he decides to withdraw, allowing Sissy to become Louisa's saviour. The resolution of the father–daughter relationship is, indeed, an interrupted melodrama, one that shades into a domestic tale. We watch, partially through Mrs Sparsit's jealous eyes, as Louisa is apparently seduced by the diabolical dandy James Harthouse. Preyed upon by husband, brother, and lover, Louisa is seen descending a gothic staircase of dishonour in Mrs Sparsit's imagination. At the last moment, however, in true melodramatic fashion, Louisa summons the strength to escape her seducer and seek her father's protection. But in the scene of recognition and reconciliation between father and daughter, *Hard Times* departs from the conventions of melodrama. Louisa does confront her father and reveal her 'true self' to him, and Gradgrind does recognise his daughter at that moment for the first time. According to the conventions, this scene should close with a tableau: the newfound daughter firmly supported in her father's strong arms. Louisa however, has never suffered from her father's neglect; rather, she has had too much attention from him, and it has been the wrong kind of attention; 'If you had only neglected me,' she tells him, 'what a much better and much happier creature I should have been this day' (p. 165). Recognition is completed in this scene, but reconciliation does not follow automatically; the old destructive bond must be broken first. The scene's final tableau represents not union but separation:

> He tightened his hold in time to prevent her sinking on the floor, but she cried out in a terrible voice, 'I shall die if you hold me! Let me fall upon the ground!' And he laid her down there and saw the pride of his heart and the triumph of his system, lying, an insensible heap, at his feet.
>
> (p. 167)

Gradgrind helps save his daughter by letting go of her. In their next conversation, he explains to Louisa why he is delegating his parental responsibility to Sissy Jupe:

> 'I am far from feeling convinced now ... that I am fit for the trust you
> repose in me; that I know how to respond to the appeal you have
> come home to make to me; that I have the right instinct how to help
> you, and to set you right, my child.'
>
> (p. 169)

Gradgrind turns Louisa over to someone with the 'right instinct',
and Louisa is reclaimed by the innocent child-woman. As in a domestic tale, Sissy becomes an object of adoration and a surrogate
mother for Louisa.

> [Louisa] fell upon her knees, and clinging to this stroller's child
> looked up at her almost with veneration.
>   'Forgive me, pity me, help me! Have compassion on my great need,
> and let me lay this head of mine upon a loving heart!'
>   'O lay it here!' cried Sissy. 'Lay it here, my dear'.
>
> (p. 172)

Louisa sinks to her knees and rests her head on Sissy's bosom; they
become the accepting mother and the penitent child.[8]

It is Sissy, therefore, not Gradgrind, who reclaims Louisa and
later protects her from James Harthouse. In these actions, Sissy
plays the role of a family member; but Dickens reminds us that 'this
stroller's child' is not really related to Louisa. Indeed, at the close of
Sissy's interview with Harthouse, Dickens emphasises that she is
not a Gradgrind. 'Pardon my curiosity at parting. Related to the
family?' Harthouse asks.

> 'I am only a poor girl,' returned Sissy. 'I was separated from my
> father – he was only a stroller – and taken pity on by Mr Gradgrind.
> I have lived in the house ever since.'
>
> (p. 179)

Louisa's real relatives are powerless to help her: Sissy, an abandoned child, must play the parent to Louisa.

Sissy plays a similar role in the relationship between Gradgrind
and Tom: she sets up the conditions for Tom's escape, thereby providing an occasion for Gradgrind to demonstrate his loyalty to his
son. But even this climactic act of cooperation – the conspiracy to
help Tom escape – is really an act of expulsion accomplished amid
the trappings of farce. Gradgrind, sitting 'forlorn, on the clown's
performing chair in the middle of the [circus] ring', confronts his
erring son, who is disguised as a black servant, 'with seams in his

black face, where fear and heat had started through the greasy com-position daubed all over it' (p. 215). Tom is 'grimly, detestably, ridiculously shameful', and Gradgrind is thoroughly humiliated. Tom, moreover, is not at all contrite; he is sullen toward his father and denounces Louisa outright. His conduct prompts Gradgrind to ask Sleary how he can 'get this deplorable object away'. The whole demoralising incident ends in a farcical animal act, with Bitzer, Tom's pursuer, pinned down between a dancing horse and a wrestling dog.

Indeed, family solidarity and personal fidelity are reduced to canine wonders, as Sleary attempts to broaden Gradgrind's moral horizons with an illustration of natural affection, the story of Sissy's father's dog, Merrylegs, who returned to the circus after his master's death, seeking his little mistress. Sleary concludes, 'It theemth to prethent two thingth to a perthon, don't it, Thquire?... one, that there ith a love in the world, not all thelf-intoretht after all ... ; t'other, that it hath a way of ith own of calculating or not cal-culating, with somehow or another ith at leatht ath hard to give a name to, ath the wayth of the dogth ith!' (p. 222). In this ending, exemplary family behaviour and 'the wayth of the dogth' are indis-tinguishable. Tom's escape does prove that the Gradgrinds have become a loyal clan, but it also disperses them and makes them sadly ridiculous. A close look at their pageant of solidarity thus shows it to be a grim farce culminating in separation.

The novel, therefore, contains a hopelessness about family rela-tionships, a hopelessness that makes it impossible for the Gradgrinds to become an appropriate model for a regenerated society. In *Hard Times* social paternalism's innate tendency toward public–private discontinuity is exaggerated by the novel's implicit view of family relations. The novel seems to retreat into the private realm, but that realm is itself criss-crossed by barriers. It is, there-fore, not surprising that even the reformed Gradgrinds are power-less to change Coketown. Since their family cohesion is itself fragile and ambiguous, it can hardly provide inspiration for social cohesion.

In the last chapter, which depicts the characters' futures, the Gradgrinds remain in melancholy isolation from one another and from the larger society, which goes unreformed. Louisa is never to have a family of her own, Tom is to die repentant but alone. Gradgrind's political role, we are told, will change because of his reformation as a father, but as a consequence of that reformation he will become powerless and isolated. Like most of Dickens's good fathers, Gradgrind seems to become unfit for leadership (p. 225). Bounderby, on the other hand, remains completely unreformed, but his power extends itself. Although he cuts himself off from Mrs Sparsit and Louisa, he manages to turn himself into a small crowd. At the novel's close there are twenty-five Josiah Bounderbys instead of one, all produced celibately, through the legal cloning of Bounderby's 'vain-glorious will', which stipulates that

> five-and-twenty Humbugs, past five-and-fifty years of age, each taking upon himself the name, Josiah Bounderby of Coketown, should for ever dine in Bounderby Hall, for ever lodge in Bounderby buildings, for ever attend a Bounderby chapel, for ever go to sleep under a Bounderby chaplain, for ever be supported out of a Bounderby estate, and for ever nauseate all healthy stomachs, with a vast amount of Bounderby balderdash and bluster.
>
> (p. 225)

Since the good father is impotent and the bad father unrepentant, the job of reforming society falls on Sissy's slight shoulders. Sissy's future, the last to be predicted, is the only one in which family harmony and social progress are linked. Sissy's future actions link the two metonymically, however, in the manner of domestic ideology; moreover, the connection does not seem powerful enough to bring about social change. Sissy, of course, does become a mother, 'grown learned in childish lore', and she extends her maternal care to 'her humbler fellow creatures', trying 'to beautify their lives of machinery and reality'. The narrator, though, does not suggest that Sissy's activity can materially change the harsh industrial town. The society itself is not transformed into a vast family. The final paragraph refers to 'our two fields of action' (p. 227) and recommends that the reader do his duty in each, but the hope that the two might be connected in a metaphoric transformation has been abandoned. Indeed, the 'two fields of action' are more widely divided at the end of the novel than they were at its beginning.

Despite the fact that *Hard Times* overtly celebrates family love and social cohesion, therefore, the novel actually presents a series of separations: separations between the family and society, and separations within the family itself. As we have seen, the book's tendency to sever connections arises from its use of the family–society metaphor, for separation is both implicit in the trope and exaggerated by Dickens's vision of the actively harmful relationships dominating both public and private life. Indeed, the book seems suffused with a fear of making connections in a world where relationships are almost without exception destructive.

This fear helps account for the book's metaphoric organisation: metaphors, because they generally maintain the differences between the objects they compare, can be seen as a way of avoiding the destructive proximity of literal connections. Thus, the metaphoric connection between Louisa and Stephen is beneficial in so far as it allows us to sympathise more fully with the working class by forcing us to see their suffering in terms of the suffering of oppressed children. But when Stephen and Louisa come into actual contact, their relationship becomes mutually harmful. The author's preference for metaphor is manifested in several other aspects of the novel as well; the narrator of *Hard Times* explicitly recommends making metaphors as a regenerative activity, and provides them in abundance himself. Metaphors are a hallmark of Dickens's style in all his novels, but in *Hard Times* they become a thematic preoccupation, even an obsession. This novel can, indeed, be seen as a book *about* metaphors.

It is also, however, a book in which metaphors often break down or reveal themselves to be pure illusions, mere shows that conceal (and often ill-conceal) seamy actualities.[9] In *Hard Times* even metaphoric connections are ambivalently presented. Indeed, as we will see, if the novel can be said to endorse unequivocally any connections at all, it endorses the connections made not by the fanciful narrator but by the book's most literal-minded character – the single character incapable of seeing anything in terms of anything else – Sissy Jupe. The novel, therefore, actually exhibits a distrust of its own metaphors at the same time that it explicitly recommends them.

Metaphor is introduced as an explicit theme in *Hard Times* through the book's many discussions of 'Fancy', a theme that fits neatly into the novel's paternalist scheme; Coketown's workers and Gradgrind's children are both denied 'Fancy'. They are comparable, then, because they suffer a common oppression. Moreover, the issue allows the narrator to argue explicitly in favour of making metaphors and to crowd such tropes into his own narration.[10] The book, therefore, has an excessively metaphoric style, as well as a metaphoric structure, and its style becomes one of its themes. We are told, for example, that if the little Gradgrinds had been allowed to develop metaphoric imaginations, they might have seen their teacher as an ogre (p. 7) or their schoolroom as a 'dark cavern' (p. 40). Similarly, workers with imaginative faculties would be able to see their illuminated factories as 'Fairy palaces' (p. 49). But the emphasis on fact in Coketown allows no such fanciful escapes for workers or children. The narrator, as if to compensate for the poverty of indigenous Coketown metaphors, supplies an abundance of his own. In a single paragraph, for example, Coketown's brick is compared to 'the painted face of a savage': the factory chimneys discharge 'interminable serpents of smoke'; and the piston of the steam engine is the 'head of an elephant in a state of melancholy madness' (p. 17). These separate metaphors and similes coalesce into a single image of Coketown as a jungle, an image that was used by advocates of 'internal missions', and one that resonates with echoes of the worker–slave metaphor. Paragraphs like this one illustrate the narrator's metaphoric excesses and demonstrate his already explicitly stated commitment to that trope.

The narrator, moreover, is not the novel's only locus of fanciful activity. The circus embodies fancy, and its members dramatise the social paternalists' trope: the family–society metaphor. The unrelated individuals of the circus society come together and behave like a loyal family. Most comically and grotesquely emblematic of this sort of family role-playing is the relationship between E. W. B. Childers, the Wild Huntsman of the North American prairies, and Master Kidderminster, a dwarf who 'assisted as his infant son: being carried upside down over his father's shoulder, by one foot, and held by the crown of his head, heels upward, in the palm of his father's hand, according to the violent paternal manner in which wild huntsmen may be observed to fondle their offspring' (p. 23). The more normal members of the company are also described as 'sisters', 'mothers', and 'fathers', and the whole group interacts as an extended family. In the following description, for example, family roles are emphasised and the interlocking system of support between families is expressed in the image of the pyramid: 'the father of one of the families was in the habit of balancing the father of another of the families on the top of a great pole; the father of a third family often made a pyramid of both those fathers, with Master Kidderminster for the apex, and himself the base' (p. 27). The familial nature of the circus is again stressed when Sleary explains to Sissy Jupe the advantages of staying with the troupe: 'Emma Gordon in whothe lap you're a lying at prethent, would be a mother to you and Jothphine would be a thithter to you' (p. 29).

The circus, then, is both a metaphor in itself and the novel's major symbol of fancy, the metaphor-making faculty. The circus master, Sleary, is adept at turning one thing into another. In his most important act of transformation, he helps young Tom escape by turning him into a black servant and then into a country bumpkin. The transforming power of fancy literally saves the Gradgrinds in the end. However, as we have already seen, the Gradgrinds' salvation is full of ambiguity: it entails an illegal act that cuts them off from society, and it disperses and humiliates them. If we look closer at the circus and its illusions, we can see that they, too, are ambiguously presented.[11]

The narrator first describes the circus as a place of harmless but nevertheless ridiculous ostentation, emphasising the puffery of the playbills:

> [Signor Jupe] was ... to exhibit 'his astounding feat of throwing seventy-five hundredweight in rapid succession backhanded over his head, thus forming a fountain of solid iron in mid-air, a feat never before attempted in this or any other country and which having elicited such rapturous plaudits from enthusiastic throngs it cannot be withdrawn.'
>
> (p. 9)

Sleary himself is an icon of modern commercialism: 'Sleary ... a stout modern statue with a moneybox at its elbow, in an ecclesiastical niche of early Gothic architecture, took the money.' The narrator delights in exposing the circus' illusions, in revealing the often shabby reality behind the fanciful show. Master Kidderminster, the dwarf, is unmasked as he is described:

> Made up with curls, wreaths, wings, white bismuth, and carmine, this hopeful young person soared into so pleasing a Cupid as to constitute the chief delight of the maternal part of the spectators: but in private, where his characteristics were a precocious cutaway coat and an extremely gruff voice, he became the Turf, turfy.
>
> (p. 23)

And Kidderminster, like Sleary, is an unabashed mercenary: 'If you want to cheek us', he exclaims to Bounderby, 'pay your ochre at the doors' (p. 23).

Indeed, the ostentatious puffery of Kidderminster and Sleary closely resembles Mr Bounderby's boastful lies. When Bounderby and Gradgrind visit the circus people at the Pegasus's Arms,

Bounderby repeatedly compares himself to them, and even though he tries to emphasise the differences, the likenesses emerge. In his false description of his own childhood, he declares, 'There was no rope-dancing for me; I danced on the bare ground and was larruped with the rope' (p. 20). The image of Bounderby as a circus performer sharpens as the conversation continues, and Kidderminster and Bounderby begin trading insults and blustering at one another. The circus people, professional humbugs themselves, see through Bounderby's show. Bounderby describes himself as a self-made man several times during the scene; and he is, it turns out, a self-made man in the same sense that Kidderminster is a self-made Cupid, for Bounderby, too, makes himself up. There is even an inverted similarity in their most extreme pretences: Kidderminster pretends to be Childers's son; Bounderby pretends not to be his mother's child.

In the circus, therefore, Fancy and its major mode, the metaphoric transformation, often produce showy illusions that are akin to the self-aggrandising mendacity depicted in the novel. There are, moreover, other indications in the novel that metaphors, especially metaphors that attempt to disguise an ugly reality, are useless or even pernicious things. When the narrator first asserts that factories look like fairy castles, for example, he immediately casts an ironic reflection on the analogy, attributing it to 'travellers by express-train' (p. 49) through the manufacturing districts. Only a distant observer who never stops to investigate the reality of a factory would make the fanciful comparison. It is an outsider's metaphor, a falsification that perpetuates ignorance of a reality that, according to the novel's own statements, needs confronting.

The narrator even creates ambivalence about the worker–child metaphor, implying that it, too, can be a pernicious falsification. He uses the metaphor and simultaneously abuses others for using it, he begins one paragraph:

> Now, besides very many babies just able to walk, there happened to be in Coketown a considerable population of babies who had been walking against time towards the infinite world, twenty, thirty, forty, fifty years and more. These portentous infants being alarming creatures to stalk about in any human society, the eighteen denominations incessantly scratched one another's faces and pulled one another's hair by way of agreeing on the steps to be taken for their improvement.
>
> (p. 38)

Even in these opening sentences, where the worker–infant metaphor is apparently the narrator's own, he makes it seem mildly ridiculous. And as the passage proceeds, the practice of seeing workers as babies comes to seem truly destructive, for it authorises the arrogant pronouncements of Coketown's 'eighteen denominations':

> Body number one said they must take everything on trust. Body number two, said they must take everything on political economy. Body number three, wrote leaden little books for them, showing how the good grown-up baby invariably got to the savings-bank, and the bad grown-up baby invariably got transported.

> (p. 38)

By thus satirising the worker–infant metaphor, which is itself a *reductio ad absurdum* of the paternalists' worker–child analogy, the narrator ironically undercuts the metaphoric structure of the entire novel.

Although the narrator overtly recommends that the workers' 'Lives of machinery and reality' can be 'beautified' by the indulgence of 'innocent and pretty' fantasies (p. 226), he also hints that 'pretty' fantasies about industrial life are seldom really innocent. The metaphors the narrator uses most seriously are those which intensify descriptions of the bleakness and horror of both the workers' and the children's lives. Coketown is alternately a devouring monster with 'smokey jaws' and a strangely monotonous jungle in which only two kinds of savage animals perform endlessly repetitive movements: the smokey snakes and the metallic elephants constantly coil and bob: it is, pre-eminently, the 'citadel' of 'an unnatural family' in which the very buildings are 'shouldering, and trampling, and pressing one another to death' (p. 48). In that other citadel of an 'unnatural family', Gradgrind's Stone Lodge, the inmates also torture one another; Gradgrind himself is an ogre, 'a monster in a lecturing castle, with Heaven knows how many heads manipulated into one, taking childhood captive, and dragging it into gloomy statistical dens by the hair' (p. 7). 'Reason' is the Gradgrinds' 'grim Idol, cruel and cold, with its victims bound hand to foot, and its big dumb shape set up with a sightless stare, never to be moved by anything but so many calculated tons of leverage' (p. 151).

These are, indeed, metaphoric transformations, the works of Fancy, and they help uncover an additional, submerged meaning of the word. To fancy something is to desire it, and the narrator's fanciful descriptions of Coketown and the Gradgrinds often depict a world driven by rapacious desires, especially the desires of an incestuous, 'unnatural' family. The would-be fathers in the book, the upper-class men, do not neglect their metaphoric children; they try, rather, to consume them. The sexual exploitation of Louisa exposes the sexual anxiety stimulated by the social paternalists' metaphor, for if society is one big family, then fancy and incest are practically inextricable. The metaphors used suggest such destructive connections do not contain the 'imaginative graces' prescribed by the narrator to 'beautify' reality (p. 226). The kinds of metaphors the narrator explicitly recommends, the fanciful 'garden[s] in the stormy ways of this world' (p. 15), prove in practice to be either inappropriate or destructive falsifications. The metaphors that reveal the book's truths, however, reveal its fear of fancy.

Thus, in this novel, where metaphor is an explicit theme, metaphoric connections are actually ambiguously presented. The circus, the 'travellers by express-train', and the 'eighteen denominations of Coketown' all produce self-interested falsifications, whereas the narrator's own metaphors tend to darken his already gloomy vision of the literal connections among Coketown's inhabitants and to reveal the burden of illicit sexuality carried by the social paternalists' metaphor. In the novel's practice, metaphoric connection never becomes a way of escaping those destructive relationships or converting them into relationships of loving support.

Indeed, the one character in the novel who can bring about positive relationship is the completely literal-minded Sissy Jupe. Since Sissy has long been seen by critics as a mere remnant of the circus left behind in Coketown,[12] it is necessary to establish the fact that she acts as a literal-minded foil to the falsifications of both the circus and Gradgrind's school. Sissy refuses to see one thing in terms of another – not because she is totally unimaginative, but because she insists on the priority of literal relationships. When Sleary offers her the metaphoric family of the circus to replace her lost relationship with her father, she declines it. Preferring to carry out what she believes are her father's intentions, she gives herself instead to the Gradgrind household in the hope that her father will reclaim her there. She stubbornly holds onto the bottle of 'nine oils' that her father sent her to buy just before he abandoned her, insisting that if he sent her for it, he must literally have needed it (p. 31). Later in the book, when

Sissy discusses her past life, she explains that she alone saw through her father's clownish appearance to the truly shy and pathetic man. The other members of Sleary's circus were taken in by the clown's theatrical persona: 'Sometimes they played tricks upon him; but they never knew how he felt them, and shrunk up, when he was alone with me. He was far, far timider than they thought!' (p. 45). Sissy, who is not herself a circus performer, instinctively penetrates the circus' illusions. She tries to cheer her father by reading him *The Arabian Nights*, but her own imagination is far from fantastic: her mind is filled with the literal and the mundane.

Her literal-mindedness, the quality that sets her apart from the circus company, also sets her apart from the products of the Gradgrind school. Sissy is too mired in literal particulars to be able to transform the events of life into generalisations. Her imagination is too literal, for example, to allow for the *figurative* representations of statistics, as we learn when she tells Louisa about her academic failure.

> 'And I find (Mr M'Choakumchild said) that in a given time a hundred thousand persons went to sea on long voyages, and only five hundred of them were drowned or burnt to death. What is the percentage? And I said, Miss'; here Sissy fairly sobbed as confessing with extreme contrition to her greatest error: 'I said it was nothing.'
> 'Nothing, Sissy?'
> 'Nothing, Miss – to the relations and friends of the people who were killed.'
>
> (p. 44)

Sissy's attitude allows us to see that statistics resemble many of the book's other figurative operations which distance and disguise painful realities.[13]

Sissy, moreover, is able to save Louisa not by creating fanciful escapes, but by accepting the ugly reality of the young Mrs Bounderby's life. Sissy's refusal to be repelled by the unembellished facts of Louisa's life constitutes the whole of the saving action:

> 'First, Sissy, do you know what I am? I am so proud, so confused and troubled, so resentful and unjust to everyone and to myself, that everything is stormy, dark and wicked to me. Does not that repel you?'
> 'No!'

> 'I am so unhappy, and all that should have made me otherwise is so laid waste, that if I had been bereft of sense this hour, and instead of being so learned as you think me, had to begin to acquire the simplest truths, I could not want a guide to peace, contentment, honour, all the good of which I am quite devoid, more abjectly than I do. Does not that repel you?'
> 'No!'

(p. 172)

The relationship between Sissy and Louisa is built on this foundation of explicitly stated and accepted facts.

Sissy also uses her literal-mindedness to protect Louisa from James Harthouse. Harthouse tries to evade Sissy's prohibition on his seeing Louisa, but Sissy simply repeats her message, 'You may be sure, Sir, you will never see her again as long as you live' (p. 175). Harthouse, the narrator emphasises, is vanquished by this simple matter-of-factness, by the 'child-like ingenuousness with which his visitor spoke, her modest fearlessness, her truthfulness which put all artifice aside, her entire forgetfulness of herself in her earnest quiet holding to the object with which she had come' (pp. 175–6). Similarly, Sissy insists that Harthouse 'leave [Coketown] immediately and finally' (p. 177), and none of his artful manoeuvres sway her from a strict construction of those words. Harthouse finally follows her instructions to the letter.

For all its talk about fancy, and for all its own metaphors, *Hard Times* finally cannot be said to endorse metaphoric connections. The saving relationships are made by the literal-minded Sissy. Even though we are told on the last page that Sissy provides the workers with 'imaginative graces and delights' (p. 226), nothing we know of her makes this a credible claim. We are told in the same sentence, moreover, that Sissy is 'holding this course as part of no fantastic vow, or bond, or brotherhood, or sisterhood, or pledge, or covenant, or fancy dress, or fancy fair; but simply as a duty to be done' (pp. 226–7). This description of Sissy's charitable activities constitutes yet another covert negation of the metaphoric activities the book overtly endorses: she does not do them as a member of a metaphoric family (a 'brotherhood' or 'sisterhood') or as a participant in a fanciful pageant (a 'fancy dress, or fancy fair'). Up to its very last page, *Hard Times* is a book that simultaneously flaunts and discredits its metaphoricality, calling into question both the possibility of paternalist reform and the validity of its own narrative practice.

From Catherine Gallagher, *The Industrial Reformation of English Fiction, 1832–1867* (Chicago, 1985), pp. 147–66.

NOTES

[Catherine Gallagher's essay is taken from her book *The Industrial Reformation of English Fiction*, in which she looks at the 'industrial novels' of Gaskell, Kingsley, Disraeli, Dickens and Eliot, examining the relationship between social change and change in literary form. In this section, Gallagher focuses on the desire for social cohesion in *Hard Times* (and, in the original chapter in the book, *North and South* by Elizabeth Gaskell), a cohesion which will be achieved by changing the relationship between family and society, by introducing cooperative behaviour, as seen in private life, into the public realm. What Gallagher stresses, however, are the contradictions inherent in social paternalism and domestic ideology; both *Hard Times* and *North and South*, she suggests, ultimately propose the isolation of families from the larger society. Perhaps the most important thing for the reader to note about the method of Gallagher's essay, which combines deconstruction and New Historicism, is its focus on the language of the text, specifically Dickens's use of metaphor in *Hard Times*. It is primarily a family–society metaphor that Dickens employs, but it is shown to break down, for the Gradgrinds only become a model family by symbolically betraying the working class and breaking society's laws (although young Tom is ultimately responsible for Stephen's death, the Gradgrind family rallies to his defence). The text as such reflects a fundamental Victorian problem: they extolled the family, maintaining that its values could be echoed in a paternalist reform of society, but, in advocating the isolation of the family, social paternalists reconstituted the very disjunction between the public and private spheres they set out to overcome.

Gallagher's essay, along with others in this collection, demands some consideration of the concept of ideology: the beliefs, values, and ways of thinking and feeling through which human beings perceive, and by which they explain, what they take to be reality. An ideology is always the product of the position and interests of a particular class. In any era, the dominant ideology embodies, and serves to legitimise and perpetuate, the interests of the dominant economic and social class. The issue is more complicated than this, with Marxist critics in particular consistently adding to and modifying our understanding of the meaning of ideology, but the significant point to grasp in relation to both *David Copperfield* and *Hard Times* is the way in which both novels associate themselves with a developing middle-class discourse, yet both, in adopting the voice of the liberal, humane wing within that society, at the same time reveal the contradictions and inconsistencies in a vision of social cohesion, family values and responsible individualism. Ed.]

1. See 'The Preston Strike: A History', in the *Annual Register* (May 1854), reprinted in *Hard Times,* ed. George Ford and Sylvère Monod (New York, 1966), pp. 279–82.

2. [In the previous chapter of her book, pp. 127–46, Gallagher discusses popular industrial narratives, in particular cheap magazine stories about women workers, focusing on the work of J. M. Rymer and G. W. M. Reynolds. Ed.]

3. Humphry House has noticed and discussed Dickens's social paternalism and has suggested that the novels should be read in the context of such books as Arthur Helps, *The Claims of Labour*. See *The Dickens World* (London, 1941), p. 45. Dickens, of course, knew Helps; it was Helps who arranged Dickens's 1865 interview with Queen Victoria. Helps was then Clerk of the Privy Council. See Edgar Johnson, *Charles Dickens: His Tragedy and Triumph*, revised edn (London, 1976), p. 574.

4. Of these novels, Raymond Williams says, 'Recognition of evil was balanced by fear of becoming involved. Sympathy was transformed, not into action, but into withdrawal' (*Culture and Society: 1780–1950* [New York, 1966], p. 109). According to Williams, *Hard Times* withdraws into personal feeling, into an innocence that 'shames the adult world, but also essentially rejects it' (p. 96). In *North and South,* Williams notes, there is a more serious attempt to come to terms with industrial society, but he believes Margaret's legacy and her marriage to Thornton to be forms of escape: 'Once again Mrs Gaskell works out her reaction to the insupportable situation by going – in part adventitiously – outside it' (p. 94). In his essay 'The Early Victorian Social-Problem Novel', in *From Dickens to Hardy*, vol. 6 of *The Pelican Guide to English Literature* (Baltimore, 1973), pp. 169–87, Arnold Kettle blames the difficulties of the industrial novels on the 'abstraction' that comes from seeing 'a living complex of forces and people as a 'problem'. He specifically exempts *Hard Times* from this charge, but the ending of *North and South* seems to Kettle a tepid compromise of a conflict that was never fully ripe emotionally.

5. Charles Dickens, *Hard Times*, ed. George Ford and Sylvère Monod (New York, 1966), p. 9. All further references in the text are to this edition.

6. In ' "Divorce and Matrimonial Causes" ': An Aspect of *Hard Times',* *Victorian Studies*, 20 (1977), 401–12, John D. Baird argues persuasively for Dickens's use of actual cases in his portrait of Stephen Blackpool, whose wife, Baird suggests, is not only alcoholic but adulterous and syphilitic as well. Nevertheless, under then-current divorce laws, Stephen's only remedy lies in the procedure Bounderby outlines – three separate lawsuits and a private act of Parliament, at an estimated cost of two thousand pounds – in order to be free to marry Rachael.

So, with his fellow 'average Englishman', Stephen is, as Baird points out, 'more likely to be struck by lightning than to be divorced'.

7. Carlyle's influence is partly responsible for this pessimism, but a number of other factors contribute to the book's bleak outlook. Edgar Johnson attributes the darkness of vision in *Hard Times* to Dickens's earlier experience in the north of England: 'the roots of the story ... were twisted in the flaring gloom of the Black Country and his first horrified vision, sixteen years ago, of mines like underground dungeons and mills filled with clamour and cruelty. He had sworn then "to strike the heaviest blow in my power" for their victims' (*Charles Dickens*, p. 404). Dickens's own family troubles must also have contributed to the novel's advocacy of easier divorces and to its general pessimism about family life. The dispersal of the Gradgrinds at the end of the book may be related to the author's own restlessness during the period of composition. 'I am in a state of restlessness,' he wrote in a letter, 'impossible to be described – impossible to be imagined – wearing and tearing to be experienced' (quoted in Johnson, *Charles Dickens*, p. 422).

8. Such scenes were staples of didactic domestic tales, which frequently portray the redemption of women by other women. In *Lucy Dean,* for example, Mary Austen saves the fallen Nelly Dean by the same means that Sissy uses to save Louisa. The two scenes are strikingly similar:

> For a moment, the wretched girl, with a sort of blind ferocity, strove to elude the restraining arms, and in the struggle, gripped them as a vice its wedge or nail; then as the voice entreated once again, crouched like a hound beneath the keeper's lash; and then at last, all woman, fell weeping down before the feet of her, who of all women, most could save and most could pity. 'My poor one, my unhappy one,' spoke Mary, half kneeling too in the fervency of her extreme pity. 'I know you ... and I must save you if I can.'
>
> (Silverpen [Eliza Meteyard], *Lucy Dean: The Noble Needlewoman,* in *Eliza Cook's Journal,* 3 [1850–1], 361.)

9. John D. Baird traces interesting ironic inverse parallels between the non-marriages of Bounderby and Stephen Blackpool in ' "Divorce and Matrimonial Causes" ': An Aspect of *Hard Times*', see above, 410–12.

10. For a discussion of Dickens's own perceptions and manipulations of fact, fancy, and public opinion, see Joseph Butwin, '*Hard Times*: The News and the Novel', in *Nineteenth-Century Fiction*, 32 (1977), 166–87.

11. To contend, as F. R. Leavis has in '*Hard Times:* An Analytic Note', in *The Great Tradition* (London, 1960), pp. 227–48, that the circus is unambiguously depicted as a centre of vitality and human sympathy is to ignore much of the evidence of the text. For a full discussion of the ambiguity of the circus in *Hard Times*, see Joseph Butwin's 'The

Paradox of the Clown in Dickens', in *Dickens Studies Annual*, 5 (1967), 115–32.

12. Leavis's discussion of Sissy, which stresses her vitality, makes her seem a representative member of Sleary's troupe. See *The Great Tradition*, pp. 230–5.

13. Dickens is here playing off the growing Victorian mania for statistical data in aid of scientific authority. According to the London Statistical Society Report of 1836, 'The spirit of the present age has an evident tendency to confront the figures of speech with the figures of arithmetic … in the business of social science principles are valid for application only inasmuch as they are legitimate inductions from facts, accurately observed and methodically qualified' (quoted in T. S. Ashton, *Economic and Social Investigations in Manchester, 1833–1933: A Centenary History of the Manchester Statistical Society* [Manchester, 1934]).

9

Writing as a Woman: Dickens, *Hard Times*, and Feminine Discourses

JEAN FERGUSON CARR

In his 1872 retrospective essay on Dickens, George Henry Lewes presents Dickens as an exemplary figure whose career has upset the balance between popular taste and critical judgement.[1] The essay depends on what seems initially an aesthetic opposition between show and Art, between 'fanciful flight' and Literature, but these critical terms also demark class and gender boundaries that preserve the dominant literary culture. Dickens becomes 'the showman beating on the drum', who appeals to the 'savage' not the 'educated eye', to 'readers to whom all the refinements of Art and Literature are as meaningless hieroglyphs'. He works in 'delf, not in porcelain', mass producing inexpensive pleasure for the undiscerning reader, but is found wanting by the 'cultivated' reader of 'fastidious' taste. The essay attempts to contain Dickens's impact by identifying him as lower-class, uneducated, and aligned with feminine discourses, but it also suggests the difficulty of accounting for Dickens's influence and the importance of investigating the 'sources of that power'. Despite Lewes's isolation of Dickens as a 'novelty' or as a madman, he concedes that he 'impressed a new direction on popular writing, and modified the Literature of his age, in its spirit no less than in its form'.[2]

Dickens's admirers, following John Forster, have responded to the essay as mistaken and insulting.[3] As John Gross wrote, the essay 'still has the power to irritate', with its innuendo about hallucinations and lower-class vulgarity, and its casual anecdotes about the author's inadequate library.[4] Lewes's class bias and his narrow definition of education have undermined the influence of his critique of Dickens for modern readers, but his subtle positioning of Dickens in relation to women writers and his articulation of the categories by which novels will be judged has been more durable. When, for example, Gordon Haight concludes that 'Dickens was a man of emotion, sentimental throughout; Lewes was a man of intellect, philosophical and scientific',[5] he is echoing the gender-based oppositions of Lewes's argument.

The essay on Dickens is part of the broader attempt begun by Lewes in the 1840s to serve as arbiter of the emergent literary class and of its premier form, the novel. Like Lewes's 1852 essay 'The Lady Novelist', it seeks to position those literary newcomers who threaten the status and boundaries of nineteenth-century literary territory, to control the impact of a broader-based literacy and of women's emergence into more public spheres.[6] The critique of Dickens depends on polarities that usually mark gender differences in nineteenth-century criticism, as, for example, the difference between feeling and thinking, between observing details and formulating generalisations. 'Dickens sees and feels', Lewes intones.

> but the logic of feeling seems the only logic he can manage. Thought is strangely absent from his works ... [K]eenly as he observes the objects before him he never connects his observations into a general expression, never seems interested in general relations of things.[7]

Lewes makes still more explicit his identification of Dickens with this secondary realm of women's writing in this backhanded compliment:

> With a fine felicity of instinct he seized upon situations having an irresistible hold over the domestic affections and ordinary sympathies. He spoke in the mother-tongue of the heart, and was always sure of ready listeners.[8]

Dickens is thus identified with the feminine, as instinctual and fortunate, as seizing rather than analysing, as interested in 'domestic affections and ordinary sympathies'. He 'painted nothing ideal, heroic', Lewes explains. 'The world of thought and passion lay beyond his horizon'.[9]

Lewes evokes many of the same oppositions when instructing Charlotte Brontë on the 'proper' realm for women writers, when cataloguing the 'lady novelists' of the day, or when marking the novel as the particular 'department' of women, the form that values '*finesse* of detail ... pathos and sentiment'.[10] His acknowledgement that Dickens is 'always sure of ready listeners' rehearses a charge often made against nineteenth-century women writers, that the financial success and popularity of their work, its very attentiveness to audience concerns, marks it as 'anti-' or 'sub-literary', concerned with sales not posterity. Dickens thus joins the company of writers like Fanny Fern and Mary Elizabeth Braddon who, as one critic put it, discovered: 'a profitable market among the half-educated ... giving the undiscriminating what they wanted to read.'[11] The use of a category like the 'subliterary' works to regulate the effects of the novel as a newly-positioned literary discourse that challenges the cultural hegemony of upper-class men of letters.

In July 1845, Dickens described the aim and rhetorical stance of a proposed journal, *The Cricket*: 'I would at once sit down upon their very hobs; and take a personal and confidential position with them.'[12] In 1850, he finally established a periodical to fulfil the role of domestic comrade, that aspired 'to live in the Household affections, and to be numbered among the Household thoughts, of our readers.'[13] In establishing a journal to be 'familiar in their mouths as Household Words' (as the motto read), Dickens was making use of a feminine guise, privileging the intimate, private, and informal qualities usually associated with women over the social, public, and authoritative powers usually associated with men. But he was also disrupting the conventional wisdom that sharply divided the domestic and public spheres, for his journal insisted on the interpenetration of these realms.[14]

This gesture of cultural cross-dressing is part of a recurring exploration by Dickens in the 1850s of the discourses usually identified as feminine.[15] Michael Slater has argued that in the decade 1847 to 1857 Dickens was 'apparently preoccupied with women as the insulted and injured of mid-Victorian England', and that the novels in this period feature more women characters in more prominent positions than do other of his novels. But he also sees Dickens as 'voicing no general condemnation of prevailing patriarchal beliefs and attitudes'.[16] I do not find it surprising that Dickens did not 'voice' a 'general condemnation' of the ideology within which he wrote. What I want to investigate is why his interest hovers at the edge of articulation, why it goes so far and then retreats, or goes so far and then is silent. Why is Dickens simultaneously empathetic with oppressed women and insistent on the constraints and stereotypes that restrict them? What does his practice suggest about how women are rendered silent in Victorian culture and novels, how their perspective is undermined or pre-empted? To use Pierre Macherey's terms, such issues become part of what is 'unvoiced', 'unspoken' both in the novels and in Dickens's public postures.[17] The issue is not so much, then, whether Dickens crafted complex psychological women characters along the lines of George Eliot or Charlotte Brontë, but how women are positioned in the powerful discourses of the novels as in contemporary social practices. In Dickens's novels, the notion of 'writing as a woman' is problematic, as opposed to the confident assumptions Lewes makes of what it means 'to write as women', of what the 'real office' is that women 'have to perform', of the 'genuine female experience'.[18] Dickens's experimentation suggests that much is unknown, even to the women who 'experience' their lives and desires, that there is no ready language for what women wish to 'write'. Although Dickens himself certainly does not articulate a programme of women's liberation, and indeed deploys many cultural tropes that restrict women as 'relative creatures', his novels often make the 'commonsense' notions of Lewes untenable.[19]

The proliferation of child-wives in his novels and his portrait of Esther Summerson's strained narrative have often been cited by critics as signs of Dickens's preference for coy, idealised, and subservient women. His advocacy of the domestic values of hearth and home has similarly been dismissed as a sign of a peculiar weakness, a bourgeois sentimentality aimed at pleasing or appeasing his readers. Along with his taste for melodrama and Christmas morality, such quirks are explained away as a cultural disguise the master assumed to protect his more radical designs. The more critically acceptable Dickens provides cynical and witty analysis of cultural conventions and hypocrisies from a disengaged positon. In other words, Dickens is valued as a prototype of the (male) modern artist as rebel and cultural critic; he is embarrassing in his assumption of what we label (female) 'Victorian' values. Like Lewes, then, we perpetuate the stigma of writing as a woman, associating feminine discourse with a lack of analysis and rigour, with pandering to 'cheap' tastes. And we resist identifying Dickens with either its problems or its effects.

When Dickens's experimentation with 'writing as a woman' is examined within this contest for literary territory and power, it involves more than merely being a woman writer or adopting a feminine persona.[20] By aligning himself with terms and oppositions usually associated with women (for example, fancy vs reason or fact, the personal vs the institutional), Dickens, in effect, explores how his own position as a writer of fiction is marked off as suspect or inferior.[21] He experiments with writing that traverses opposed realms and deploys narrative tropes that mark breaks in discursive power – stuttering, deception, metaphor, eccentricity, strain of voice or prose, interruptions. In this context, for example, Dickens's insistence on a linkage between 'romance' and familiar things is more than a personal credo or a rehearsal of a romantic ethos.[22] The preference in *Hard Times* of the devalued term 'fancy' over the more culturally respectable term 'imagination' locates his argument in a contemporary ideological contest, rather than as a repetition of an earlier aesthetic debate. The problematic position of women characters and writers functions as a figure of Dickens's own position in a culture suspicious of fancy and wary of claims to 'domestic' power. Deflecting the unease of his position onto women as an oppressed class allows Dickens to be more extreme and critical than he could if he were evaluating his own position directly.[23]

I would like to focus on what has usually been cited as a negative portrait of women, the failure to create a strong, likeable heroine or a credible mother figure in *Hard Times* (1854). The novel itself is an instance of the conditions of feminine discourse, written not in any expansive artistic mode, but under the urgency of periodical publishing, as a project his printers hoped would attract readers to *Household Words*. Dickens disliked the conditions of weekly publication and deplored as 'CRUSHING' the consequent lack of 'elbow-room' and 'open places in perspective'.[24] But the process must have underscored the constraints embedded in the social and material production of discourse. Indeed much of the novel explores what cannot be said or explained, what cannot be portrayed. The women of this fictional world in particular are restricted by and to their social positions, defined within narrow ideological bounds that afford little relief. The characters do not operate primarily in personal relationships to each other, nor do they 'forget' their social positioning, or the polarities that operate in Coketown. They are constructed in oppositions, as women and men, mothers and daughters, middle-class thinkers and lower-class workers. The usual cultural positions for women remain curiously unpopulated, incomplete, present but not functioning as they ought. This schematic underdevelopment need not be explained away as a technological effect of the novel's weekly form, or as a style of abstraction.[25] The ideological and technical constraints also create the possibility for Dickens to write as if from within the realm that Lewes marks off for women writers – a realm of fancy, romance, ordinary events, and mass production; a realm that remains apart from what fastidious or learned readers will value.

The novel is constrained from the beginning by the powerful social discourse of the Gradgrind system, which exists in the novel as what Bakhtin called 'the word of the fathers'. Bakhtin argues that such a word need not be repeated or reinforced or even made persuasive, but has 'its authority already fused to it':

> The authoritative word demands that we acknowledge it, that we make it our own; it binds us, quite independent of any power it might have to persuade us internally; we encounter it with its authority already fused to it. ... It is, so to speak, the word of the fathers. Its authority was already *acknowledged* in the past. It is a *prior* discourse. It is therefore not a question of choosing it from among other possible discourses that are its equal.[26]

Against such a word, opposition or argument is already preempted, made secondary or unhearable. Unlike the opposing terms of 'wonder' and 'fancy', which require constant justification in the novel, the simplest reference to 'fact' evokes the authority of learning and scientific knowledge. The effect of such an authority is to make all private exchanges in the book dependent on arguments that cannot be imagined within the novel's authorised categories, so that the characters speak a kind of shadow dialogue.

The effect of this social construction is especially destructive to the transparent figure who serves as the heroine's mother. In a more self-consciously 'feminist' novel, Mrs Gradgrind might be expected to suggest the alternative to patriarchal discourses. In *Hard Times*, the mother is comically ineffectual and trivial, represented not as a person but as an object, as a 'feminine dormouse' (p. 102), and a 'bundle of shawls' (p. 59). Yet she is not even a particularly satisfactory object. Her central representation, repeated three times, is as a 'faint transparency' that is 'presented' to its audience in various unimpressive attitudes:[27]

> Mrs Gradgrind, weakly smiling and giving no other sign of vitality, looked (as she always did) like an indifferently executed transparency of a small female figure, without enough light behind it.
>
> (p. 60)

A transparency is an art form popularised by the dioramas in which a translucent image painted on cloth is made visible by backlighting.[28] Its fragility and potential for varying production make the transparency a felicitious medium to suggest Mrs Gradgrind's ambivalent positioning. The failure of the transparency renders her almost invisible in the novel, making her neither a pleasing image nor one that is easily readable. But the particularity of the image insists on a producer as well as a product, raising the issue of what painter 'executes' her so indifferently, what producer withholds the light that might have made her more substantial, in other words, why she has been neglected as a cultural formation. Vaguely discernible through the translucent object, the producer remains a shadowy, unnamed, prior force, whom we know by traces and effects. At Mrs Gradgrind's death, for example, we are told of an effect, but not of a cause – 'the light that had always been feeble and dim behind the weak transparency, went out' (p. 226). And the physical depiction of her as recumbent, 'stunned by some weighty piece of fact tumbling on her' (p. 59; see also pp. 60, 62, 137) leaves unnamed the force that stuns her with its weight and carelessness. We are left with an authorless piece of evidence, a 'piece of fact'; but in *Hard Times* 'fact' is easily traced back to the Gradgrind system. When we are told that finding herself alone with Gradgrind and Mr Bounderby is 'sufficient to stun this admirable lady again, without collision between herself and any other fact' (p. 62), we know what constitutes her as an object of its gaze. It is under her husband's 'wintry' eye that Mrs Gradgrind becomes 'torpid again' (p. 102); under Sissy Jupe's care or even in Louisa's presence, she can be 'rendered almost energetic' (p. 94). Both fact and its proponents are equally capable of rendering Mrs Gradgrind non-existent, a product of a careless fancy: 'So, she once more died away, and nobody minded her' (p. 62).

Mrs Gradgrind has been so slighted as a 'subject' that she is surprised when Louisa asks about her: 'You want to hear of me, my dear? That's something new, I am sure, when anybody wants to hear of me' (p. 224). And the outcome of such a lifetime of being constituted by others is that she cannot even claim to feel her own pain; when Louisa asks after her health, she answers with what the narrator calls 'this strange speech': 'I think there's a pain somewhere in the room ... but I couldn't positively say that I have got it' (p. 224). She is certainly slighted by Dickens, appearing in only five of the novel's thirty-seven chapters, and then usually in the final pages or paragraphs. Even her introduction seems almost an after-thought, located not in the chapter with Mr Gradgrind, the children, or even the house (ch. 3), but in a parenthetical position as audience for Mr Bounderby (ch. 4).[29] But if Dickens is cavalier about her pres-ence, he strongly marks her absence from that nineteenth-century site for Mother, as idealised figure in her children's memories or in their imaginative dreams of virtue.[30] Mrs Gradgrind's expected place as her children's earliest memory has been usurped by the father who appears as a 'dry Ogre chalking ghastly white figures' on a 'large black board' (p. 54). Louisa's return 'home' for her mother's death evokes none of the 'dreams of childhood – its airy fables' and 'im-possible adornments' that Dickens describes as 'the best influences of old home'; such dreams are only evoked as a lengthy litany of what her mother has *not* provided for her child (p. 223).

Mrs Gradgrind does not offer a counter position – covert or oth-erwise – to the world of fact and ashes. She cannot overtly defy her husband, nor can she save herself from her daughter's scorn. Her advice to Louisa reflects this helplessness, and its incomprehension of the accepted referents makes her ridiculous in her child's eyes: 'Go and be somethingological directly', she says (p. 61), and 'turn all your ological studies to good account' (p. 137). When she is dying, Mrs Gradgrind tries to express her loss – of something and of words with which to articulate it – to her daughter:

> But there is something – not an Ology at all – that your father has missed, or forgotten, Louisa. I don't know what it is. ... I shall never get its name now. But your father may. It makes me restless. I want to write to him, to find out for God's sake, what it is. Give me a pen, give me a pen.
>
> (p. 225)

To the transparent Mrs Gradgrind, all authoritative knowledge must come from the father, yet she worries that he has missed or forgotten something. She does not imagine herself finding or naming it, but remembers it as unsaid. The outcome of this 'insight' is invisible to the patriarchal eye; it disappears as 'figures of won-derful no-meaning she began to trace upon her wrappers' (pp. 225–6). When Louisa tries to fashion a meaning of her mother's words, her aim is to 'link such faint and broken sounds into any chain of connexion' (p. 225), in other words, to translate her mother into the Gradgrind discourse. Mrs Gradgrind emerges 'from the shadow' and takes 'upon her the dread solemnity of the sages and patriarchs' (p. 226) – she 'hears the last of it' – only by dying, not as a living speaker addressing her daughter knowingly and directly. She remains stubbornly unincorporated by the novel's powerful discourses, a no-meaning that can be neither heard nor reformed.

But the mother is ridiculous, rather than tragic, only within the father's terms of judgement – terms which a society divided into opposites cannot unimagine or unspeak, and against which the lower-class opposition of fancy and heart will have little impact. The mother's very imprecision undercuts the authority of the father's discourses, making them a lesson imperfectly learned and badly recited. The novel cannot construct an imagined alternate culture, in which Mrs Gradgrind would 'discover' the language to define the 'something missing', in which 'ological' would not be required as an ending that validates an object's existence. Instead it unfolds the boundaries and effects of such a system. Louisa learns painfully that Mrs Gradgrind's point-of-view has been confined to its position of 'no-meaning' (p. 225) by concerted efforts by her father and his system of definition. Towards the end of the novel, Louisa reverses the charge of 'no-meaning' and demands that her father justify instead what his 'meaning' has produced: 'Where are the graces of my soul? Where are the sentiments of my heart? What have you done, O father, what have you done, with the garden that should have bloomed once, in this great wilderness here!' (p. 239). In this confrontation, Louisa recognises the contest her father has suppressed and her mother has barely suggested, a contest for how to determine the shape and value of the social realms:

> I have grown up, battling every inch of my way. ... What I have learned has left me doubting, misbelieving, despising, regretting, what I have not learned; and my dismal resource has been to think that life would soon go by, and that nothing in it could be worth the pain and trouble of a contest.
>
> (pp. 240–1)

The novel presents several scenes between Louisa and her father in which this authority is examined and questioned, scenes which pointedly exclude Mrs Gradgrind, as someone whose objections or interests are irrelevant. The chapter 'Father and Daughter' opens with an oblique questioning of the absolute value of such authority (pp. 131–2), but only once the 'business' is resolved does Gradgrind suggest, 'now, let us go and find your mother' (p. 137). Yet the exploration of Gradgrind's power makes an obscure and unacknowledged connection between his power and her mother's 'death' from the novel. By what seems a frivolous word-game on the part of the narrator, Gradgrind's governmental blue books (the emblem of his power) are associated with an infamous wife-killer: 'Athough Mr Gradgrind did not take after Blue Beard, his room was quite a blue chamber in its abundance of blue books' (p. 131). The narrator denies that this 'error' has any meaning, thus resisting the implication that Gradgrind's intellectual system of power has something to do with the oppressed status of his wife. The blue books are accorded the power of fact, which is to prove 'usually anything you like', but the narrator's flight of fancy is not to prove anything. It refers, not to the authoritative realms of statistics and science, but to fairy-tales: it is not a 'fact' derived from texts, but is 'something missing', an association produced by the unconscious. It remains, at best, as a kind of insider's joke, in which readers can remember that its 'power' derives from texts with which Dickens was aligned, both in general (fiction and fairy-tale), and explicitly (Blue Beard is the basis for Dickens's Captain Murderer, whose tale he published in 1860 as one of his 'Nurse's Stories').[31]

The reference to the wife-killer, Blue Beard, who charms all with his show of courtesy and devotion before devouring his wives in the privacy of their home, is an 'error' that suggests the gap between public and private, between acknowledged power and covert violence. Like the marginalised tensions created by Mrs Gradgrind throughout the novel, this slip of the pen provokes despite its claim to marginality. The error is allowed to stand, thereby suggesting what would otherwise be too bizarre to consider. It reminds us that Gradgrind has been a social 'wife-killer', obliterating his wife's role as mother to her daughter and keeping her from fuller participation in the daughter's narrative. He has 'formed his daughter on his own model' (p. 168), and she is known to all as 'Tom Gradgrind's daughter' (p. 143). He has isolated Louisa in his masculine realm, depriving her of any of the usual female resources with which to oppose his power; as Tom mentions with devastating casualness, Louisa 'used to complain to me that she had nothing to fall back upon, that girls usually fall back upon' (p. 168). The reference to Blue Beard reminds us that Gradgrind's realm is *not* absolute except by force and mystification, that his 'charmed apartment' depends on the exclusion of a more powerful, more resistant 'other'. The rest of the chapter teases out the possibilities that his power can be questioned. Through a series of fanciful images – that make the narrator not an unworthy companion of Mrs Gradgrind – the absolute value of his authority is obliquely undermined. Gradgrind is presented as needing to enforce his positions with military might, relying on his books as an 'army constantly strengthening by the arrival of new recruits'. His solutions persist because they are isolated within a necromancer's circle, protected from critique or even outside knowledge. From his enclosed, abstracted fortress, he orders the world as if 'the astronomer within should arrange the starry universe solely by pen, ink and paper, ... could settle all their destinies on a slate, and wipe out all their tears with one dirty little bit of sponge' (pp. 131–2). All these questions about Gradgrind's power are delivered as amusing details, as arguments the novelist is not able to give serious articulation. Yet the details attack not the effect of Gradgrind's power, as Louisa does with hopeless inertia, but the claim to power, its genealogy and maintenance.

It is not surprising that Louisa and her mother, and even Dickens, cannot find words for what is missing from their lives, words having been usurped as the tools of the Gradgrind system, defined and delimited by male authority. Mrs Gradgrind does not articulate an opposition, nor does the novel openly pursue the traces of her petulant complaints. *She* remains unaware that her headaches and worries are symptoms of a cultural dissatisfaction, although she knows that her head began 'to split' as soon as she was married (p. 137). She complains to Louisa about the trouble that comes from speaking – 'You must remember, my dear, that whenever I have said anything, on any subject, I have never heard the last of it; and consequently, that I have long left off saying anything' (p. 225), but the ideological implications of these remarks are shortcircuited by the personal contexts in which she declines to speak. These scenes do not transform Mrs Gradgrind into a covert rebel, but represent her as wilful and self-absorbed, betraying Sissy and Louisa by her silence and diverting attention from their more pressing needs.

In fact, Mrs Gradgrind seems to exist primarily as the cautionary exemplum of the Gradgrind system, having been married for the 'purity' of being as free from nonsense 'as any human being not arrived at the perfection of an absolute idiot, ever was' (p. 62). She proves her usefulness to the system, admirably serving as the negative against which the father seems more caring, more responsive than he seems in isolation. Her mother seems unsympathetic to Louisa's discontent, worrying over it as 'one of those subjects I shall never hear the last of' (p. 138). And she serves as the agent who reinscribes the ideological positions of the Gradgrind system, who insists on reality being defined as what is kept 'in cabinets' or about which one can 'attend lectures' (p. 61). Louisa is scolded for running off to look at the forbidden circus by her mother, not by the father whose prohibition it is and who has caught her in the crime. The hapless Mrs Gradgrind 'whimpers' to her daughter; 'I wonder at you. I declare you're enough to make one regret ever having had a family at all. I have a great mind to say I wish I hadn't. *Then* what would you have done. I should like to know' (p. 61). Yet in this pathetic effort to enforce her husband's laws, Mrs Gradgrind has unknowingly allied herself with her child's rebellion. Her words give her away: she has 'wondered' (a crime against reason), she has 'regretted' (a crime against fact), and she has 'wished' (a crime against her husband). Dickens notes that 'Mr Gradgrind did not seem favourably impressed by these cogent remarks'. Yet what seems initially a silly, self-indulgent speech has deflected the father's wrath from his daughter and has suggested the terms for opposition – wonder, regret, desire.

Hard Times appears to authorise an oppositional discourse of fancy, which is lisped by the circus-master Sleary and represented in Sissy Jupe, the substitute mother whom Gradgrind praises as the 'good fairy in his house' who can 'effect' what 10,000 pounds cannot (p. 294). Gradgrind's approval, and the conventionality of Sissy's depiction as a house fairy, devalues her status as an opposition figure. Indeed Sissy rarely speaks in opposition, or at all. Her power is cited by men like Harthouse and Gradgrind, and by the narrator. Unlike Mrs Gradgrind, Sissy cannot be mocked for 'cogent remarks', but simply *looks* at Louisa 'in wonder, in pity, in sorrow, in doubt, in a multitude of emotions' (p. 138). Her effect is largely due to the novelty of her discourse, a novelty produced by her status as an outsider who does not understand the conventions of the system. 'Possessed of no facts' (p. 49), girl number twenty does not recognise that 'fancy' is a significant term, but uses it unthinkingly. She silences the cynical Harthouse by presenting 'something in which he was so inexperienced, and against which he knew any of his usual weapons would fall so powerless; that not a word could he rally to his relief'. Sissy insists on her words to Harthouse remaining a 'secret' and relies on a 'child-like ingenuousness' to sway her listener. And what Harthouse notices is her 'most confiding eyes' and her 'most earnest (though so quiet)' voice (pp. 252–7). Sissy's 'wonder' is powerful only as long as she does not 'speak' it in her own right, but presents it in her disengaged role as go-between. Her 'power' depends on 'her entire forgetfulness of herself in her earnest quiet holding to the object' (p. 253) – depends, in other words, on a strenuous denial of herself as a contestant for power. The narrator comments that 'if she had shown, or felt the slightest trace of any sensitiveness to his ridicule or astonishment, or any remonstrance he might offer, he would have carried it against her at this point' (p. 255).

Sissy's discourse derives its power, not from any essential woman's knowledge that Louisa and her mother could share, but from her experience as a working-class child who knows counter examples and a different word than 'fact'. Louisa acquires from Sissy not the power to be 'a mother – lovingly watchful of her children' but to be 'learned in childish lore; thinking no innocent and pretty fancy ever to be despised' (p. 313). The opposition Sissy seems to represent – of imagination, emotion, questioning of patriarchal discourses – stands like the circus-master's fancy, a fantastic dream that amuses children but does not displace Gradgrindian fact. It has no ability to construct a shared feminine discourse that can alter the rigid polarities of fact and fancy, meaning and no-meaning. When Louisa tries to inquire about such forbidden topics as love, she is on her own, pursuing a 'strong wild, wandering interest peculiar to her; an interest gone astray like a banished creature, and hiding in solitary places' (p. 98).

In her dramatic confrontation with her father (pp. 238–42), Louisa tries to construct a realm outside the powerful sway of reason and logic. Yet she can imagine this realm only as the 'immaterial part of my life', marking it as that which has no material existence or is irrelevant. She thereby perpetuates the construction of her world as absolute in its polarities – as a world that is either material or immaterial, fact or fancy, reason or nonsense.[32] To use Bakhtin's terms, she remains 'bound' to 'the authoritative word' in its totality; she cannot 'divide it up', or 'play with the context framing it' or 'play with its borders'.[33] She suggests she might have come closer to a desired end 'if I had been stone blind, if I had groped my way by my sense of touch, and had been free, while I knew the shapes and surfaces of things, to exercise my fancy somewhat, in regard to them' (p. 240). Passionate as this scene is, Louisa's specific argument shows the difficulty of evading the power of patriarchal discourse; she can only 'prove' the worth of an oppositional realm by the tools she has learned from her father. Her vision remains defined as 'no-meaning', as existing only in opposition to what persists as 'meaning'. Louisa tries to imagine a realm 'defying all the calculations ever made by man, and no more known to his arithmetic than his Creator is', but ends up describing herself as 'a million times wiser, happier'. Like her mother, her power lies in speaking the father's word imperfectly, making her father's statistical practices meaningless by her exaggerated application. Like her mother, Louisa's complaints refer only to 'something' missing; there are no words for what might be gained. The Gradgrind system is too powerful to allow Louisa or her mother to break away or to communicate very well with each other. All they can do, in their separate ways and unbeknownst to each other, is to disrupt the functioning of the father's word, and to indicate a lack, an incompleteness.

The schematic quality of *Hard Times* indicates a broader lack or incompleteness in the authoritative discourses of Dickens's social and literary world. Like Louisa and Mrs Gradgrind, Dickens must articulate his valuing of 'fancy' and his concern about crossing proscribed boundaries in language devalued by the patriarchal discourses of reason and fact. That Lewes sees him as hallucinating a world no wise man would recognise indicates the disturbing effect of this crossing of boundaries. Both Lewes and Dickens identify the disturbance as somehow connected with women, seeing women as touched by issues that more successfully acculturated males do not notice. Lewes saw much of Dickens's power – and what made him a disturbing novelist – as the ability to represent something that could not otherwise be acknowledged. 'What seems preposterous, impossible to us', he wrote in 1872, 'seemed to him simple fact of observation'.[34] Writing as a woman places Dickens in a position to observe what seems 'preposterous, impossible'.

At the same time, of course, for a powerful male novelist like Dickens, the position of outsider is exaggerated. Dickens can be seen as exploiting the exclusion and material oppression of women and the poor when they serve as analogies for his own more temperate marginality as a lower-middle class writer of fiction in a literary culture that preferred educated reason over experienced fancy. For male writers like Dickens and Trollope, writing 'as a woman' brought literary respect and considerable financial return, whereas a writer like Charlotte Brontë was censured for her un-womanly productions and underpaid by her publisher.[35] Unlike women who transgress the boundaries of the literary establishment, Dickens could signal his difference as significant rather than ridicu-lous. Unlike the poor with whom he was so closely identified, Dickens had access to the means of publication; he had the influence and position to pressure contemporary methods of pro-duction and dissemination of literary and social discourse. Such was his influence as spokesman of social discontent, that women writers of the nineteenth century, in both England and America, had to come to terms with his boundaries and codes, with his literary con-ventions for observing the social world and its institutions. Writers like Mary Elizabeth Braddon, Elizabeth Gaskell, Elizabeth Stuart Phelps, and Rebecca Harding Davis both quote and revise his por-trayal of women's writing and social position. Their attempts to write as women are circumscribed within Dickens's example and within the audience that he so powerfully swayed.

This assessment of Dickens's sympathetic identification with fem-inine discourses in the 1850s returns to the intertwined, ideological interests involved in any attempt to write 'as a woman', in any project that *assumes* the position of an outsider, of an other. Dickens's experimentation with excluded positions of women and the poor provided him with a way of disrupting the status quo of the literary establishment. But, ironically, his experimentation also helped him capitalise on his status as an outsider in that literary realm. The inarticulate masses became, in effect, his constituency and his subject matter, supporting his powerful position within the literary and social establishment as arbiter of how to write about cultural exclusion. Dickens's growing influence as an editor and public spokesman for the literary world make his representations of women's writing dominate the literary scene. His example carves out a possible space for women writers in his culture, but it also takes over that space as its own. His assumed position as outsider complicates assumptions about gender difference in writing and problematises what Lewes so confidently called 'genuine female ex-perience'. It disrupts and forces out into the open the literary estab-lishment's defensive cultural narratives, and, in the process, constructs its own protective practices and standards. In writing as a woman, in speaking for a silenced group, Dickens both makes possible and makes complicated a challenge to 'the father's word' by those who use 'the mother-tongue'.

From *Dickens Studies Annual*, 18 (1989), 161–78.

NOTES

[Jean Ferguson Carr's essay starts with a consideration of George Henry Lewes's 1872 essay on Dickens. Lewes sees Dickens as a phenomenon: lower-class, uneducated and aligned with feminine discourses. A number of the essays in this volume explore Dickens's problematic relationship with middle-class values and middle-class discourse, but when, as here, Dickens is placed alongside a solidly middle-class figure like Lewes, we perhaps become more aware of the subversive elements in his writing. It is easy to criticise Dickens, for example, on the basis of how many of his women (such as Dora and Agnes in *David Copperfield*) are male fantasy figures, but Lewes, almost inadvertently, indicates something more fundamentally disruptive: the way in which Dickens is aligned with a feminine voice. Carr, in turn, focuses on a delicate balance in Dickens: how he is empathetic with oppressed women yet also insistent on the constraints and stereotypes that restrict them. The issue, as Carr puts it, is how women are positioned in the powerful discourses of the novels as in contemporary social practices. We see in her essay, therefore, a mixture of elements: an interest in the dominant discourse of Dickens's day, an examination of how he relates to this discourse, and, more specifically, a consideration of how he is at one with the values of his period yet also critical. The issue is pursued on the basis of the linguistic evidence of the text, with gender providing a useful focus for a broad debate about the entire structure and direction of Victorian society. At the same time, Carr does not pretend that this is an objective historical reconstruction; her discussion inevitably and necessarily takes account of what matters to the modern reader. In Carr's essay, the powerful social discourse of the Gradgrind system is identified with the 'word of the fathers'; any opposition to it is not only going to prove secondary but essentially untenable. Mrs Gradgrind, therefore, who might suggest an alternative to patriarchal discourses, is comically ineffectual and trivial. There are, however, several scenes between Louisa and her father where his authority is examined and questioned, but Louisa cannot find words for what is missing from her life; and Sissy Jupe rarely speaks in opposition, or at all. The point is that Dickens offers an astute analysis of the ideology of his day by showing the impossibility of articulating an opposing position. There are critics who have attacked Dickens's fictional notion of fancy and the falseness of his circus-world, but what Carr enables us to see is a far more deeply-rooted problem in the novel, a problem that reflects the reality of the society in which Dickens was writing. As is the case with the other critics in this volume, she looks behind the surface pattern and identifies a deeper tension: in this instance, it is the tension between the dominant discourse and the marginalised or silenced discourses of the period. The final, and most telling, illustration of this appears in the closing paragraphs of Carr's essay, where she shows how Dickens, for all his sympathetic identification with an alternative standpoint, remains a powerful male novelist: 'The inarticulate masses became, in effect, his constituency and his subject matter, supporting his powerful position within the literary and social establishment as arbiter of how to write about cultural exclusion.' The contradiction emphasises again the complex relationship between ideology and literary form. Ed.]

1. 'Dickens in Relation to Criticism', *Fortnightly Review,* 17 (1872), 141–54. Lewes had written in *The Leader* in 1852 about *Bleak House* and had engaged with Dickens in a debate about the scientific basis for spontaneous combustion. For an early summary of the relationship between the two, see Gordon S. Haight. 'Dickens and Lewes', *PMLA,* 71 (1956), 166–79.

2. Lewes, 'Dickens in Relation to Criticism', 143.

3. See Forster's rebuttal of Lewes's essay in *The Life of Charles Dickens* (1872–4), ed. A. J. Hoppé, 2 vols (London, 1966), vol. 2, pp. 267–79. Forster argued: 'When the characters in a play are puppets, and the audiences of the theatre fools or children, no wise man forfeits his wisdom by proceeding to admit that ... through his puppets, he spoke "in the mother-tongue of the heart"' (2, p. 270). See also the excellent discussion of Lewes's essay by George H. Ford, in *Dickens and His Readers: Aspects of Novel-Criticism Since 1836* (1955; rpt New York, 1965), pp. 149–54, which focuses on Lewes's concern about 'realism' and his derogation of Dickens's imagination. Ford describes the essay as 'an extremely sophisticated piece of irony' (p. 151) and as 'the most effective attack on Dickens ever written' (p. 154). 'Like the walrus and the carpenter,' he concludes, 'Lewes weeps over the oysters he is consuming, and he assures his victim and his audience that it is all for the best' (p. 154).

4. *The Rise and Fall of the Man of Letters* (London, 1969), p. 73. Gross discusses Lewes's career as writer and editor of periodicals but does not mention his influence on any women writers except George Eliot. For other discussions of Lewes's influence as a critic, see Monika Brown, 'George Henry Lewes', *DLB 55: Victorian Prose Writers before 1867*, ed. William B. Thesing (Detroit, 1987), pp. 128–41; Harold Orel, *Victorian Literary Critics* (New York, 1984), pp. 5–30; Edgar W. Hirshberg, *George Henry Lewes* (New York, 1970); Alice R. Kaminsky, 'George Eliot, George Henry Lewes, and the Novel', *PMLA,* 70 (1955), 997–1013; Morris Greenhut, 'George Henry Lewes as a Critic of the Novel', *Studies in Philology,* 45 (1948), 491–511.

5. Haight, 'Dickens and Lewes', 167.

6. In 'The Principles of Success in Literature', a six-part essay appearing 'by the editor' of the new *Fortnightly Review* in 1865, Lewes discussed the 'profession' of literature, and the necessity to protect it from the 'incompetent aspirants, without seriousness of aim, without the faculties demanded by their work', those who 'follow Literature simply because they see no other opening for their incompetence; just as forlorn widows and ignorant old maids thrown suddenly on their own resources open a school' (1 [1865], 86). As he did of his letters and reviews of Brontë, Lewes saw this essay as furnishing 'nothing more than help and encouragement' (86). Lewes's defence of literature is generous in comparison to the vituperative review of *A Tale of Two Cities* by James Fitzjames Stephen, who blamed Dickens for 'infect[ing] the literature of his country with a disease' and promoting instead an 'incurable vulgarity of mind and of taste, and intolerable arrogance of temper'. He charged him with a 'complete disregard of the rules of literary composition' and a lack of 'intellectual excellence' or concern for 'the higher pleasures' of fiction (*Saturday Review*, 8 [17 December 1859], 741–3).

7. Lewes, 'Dickens in Relation to Criticism', 151.

8. Ibid., 146–7.

9. Ibid., 147.

10. 'The Lady Novelists', *Westminster Review*, 58 (1852), 72. See also 'The Principles of Success in Literature' and his reviews of Brontë's *Jane Eyre*, *Shirley*, and *Villette*. Only Brontë's side of their correspondence seems to have survived, but her letters to Lewes and her friend W. S. Williams discuss what Lewes wrote to her; see Clement Shorter, *The Brontës: Life and Letters*, 2 vols (1908; rpt New York, 1969). In a letter to her 'mentor' (6 Nov. 1847), Brontë recites the terms of Lewes's advice, his warning to 'beware of melodrama', his exhortation to 'adhere to the real', and describes her early adherence to such 'principles': 'I restrained imagination, eschewed romance, repressed excitement. ... sought to produce something which should be soft, grave, and true'. But she also questions the authority of his views: 'when [imagination] is eloquent, and speaks rapidly and urgently in our ear, are we not to write to her dictation?' (vol. 1, pp. 365–6). In her letter of 12 Jan. 1848, following Lewes's review of *Jane Eyre*, Brontë writes, 'If I ever *do* write another book, I think I will have nothing of what you call "melodrama"; I *think* so, but I am not sure' (vol. 1, p. 386). Brontë was furious at Lewes's published 'discovery' that she was a woman, especially after she had requested that he avoid the issue. She wrote to him on 19 Jan. 1850: 'after I had said earnestly that I wished critics would judge me as an *author*, not as a woman, you so roughly – I even thought so cruelly – handled the question of sex' (vol. 2, p. 106). I am

indebted to Margaret L. Shaw's discussion of Lewes's effect on Charlotte Brontë and his efforts to consolidate the emerging category of the 'man of letters' (PhD dissertation, University of Pittsburgh, 1988). See also Franklin Gary, 'Charlotte Brontë and George Henry Lewes', *PMLA*, 51 (1936), 518–42.

11. Jay B. Hubbell, *Who Are the Major American Writers?* (North Carolina, 1972) p. 79. Hubbell was specifically discussing the 'decline' of literature in the 1870s in America. In the 1872 essay Lewes argued that unknowledgeable readers 'were at once laid hold of by the reproduction of their own feelings, their own experiences, their own prejudices' (151).

12. Letter to John Forster, *The Letters of Charles Dickens*, ed. Madeline House and Graham Storey, The Pilgrim Edition, Vol. 4 (Oxford, 1965–88), p. 328.

13. Charles Dickens, 'Preliminary Word', *Household Words*, 1 (March 1850), I.

14. For the details of Dickens's periodical experimentation, see Anne Lohrli (ed.), *Household Words* (Toronto, 1973), and Harry Stone (ed.), *Charles Dickens' Uncollected Writings from Household Words*, 2 vols (Bloomington, 1968).

15. In 'Critical Cross-Dressing: Male Feminists and the Woman of the Year', *Raritan*, 3 (1983), 130–49, Elaine Showalter considers whether the fashion in the 1980s to address the 'woman question' is a disguished form of 'power play': 'Is male feminism a form of critical cross-dressing, ... or is it the result of a genuine shift in critical, cultural, and sexual paradigms ... ?' (131, 134).

16. *Dickens and Women* (Stanford, 1983), pp. 243–4. In her essay, 'Writing in a "Womanly" Way and the Double Vision of *Bleak House*', *Dickens Quarterly*, 4 (1987), 3–15, Suzanne Graver makes a compelling argument for Dickens's 'masculine stake' in discerning contemporary gender relations, in representing the value and authority of women's knowledge. Although she argues for Dickens's 'remarkably insightful portrait of a woman experiencing her knowing self as not-knowing' (10), she also charges him with using 'Esther's obliqueness not to subvert Victorian womanly ideals but to celebrate a dutifully willed acceptance of them' (4).

17. *A Theory of Literary Production*, trans. Geoffrey Wall (1966; London, 1978); see especially pp. 82–9.

18. 'The Lady Novelists' (1852), p. 72.

19. The phrase 'relative creatures' is from Sarah Stickney Ellis's influential advice book, *The Women of England* (London, 1838; rpt Philadelphia, 1841) p. 100. See Dianne Sadoff's discussion of women

characters in *Monsters of Affection: Dickens, Eliot and Brontë' on Fatherhood* (Baltimore, 1982), pp. 58–64. See also Anne Robinson Taylor's discussion of Esther, 'The Author as Female Child', in *Male Novelists and Their Female Voices: Literary Masquerades* (Troy, 1981), pp. 121–56.

20. See Peggy Kamuf, 'Writing like a Woman', in *Women and Language in Literature and Society*, ed. Sally McConnell-Ginet, Ruth Borker, and Nelly Furman (New York, 1980), pp. 284–99, for an argument against an essentialist 'female writing' (as proposed in Patricia Spacks's *The Female Imagination*, 1972) and her warning about seeing literature as 'expressions, simple and direct, of individual experience' (p. 286).

21. In 'Patriarchy Against Itself – The Young Manhood of Wallace Stevens', *Critical Inquiry*, 13 (1987), 742–86, Frank Lentricchia discusses Stevens's sense of poetry as a 'lady-like' habit, his 'feminisation of the literary life' and his 'struggle to overcome this feminisation' which his culture equated with 'the trivialisation of literature and the literary impulse' (751). He argues for 'the cultural powerlessness of poetry in a society that masculinised the economic while it feminised the literary' (766).

22. In *Bleak House* (1852), for example, his preface proposes to explore 'the romantic side of familiar things', and the opening number of *Household Words* insists 'that in all familiar things, even in those which are repellent on the surface, there is Romance enough, if we will find it out' (1 [1850], 1).

23. For an analysis of Dickens's habit of deflecting self-critique, see Jean Ferguson Carr, 'Dickens and Autobiography: A Wild Beast and his Keeper', *English Literary History*, 52 (1985), 447–69. See also Carr, 'The Polemics of Incomprehension: Mother and Daughter in *Pride and Prejudice*', in *Traditions and the Talents of Women*, ed. Florence Howe (Champaign, 1989).

24. Letter to John Forster, February 1854, *The Letters of Charles Dickens*, ed. Walter Dexter, vol. 2 (London, 1937–8) p. 543. To Mrs Richard Watson, 1 Nov. 1854, he wrote that he felt '"used up" after *Hard Times*' and that 'the compression and close condensation necessary for that disjointed form of publication gave me perpetual trouble' (vol. 2, p. 602). See his letter to Miss Coutts, 23 Jan. 1854 (vol. 2, p. 537) for a description of his printers' urging to write the novel. In *Dickens' Working Notes for his Novels* (Chicago, 1987), Harry Stone discusses Dickens's efforts to accommodate his working procedures to the constraints of weekly serialisation (p. 249), and the plans show his calculations for the unfamiliar size of a weekly part (pp. 251–3).

25. See, for example, David Craig's discussion of the novel's 'simplifying mode', in his introduction to *Hard Times: For These Times*

(Harmondsworth, 1969), p. 28. All following page references are to the Penguin edition.

26. M. M. Bakhtin, *The Dialogic Imagination*, ed. Michael Holquist, trans. Caryl Emerson and Michael Holquist (Austin and London, 1981), p. 342.

27. See also pp. 137, 224. This passage is one of the references to Mrs Gradgrind in Dickens's working plans for the novel (Stone, *Dickens' Working Notes*, p. 253): 'Mrs Gradgrind – badly done transparency, without enough light behind'.

28. In *The Shows of London* (Cambridge, 1978), Richard D. Altick defines transparencies as 'pictures made with translucent paints on materials like calico, linen, or oiled paper and lighted from behind in the manner of stained glass' (p. 95) and discusses their popularity in the Chinese shadow and magic-lantern shows of the 1770s (p. 119) and in the dioramas of the 1820s (on pp. 169–70). In Daguerre's 'double-effect' technique, transparencies were painted on both sides, their appearance transformed by the amount and angle of light shown through the image (pp. 169–70). Transparencies, or lithophanes as they were sometimes called, could also be small porcelain figures held against a light.

29. Dickens changed his mind about its positioning, marking in his working plans its postponement from ch. 3 (*'No not yet'*) to ch. 4 (*'Now, Mrs Gradgrind'*) (Stone, *Dickens' Working Notes*, p. 253).

30. His working plans indicate an early decision about whether to make it 'Mrs Gradgrind – or Miss? Wife or sister? *Wife*' (Stone, *Dickens' Working Notes*, p. 253). In *Dickens at Work* (London, 1957), John Butt and Kathleen Tillotson argue that the choice of 'wife' over 'sister' emphasises 'more powerfully' the absolute influence of Gradgrind over his children (p. 206).

31. Reprinted in *Charles Dickens: Selected Short Fiction*, ed. Deborah A. Thomas (New York, 1976), pp. 218–29. The naïve narrator of the tale assumes Captain Murderer 'must have been an offshoot of the Blue Beard family, but I had no suspicion of the consanguinity in those times'. Like Gradgrind, Captain Murderer's 'warning name would seem to have awakened no general prejudice against him, for he was admitted into the best society and possessed immense wealth' (p. 221). And, like Gradgrind, much of his power comes from being the determiner of meanings and names.

32. Several of Dickens's initial titles in his working plans for the novel reflect this insistence on polarity: 'Hard heads and soft hearts', 'Heads and Tales', and 'Black and White' (Stone, *Dickens' Working Notes*, p. 251).

33. Bakhtin, *The Dialogic Imagination*, p. 343.

34. Lewes, 'Dickens in Relation to Criticism, 145.

35. See Margot Peters's discussion of the inequity of publishers' payments, in *Unquiet Soul: A Biography of Charlotte Brontë* (1975; rpt New York), pp. 355–6. Brontë received the same unsatisfying sum of £500 for her third novel *Villette* as she had for the first two, as compared to Thackeray's £4200 for *The Virginians* or the £1000 Dickens could command for a short story. Peters quotes George Gissing's telling comment about author-publisher relations:

> A big, blusterous, genial brute of a Trollope could very fairly hold his own, and exact at all events an acceptable share in the profits of his work. A shrewd and vigorous man of business such as Dickens ... could do even better ... But pray, what of Charlotte Brontë? Think of that grey, pinched life, ... which would have been so brightened had [she] received but ... one-third of what in the same space of time, the publisher gained by her books.
>
> (pp. 355–6)

10

Wonderful No-Meaning: Language and the Psychopathology of the Family in *Hard Times*

RICHARD FABRIZIO

I THE ARGUMENT

'People live now in a way that I don't comprehend.'
(Roger Carbury in Trollope,
The Way We Live Now [1875])

Usually thought of as a satiric portrait of industrialisation, weak in drama and feeble in characterisation,[1] *Hard Times* is more fundamentally a keen description of the psyche forged out of socioeconomic conditions. It exposes personality types, their emotive and reactive make-up, and the origin and process of their symptoms. The language its characters rehearse and particularly the poses they strike result from the mind's accommodation to a new familial environment, a by-product of the machine – the great power loom. Their linguistic and paralinguistic adaptations result in a dialectic where love dominates life in the absence of its direct expression, fancy preoccupies the mind while it is ridiculed, and feeling – particularly in the male – is glorified while it is denigrated. In the fictive time-space of mid-nineteenth-century Coketown both a psychopathology of the family and its rhetorical expression is voiced.

Dickens had to describe a psychic condition with a vocabulary that itself was a symptom of the disease.

He saw his fictive society against a backdrop of an earlier agricultural state, thus naming the parts of his novel sowing, reaping, and garnering, and framing its time in spring (I:4, 11), summer (II:8, 137), and autumn (III:6, 201). Winter is absent; the great question mark at the end. These are growth stages, psychological as well as vegetative. How do agricultural and industrial growth differ? How do people, particularly the family unit, psychically grow, mature, and die in the age of steam? After the Reformation the nature of the family radically changed, according to some becoming sternly 'patriarchal', according to others richly 'affective'.[2] No such elemental split seems to have occurred; rather power (the patriarchal) and love (the affective) became fixed in an uneasy bondage within the family, the terms Wife, Husband, Mother, and especially Father undergoing redefinition. Robbed of the rich 'network' of legal and social services held by the family in ancient and medieval times,[3] and now provided by the State, the family was thrown back upon itself, had to justify itself as an entity tied together only by the cords of the emotions. Law and state replaced religion and family as the cement that held society together. Crime was divorced from sin, and punishment from family action. Entertainment which had taken place in the public arena was forced from the marketplace, tavern, or pilgrimage[4] into the confines of the home and family.

In the age of nascent capitalism, after 1750, there is a stress on the 'inner life' of the family, which is signalled by a lowering of the marriage age and a slight increase in family size.[5] Gradgrind has five children – often thought pointless for only two have an active role in the novel; Louisa marries at just over nineteen (I:3, 10–11; I:15, 75) to a much older man – while pre-industrial marriage generally took place between those of the same age.[6] Wherever technology is found, the nuclear rather than the extended family is found, with a stress on children rather than relations. The family changed from a more functional to a more affective unit. As it weakened politically and economically, it changed psychically. With the narrowing of its activity in public space came an expansion of its inner life in the private space of the home, what historians have labelled its domestication but which Dickens in *Hard Times* describes as its dislocation. The shift in the nature of the family is marked by redefinition in vocabulary. The very word economics, for instance, derived as it is from Greek οἶκος or 'house', was no longer referred to in terms of the household unit. The family became mythologised, maintaining itself as a unit by godly commandment (paterfamilias) and supporting itself by sacrificial rite (feminine love).

Woman's function is reduced to her love; man's affection is replaced by his function. Dickens's novel for good reason centres on the industrialisation of weaving, the very sign of woman's traditional status and economic position.[7] Every Homeric woman – mortal or immortal – is never found without her distaff. Here mechanical frame and loom replace her distaff. In the fifteenth century, the water power revolution stripped her of another function, the two or three hours of grinding duties to feed her family.[8] Four centuries later the attrition of her functional value in terms of household economy was enormous. With attenuated functional value, women became aliens inside and outside the home. They were justified as moral agents, as repositories of love and beauty; that is, for themselves not for their function. After his educational system failed in Louisa, Gradgrind does not so much question its utility as its applicability to females: 'it [the educational system] would be difficult of general application to girls' (III:3, 183). Later, Louisa is praised for having no function. She 'beautifies' life precisely because she holds 'no fantastic vow, or bond, or brotherhood, or sisterhood, or pledge, or covenant' (III:9, 226). Women became the fertile matrix for great moral battles between function and love. Wives are destroyed. Marriage kills off Mrs Gradgrind, Mrs Blackpool, Mrs Jupe, and to all intents and purposes Mrs Bounderby. Sibling and romantic love are confused. Louisa malfunctions in the expression of her emotions to her brother and to her would-be lover.

Female functionalism in terms of family economics reciprocally affected male functionalism. Dickens in *Dombey and Son* (1848) had documented an earlier stage in the transition of the family from farm to firm. Mercantilism affected awkward family relations, particularly the sexual ones between husband and wife. The first Mrs Dombey is a procreating object; the second Mrs Dombey a sexual curiosity. The 'father' and 'son' of the title are equivocal terms, undergoing redefinition because of economic imperatives; a father and a son are something between partners and relatives. Emotion publicly stripped from males found clumsy expression in the family. Sons deny motherhood. Bounderby and Bitzer in *Hard Times* effectively eliminate motherhood, matricides by intent. Fatherhood is lethal. Mr Gradgrind tries to withdraw his affections from his daughter; Mr Jupe nobly parts from his.

In a wild interplay of actions and reactions among the Gradgrinds and Bounderbys, the Jupes, Sparsits, Bitzers, and Blackpools, the roles of father and mother, husband and wife, brother and sister, bachelor and spinster are psychically re-established. It is on this all too fragile, this all too unprofound psychic surface where the matter of the novel exists. It is here that we find the causes and motives for the awkward reticence, indirection, and circumlocution that mark all the relationships in the novel.[9] Characters conform to an oblique communication code. To understand the code, the pathos of the moment must be deciphered. For after all, it is of the essence that the novel is an exposé of ordinary people interacting in the daily course of daily life. For instance, the three mysteries of the novel, where is Mr Jupe? who robbed the bank? what happened to Blackpool?, are not exploited as means to uncover monumental truths but to map the characteristic ways that feeling finds expression. Mr Jupe's whereabouts is every day fixed in the pathetic pattern of Sissy's carrying about the bottle of nine-oils. The robber's identity is manifested in Louisa's pathetic doubts about her brother's complicity. Blackpool's disappearance stimulates the pathetic faith of Rachael. The structure of *Hard Times* is therefore regressive – events are not cumulative but repetitive, bound to a single psychic pattern. Its paradigm may be described as: (1) daily 'incompatibility' (Dickens's word), in which males and females are ill formed and wrongly joined; (2) daily misdirection, in which communication of all kinds between and among the sexes is oblique – a pattern of avoidance marked by the heart's silence or dumbness to its desires; (3) daily disaster, in which relationships break up and end rather than grow and resolve.

The regressive structure of the novel is a template of the repressive nature of its language; that is, a language that moves action ahead while harking back to loss. On the purely pathological level, action is impersonalised by a varied catalogue of gestures and tics, from Bitzer's parroting of formulae (echolalia) to Mrs Gradgrind's mental torpidity (bradyphrenia). A veritable pathopoiesis results, each compulsive movement manifesting a feeling in the absence of its direct expression. On the rhetorical level, Dickens creates a structure of naming. Throughout the text, he humorously plays with the designation, 'ology'. The suffix carries all the weight of its origin in λόγος, 'logos'. Logos means 'word' or 'name' but signifies a complex of values from thought and discourse to reason and conversation; in fact, it refers to all that gives meaning to existence. On her deathbed, Mrs Gradgrind wishes to find the word or name for all that is missing in Gradgrind's philosophy. She knows that the word is not a Gradgrindian 'ology'. She struggles, but before she can find the word she dies. The narrator comments: 'It matters little what figures of wonderful no-meaning she [Mrs Gradgrind] began to trace upon her wrappers' (II:9, 152–3). Dickens insists that to see into his characters it is only the 'unsaid', the 'unlogos' that will do. With no pen, Mrs Gradgrind writes no words on no paper. It is the 'wonderful no-meaning' that gives meaning to existence. It is the 'wonderful no-meaning' that is the rhetorical counterpart to the no-actions and the no-statements of all the characters. On the language level, Foucault calls a similar occurrence society's 'procedures of exclusion';[10] that is, structures society uses to avoid the expression of what it does not permit, the prohibited. Here, what is not permitted or withheld expression is nevertheless stated; it might be called a rhetoric of exclusion. The rhetoric exposes what is in the mind of characters by what is excluded in acts and words. Dickens uses exclusion as a tool to satirise the inadequacy of the linguistic formula of Gradgrind's school and Bounderby's factory. Gradgrind wishes his students to form themselves on the factory model of a language that expresses a one to one relationship with 'thingness'. Such a mathematical formulation eliminates the space between word and phenomenon, the space where ambiguity and emotion slip in at the back door. Therefore, he wishes a definition of a horse in terms of genus and differentiation, stripping language of either cultural or personal connotation. Bitzer's scientific enumeration of the qualities of a horse is preferred to Sissy's perplexity about how to define. Louisa and Tom keep 'conchological' and 'mineralogical' cabinets: 'the specimens were all arranged and labelled, and the bits of stone and ore looked as though they might have been broken from the parent substances by those tremendously hard instruments their own names' (I:3, 8). The very act of naming is then an act of destruction – of breaking reality from the word meant to explain it. In Bounderby's factory the same process occurs. At his marriage breakfast, Bounderby vaunts that he is 'a man, who when he sees a Post, says "that's a Post"' (I:16, 83). Expression is an exact equation: one word equals one thing. But what functions satisfactorily in his factory cracks in daily life. Bounderby accuses Blackpool of refusing out of fear to spy on his fellow workers. Blackpool denies the accusation not by an assertion of his reasons but by refraining to speak – 'nowt to sen'. The no-statement is filled in as the content of his psyche – ethical, human, religious. The unsaid has no meaning and all meaning. Therefore, Bounderby is constrained to respond in words that mock his own attitude about language: 'I know what you said; more than that, I know what you mean, you see. Not always the same thing, by the Lord Harry! Quite different things' (II:5, 112). It is appropriate that he swears by the Lord Harry, or the Devil, for it is the devil who represents splitting word from thing – the diabolic being even in etymology a 'carrying away' as opposed to symbolic, a 'carrying together'.

In presenting the psychic activity of a new family type, Dickens replaces expression by indirection, the frontal attack by the gesture. Language of the public space (factory and worker) was too shallow to function effectively in the private space (home and family); it detached and split rather than unified and glued the world and the self. In a linguistic *tour de force*, Dickens supported his psychological investigation with a virtual philosophical theory of language. 'Wonderful no-meaning' is hunted in 'no-naming', 'no-stating', and 'no-acting'. This notion may be refined, at least briefly, by stating a few forms into which his language falls: (1) 'no-meaning' discovers meaning when of two significations for a sign the intended one is false while the unintended is true (amphiboly). Louisa thus logically interprets the woman in Blackpool's room as his 'wife', but the woman is Rachael – not his wife but whom he wishes were his wife (II:6, 12); or Tom intends that Blackpool's appearance nightly at the bank will be logically perceived as a sign of guilt should the bank be robbed (II:6, 125–6) while the hidden truth is that innocence will be sacrificed. Signs rather than having direct meaning stand for the presuppositions of the interpreters. (2) 'No-naming' discovers meaning by the substitution of an epithet for a personal name (antonomasia). Children in the school are designated by numbers; workers in the factory are called 'hands'. The rhetoric of no-naming is fixed in the references to nicknames. Nicknames indicate not just identity but attitude. Mrs Gradgrind's perplexity about nicknaming gets at a psychic truth: the word can be a kind of medicine to relieve anxiety. Her problem is what to call Bounderby after he marries her daughter. Gradgrind won't permit nicknames (I:2, 2). If nicknames like 'Joe' aren't permitted, and she can't call him mister, and the name Josiah is 'unsupportable' to her, what shall she name him (I:5, 78–79)? Her dilemma originates because she cannot call son a man who is as old as she is; the integration into her family of such an old man upset family order and strained the available language.[11] She solves her problem by a no-name; he becomes a letter, 'J' (II:9, 151). Cecilia is Sissy, an expressive name that indicates family and social order, while 'J' indicates detachment and predicament. (3) 'No-stating' discovers meaning by the personification of the absent (prosopopeia). The personification is of psychic conditions. The Sparsit–Bounderby relationship is almost totally unexpressed in their direct conversations. Mrs Sparsit apostrophises Bounderby's portrait (II:10, 156; III:9, 224–5). What she refrains from expressing and acting out to him in person, she speaks to his portrait, thereby retrieving for us some of her hidden feelings. (4) 'No-acting' discovers meaning in unexpressed acts tied to withheld words (anastrophe). This is the most used device to capture not only suspense but all the unexpressed hopes, desires, and dreams of the characters. For example, Louisa does not know how to act in Blackpool's rooms. She says that she is ignorant of 'how to speak' (II:6, 121), but she also refrains from doing: 'She [Louisa] stretched out hers [her hands], as if she would have touched him [Blackpool]; then checked herself and remained still' (II:6, 122). Psychic content is built at the expense of expression.

Dickens chronicles by a vast psychic and linguistic system family history, or more accurately, family psychohistory in *Hard Times*. His subject is the domestic family and its intricate battle to survive under industrial capitalism, how it is welded together, how it thinks and loves, how it is perverted and dies.

II   THE PSYCHIC HISTORY

'It was now ... The Magnetic Age: the age of violent attractions, when to hear mention of love is dangerous, and to see it, a communication of disease.'

(Sir Austin in Meredith,
The Ordeal of Richard Feveral [1859])

The opening of *Hard Times* documents an act of psychic surgery. A new training ground, the school, was a prerequisite for the new ethical and emotional thinking required by the new economic and social world. Emotions, which have no practical value, would be replaced by 'facts', which can aid in economic life. The school is the training ground for the middle-class psyche; the factory is the

training ground for the working-class psyche. Bounderby is the professor of the novel's second school. The factory required altered behaviour from workers, machine teaching man its rhythm,[12] even as
Blackpool complained of the machinery working 'in his own head'
(I:10, 49). One of the most astounding side-effects of the operation
on the emotions is the surface calm of the patients. Though the
surgery is fundamentally a violent act, it is performed calmly, responded to almost silently. Silence reigns in Coketown, save for the
rhythmic beating of the power looms. They are its heartbeat. When
the second Mrs Dombey does not return home one night, Dombey
himself breaks down her locked door and thereafter strikes his
daughter who tries to comfort him. Jonas Chuzzlewit screams and
'hauls' about his wife, Mercy Pecksniff, so that she fears 'blood-
shed'.[13] But the psychological violence in *Hard Times* is executed
silently. Relationships with self, others, and even things are quietly
taut. The attempt to fashion the mind on the economic formula of
trade – quid pro quid – left the psyche distressed. Emotion evicted
from public life found uneasy expression in the family; love prohibited to males found unstable shelter in females. A side-effect of the
psychic operation is infertility – the death of the family. Tom and
Louisa will produce no children; Blackpool and Rachael will never
marry. Bounderby, Bitzer, and Harthouse personify futile bachelor-
hood.[14] In a world where the family is dislocated by economic and
social forces, where the psyche is deformed by education, characters
express themselves in twisted language and hunt their selves in
twisted relationships.

Nowhere is the psychic condition of the family better seen than in
Mr Thomas Gradgrind's relationship with wife and daughter. He is
not monolithic, impenetrable, and cold. His sentiments at time
unseat him (I:5, 20–1). He is unaccountably kind to Sissy, for instance. He excuses his feeling by the rationalisation that success
with such poor matter as she will prove his system. Reluctantly he
admits that 'he had become possessed by an idea that there was
something in this girl which could hardly be set down in tabular
form' (I:14, 71). 'Tabular form' is a stale metonymy whose origin is
the *tabula* or writing table, a flat surface or board upon which wills,
accounts, and letters were once written. So the *tabula* defines communication in terms of lists and public accounts; for instance, God's
commandments were written into a tablet. Typically in this novel,
the metaphor – Sissy being compared to what is not tabular – cata-
logues an absence: her worth is what 'could hardly be set down'.

The 'idea', the atabular, appears obliquely just beneath the surface of the action, at the point where verbal expression and psychic desire conflict. The absence defines the presence or the sum of Gradgrind's actions, his calculated existence as a public man, teacher, and MP. But he is a man 'possessed' by a formless 'idea'. The idea, the private man, peeks through. The idea is expressed even though Gradgrind has no vocabulary for it. This akinesia is typical of him when he confronts feeling; the articulate man displays a stickiness of mind. When her father left Sissy, Gradgrind had taken her in against the sound advice of Bounderby (I:8, 37). In the negotiations for her at the circus, the 'idea' appears in glances and movements. Circus folk read in Gradgrind what he does not realise is in him. Childers looks at Gradgrind with 'hope'. But most importantly the absent 'idea' forces its presence upon him when their idiom pops out of his mouth, the idiom being atabular in form: 'Why has he [Jupe] been – so very much – Goosed? asked Mr Gradgrind, forcing the word out of himself, with great solemnity and reluctance' (I:6, 24). The idea's atabular form is the common idiom of the other, the circus. Gradgrind forces the word out with 'solemnity', as if it were a word in a religious rite, an untouchable thing both magical and lethal at the same time. The socially loaded word 'goosed', meaning hissed, is really a non-word that mimics the hissing of the goose to express an attitude and feeling of disapproval. His 'reluctance' to use the word is a sign of psychic stricture. Such words are metaphoric, expressing social norms and the grey area between desire and permissibility. They are a psychic shorthand. In the same circus atmosphere, Bounderby will object to the circus word 'Cackler', and indeed Childers will have to translate the expressive particular term to its inexpressive general form 'speaker' (I:6, 24). Such linguistic acrobatics are commonplace in the novel. Feeling requiring suppression in public life is expressed over and over again by circumlocution, signs, and absence.

Gradgrind's manner in relation to females displays the silent truth beyond the surface of his words; his innate affection suffers from public image. Straight away we learn that Gradgrind 'was an affectionate father after his manner' (I:3, 8). Nothing could be more important than the modifying phrase – 'After his manner'. The sole bit of information we have about his past, his manner, is that he had sold hardware. His past is business; his manner is geared to it. The ex-hardware man has modified his character with a manner. As the idea of fatherhood became reduced in its legal, political, and economic extensions, the demand for another dimension – affection – increased.[15] For instance, the notion of a 'confidence', a trust beyond the kind of business affiliation of *Dombey and Son* was expected of the relationship. Harthouse notices that had such a confidence been present between Gradgrind and his son their relationship might have been different (II:7, 131). At one point, Louisa is in a state of tension: 'a fire with nothing to burn' (I:3, 10); something had 'crept' into her head (I:4, 14) which stunted could only grow malignantly. Again the expression takes the form of negation; a fire cannot exist unless it burns. The 'unfire', which is the fire, thus may give neither light nor heat, yet both are present. This is a psychic expression of schizophrenia, literally the broken-off mind. But her symptoms are the physical manifestation of his anxiety – his broken-off mind. Whenever she hints at tensions by broken-off words or physical ties, Gradgrind himself becomes ill at ease. He attempts to preserve his equilibrium by cutting himself off from inconvenient sentiments. But the strength with which he stops the onrush of sympathy shows the concomitant strength of the now deemed pertinent family feelings, the strength of what is absent. Louisa says to her father: 'I was tired ... I have been tired for a long time' (I:3, 10). But she doesn't know from what; exhaustion is the state resulting from the pursuit of the unknown absent. Gradgrind cuts her off, cuts off any investigation of her exhaustion, of what is too mysterious to be categorised as data, as tabular. Nevertheless, Gradgrind reacts, silently within himself. Non-statement or non-action is the sign of his state. His instincts function without his practical consent. His state and his perplexity rankle, for he is unable to get what she said (or did not say) out of his mind. He walks along 'in silence' for half-a-mile after the conversation, exactly like the meditating Abraham about to sacrifice his son Isaac. A slowness of mental activity, almost a frozen mind (bradyphrenia), marks his emotional state when it comes to family love. Finally, he 'gravely broke out'. Surely Dickens's ear was to the grindstone of the psychic expression of his period. 'Gravely' and 'broke out' conflict. The grave, what is heavy and solemn, conflicts with the eruptive and effusive 'broke out'. What breaks out is a nothing with regard to the situation. Bradyphrenia becomes bradyphrasia – his speech is slow and heavy and does not express his psychic state. He broke out not in tears or in anger, but in an appeal drawn from the language not of family but from the imperatives of public life, admonishing her to heed her friends who would think her vagueness silly (I:3, 10–11). Blunting Louisa's nascent expression of emotion, he blunts his own.

Gradgrind began the process to reduce emotional stimuli by mating years before with an unwomanly woman. Mrs Gradgrind is a non-entity, without even a first name to distinguish her as separate from her husband. She is deprived of sexual identity, being a 'transparency of a small female figure, without enough light behind it' (I:4, 12). Gradgrind's emotional bradyphrenia is the sum of her character. Like Bitzer, she involuntarily parrots the words spoken by others (echolalia), a condition frequently present in catatonic schizophrenia. For instance, she castigates Louisa by telling her to 'go and be somethingological directly' (I:4, 14) – the 'ologies' belonging to her husband's vocabulary. On the image level, Mrs Gradgrind is the final product of the early stage Louisa. Mrs Gradgrind is a 'transparency ... without enough light', while Louisa is a 'light with nothing to rest upon' (I:3, 10). Once again Dickens defines character by absence. Neither the transparency with too little light nor the light with no resting place may be seen. Mrs Gradgrind is the mother reduced to a comic and useless figure. Her symbolic symptom is a constantly 'throbbing' head (I:4, 13). Her head began to split as soon as she married Gradgrind and never stopped thereafter (I:16, 78). These headaches are attributed by Louisa to life lived in the world of facts (I:4, 14), at the tabula. The more the world, Hermia, dominated the domestic life, Hestia, the more women became displaced; the more the term motherhood is stripped of economic significance, the more it was redefined in terms of love of children and husband. 'Husband', on the other hand, originally only a Germanic term for the master of a house, now solely expressed a relationship to a woman, both legal and affective. Gradgrind attempts to reduce psychic tension – born of the growing demand for affection in marriage and fatherhood – by reducing the femaleness of his wife and daughter.

In Bounderby the same psychic conflict is almost eliminated by excess, by overabundance. The mark of his character is an abnormally rapid mental activity (tachyphrenia) marked by volubility or rapidity in speech (tachyphrasia). The hint of his conflict is, as in Gradgrind, his avoidance of femininity, but he avoids not by passivity but by intimidation. He is a 'bounder', cocksure, wielding vulgarity as a weapon, in his creation of new boundaries, limits, shapes. The narrator speaks of him as a God, one with 'Divine Right' (I:12, 61). On the linguistic level, he vulgarises the terms

family, state, hero by a process of deformation and then reformation. He creates myth or μυθός – the words out of which reality is
made. He uses myth to such a degree that he structures both world
and people by it. He builds with the fiction of his 'humility' the
other that he would be; the narrator thus calls him the Bully of
Humility. The public, other self he creates (Hermes) dominates the
private, inner self (Hestia). Bounderby is self-made; he is one who
by sheer will pulled himself up by the bootstraps out of a poor and
wicked family to become great. The myth of the self-made man, the
new hero, is tied to the death of the family. He posits this death in a
scene that has Mrs Gradgrind for its audience and his birthday for
its subject. He is so voluble that his words overwhelm her while in
his tale he attacks fictive women. Rechristening himself Bounderby,
he consciously destroys the Pegler family – his real father and
mother. This substitution of an epithet for a name (antonomasia)
discovers a withheld psychological condition. Changing his name,
he escapes meaning that proceeds from the family; at the same time
under the assumed name he self creates a new type. He is a self-
made man born of a self-made language; he is the child of his own
words. He destroys every trace of the gentle woman who is his
mother, Mrs Pegler, and of his father who is called the 'best' of husbands (II:6, 19). What Bounderby does is replace his 'ideal' family –
the gentle mother and good husband – with an ideal 'no-family' in
mythic terms. Exiling his real mother from ever seeing him (or to
put it correctly, from his seeing her), he commits a kind of matri-
cide. But Bounderby goes further. He creates and then abuses a
fictive mother and grandmother. With each retelling of his fictive
autobiography, he destroys his female side – a kind of gynecide.
The male is heroic to the degree he is a bastard, one who makes it
on his own in the same way as Gide later linked the bastardy of
Oedipus to his greatness.

Bounderby's pursuit of Louisa, young enough to be his daughter,
is a sign of his malady. Outwardly like Mrs Gradgrind, Louisa is
unfeminine, the product of a sexually egalitarian education. Yet he
proposes to her not because she is asexual but because he expects to
find in her all the feminine charms with none of the difficulties. He
seeks to release on her all his emotions. Nowhere is the split
between man and words better represented than in his ability to
talk of other things while his heart is preoccupied with Louisa: 'He
spoke of young Thomas, but he looked at Louisa' (I:4, 13). He
babbles out words (tachylalia); he talks of other things, of what is

not on his mind. His words negate his thoughts, but his body reveals them. Typically, he will say, 'Well, Louisa, that's [stemming her father's anger] worth a kiss' (I:4, 16). His training makes him speak of the kiss as an exchange for help, while emotionally he needs the fulfilment the kiss provides.

His body bursts from its shell, his head swells from its skin, his face erupts into fiery red (I:4, 11; II:5, 116). His rapid mental activity is out of bounds of his body. His tachyphrenia is so endemic that no situation in which he acts is free of it. One of the more curious, but no less typical relationships in the novel is between Bounderby and Mrs Sparsit. On the conscious level, Bounderby regards the woman as a possession. He dominates others with a flood of words that uses her nobility to quell opposition and to control behaviour (e.g. I:7, 36). Her worth is that she will be the captive nobility, the 'captive Princess' (I:7, 33), that demonstrates the captor's strength. But their relationship, like all other relationships between men and women, functions mechanically on the programme of a series of unstated assumptions. One of the best ways to see this is to compare Bounderby's telling Sparsit he will marry Louisa with Gradgrind's asking Louisa to marry Bounderby. It is curious the extent to which these two scenes run parallel. First, the subject is the same: a marriage proposal between Bounderby and Louisa. Next, the manner of handling the announcement is the same: Louisa is told to marry someone she does not want to marry; Sparsit is told she is barred from marrying someone she wants and from being his housekeeper. Both Gradgrind and Bounderby expect the women to react with emotion; neither does. Sparsit, like Louisa, outwardly accepts what she inwardly repels. That Bounderby is aware that Sparsit's attachment to him is more than professional is signalled by Bounderby himself who, though never expressing any desire for her, thinks she will faint away at news of his forthcoming marriage. He is aware of what neither verbalises: that she cares to be his wife, a feeling that puffs no doubt a side of him he doesn't acknowledge – his sexual vanity. Finally, the two scenes are alike in their effects on the males: if Gradgrind is upset by Louisa's cold response, Bounderby is 'far more disconcerted than if she [Sparsit] had thrown her box at the mirror or swooned on the hearthrug' (I:16, 80).

Her fumbling with this workbox encodes her psychic state. The box is constantly in her hands. It is a sexual symbol, a place to receive needles and pins to store the cloth of life. While Bounderby is telling her of his decision to marry, she of course has her box with her and works on a piece of cambric: 'she picked out holes for some inscrutable ornamental purpose' (I:16, 80). Her actions speak without words. She is a gross caricature of Penelope, always pictured with distaff, always waiting for her man, a man always in danger of being snared by sirens. Sparsit thinks of Bounderby as a victim, particularly of Louisa's snares. That Tom noticed in his sneering way that she wished to marry Bounderby (II:3, 104) and that she was like a mother, calling her continually 'Mother Sparsit', indicates the complexity of this relationship. She functions like a mother, taking over domestic duties, but fits into the economic framework of a housekeeper. In Freudian terms, she is the desired mother from a higher class worthy of such a son.[16] She is a sign of his inner emotional dilemma and a symbol of his outer victory over class. With her genteel sewing what better figure to represent the domestic side of cloth manufacture which his power looms have assaulted and destroyed.

Emotional and class signs and symbols that hover about this relationship are fixed in a single act: Bounderby's dismissal of Sparsit. Bounderby does not face her or himself, but nevertheless encodes in his words and acts what he would hide. He sticks 'an envelope with a cheque in it in her little basket' (III:9, 224). The cheque, an economic promise, replaces the sexual promise of the man. He deposits money in her 'box' and withdraws self.

Bitzer parallels Bounderby more than in the alliteration of their names. He is the perfected state of the new mythic hero – the Industrial Man. He is the echo of Bounderby. He acts without acting, for his actions are repetitive of others. He repeats definitions without personal imput (I:2, 3); he repeats Gradgrind's philosophy without concern for human relationships (III:8, 218–19). His language is the ideal shape of all others – a parrotlike repetition of the words spoken by others (echolalia). A Hermes, he begins as a messenger of the banking god, spying and informing on mankind for Bounderby while conniving to usurp his position. Bounderby dies of a fit in a Coketown street (III:9, 225), a final paroxysm that appropriately ends his excess of words in an excess of movement. But Bitzer continues to climb the mythic ladder (III:9, 225).

After his father dies, Bitzer – echoing his idol Bounderby – gets rid of his mother. Bounderby's myth is Bitzer's reality. He does not exile her into anonymity in the country, rather he has her shut up in the Work House. Like Bounderby, he provides her with an allowance, 'half a pound of tea a year' (II:1, 88). To the perfected type such an allowance is a weakness. To him the idea of the family is ludicrous. It is provident to be single, and it is perverse to have a family according to his ethic, for Bitzer says, 'I have only one to feed, and that's the person I most like to feed' (II:1, 90). Even 'hearing' of 'wives and family' conditions makes Bitzer 'nauseous' (II:1, 90).

The industrial ethic sought to retrain the affections, 'gratitude' for instance and its consequent 'virtues' (III:8, 219). Bitzer is simply the advanced state of what Dickens saw as the new malady – Industrial Man. The sleeping Bitzer emits a kind of 'choke' (II:8, 139). The noise is just the non-word to characterise his stifled life. The choke is a sign of tension incipiently present in him, the tension between organic desire and social mores. What he despises, intrigues him – the forbidden world of fancy. In the same way as Louisa, dragging Tom after her, is intrigued by the circus, Bitzer runs after something, a circus character – Sissy. He does not simply wish to catch her but to establish a relationship with her, his void, his unexpressed torment exposed in his need to torment her. The two were already metaphorically linked in the opening classroom scene. Now Bitzer redirects the relationship by making faces at her as any child might do. But the faces are frightening, ill-adapted to creating a relationship. They are manufactured emotions. They seem 'cruel' to Sissy, and she runs away from him (I:6, 20). His 'faces' are his ethic. Like all else about him they are imitations; they are unfeeling because there is nothing behind them. He 'knuckles' his forehead, 'blinks rapidly', 'chokes', all the non-verbal signs of his condition.

Bitzer, a Hermes figure, represents movement, mobile wealth, and public space; Sissy, a Hestia figure, represents fixed hearth, domestic affection, and private space. Educated to be a Hermes, Louisa's sex prevents fulfilment of her role. Absence dominates her. Awaiting a sign from her mother that never comes, or a kiss from her brother that proves too little, Louisa is a figure who might have become something wonderful but doesn't. At the end of the novel, the narrator characterises her future as an absence: 'a thing [wife and mother that] was never to be' (III:9, 226).

Very early, Louisa is curious about family relations, about what binds husband to wife, parent to child. Although her only extended conversation with Sissy Jupe begins with school matters, themselves inherently parental, it ends with Louisa directly asking Sissy about the emotional ties that unite a family. Louisa pointblank inquires,

'Did your [Sissy's] father love her [Sissy's mother]?' (I:9, 45). More than the words, the manner with which they are spoken reveal their intent, for 'Louisa asked these questions with a strong, wild, wandering interest peculiar to her; an interest gone astray like a banished creature, and hiding in solitary places' (I:9, 45). The differentiation between what she expresses and what seethes in her creates a charged atmosphere. The normal love essential to her being is the 'banished' monster. Love is the perversion, what 'has gone astray' to hide 'in solitary places', while cultivated conduct is accepted in its place – such emotional displacement is the very basis of the pathology of Coketown family life. Louisa here is like Florence Dombey, believing she is to blame for her father's hatred for her and thus trying to reshape 'her wrong feeling'.[17] What baffles Louisa is her own wrong feelings. She is baffled by the forms and structures of family ties expressed in the paradox of Sissy's father loving yet leaving her. Her recourse rather than to feel is to collect more data about the biography of the man so as to still by neutral facts her nascent feelings (I:9, 45–6).

Louisa's own father is near physically but distant emotionally. She has only a professional (a teacher) relationship with him. With her mother, she does not even know how to be cordial, Sissy being 'more pleasant' than Louisa 'can ever be' (I:9, 43). Love goes 'astray' with her parents and with all of Louisa's relationships. Her love for her brother, her marriage, and her attraction to a lover on both the plot and the psychic levels are one unit. The intensity of her feelings for her brother spurs her to action. Accepting a man, Bounderby, who is old enough to be her father, she first gives passive comfort to the perversion of love, to fulfilling the desires of her brother. Refusing a man, Harthouse, who is young and alluring, she next gives active vent to her confusion about love, to the man who purposely links himself with her brother, his eligible surrogate.

Professor Deneau calls the brother–sister relationship 'abnormal'.[18] As important as the label is, the manner of the malady, the shape the perversion takes is more important. Tom actively uses Louisa while passively accepting her love. She passively accepts usage while actively loving him. Whenever these active and passive forces meet, language fails. Circumlocution, indirection, and finally silence prevails. For instance, one of her most revealing statements about her relationship with Tom is a non-statement. In the scene where Tom lays his plan before her for escape from home, she interprets his words as an expression of love for her. She looks into the fire and wonders about 'you [Tom] and me grown up' (I:8, 41). She burns like a fire, at once life-giving warmth and self-destructive force. What is the content of her wonder? The precise nature of her thoughts is inexpressible, cut off from all conscious awareness. She wonders 'unmanageable thoughts' (I:8, 41). Louisa's feelings for her brother are too complex for her to handle; they are deep but inchoate. Such formlessness is that mysterious fount out of which tension universally grows. Tension exists on the level of the taboo – the desire never to be directly expressed or experienced. Louisa does not know how to distinguish sensual passion from fraternal affection.

Tom fosters the 'unmanageable' thoughts. He fosters her taking the roles of mother and wife, not because he understands what is 'unmanageable' but because he wants ease. To 'enjoy' himself, he will exploit Bounderby's willingness to do 'anything' for Louisa (I:8, 40). She is his victim, exactly like the mothers and wives in the novel are victims of their sons and husbands. When later Tom explains to Harthouse why Louisa married Bounderby, he stresses two important reasons: her having 'no other love' than the old gruff magnet, and her being left at home without her brother would be 'like staying in jail' (II:3, 103). He realises that she has no experience in love and whatever love she knows is wholly experienced for him. He induces her to marry, offering himself as consolation. Marrying this man, she and he will be 'much oftener together … Always together, almost' (I:14, 72). Knowingly, he trades Louisa to secure his pleasure. Unwillingly, he puts himself in the place of her lover, indeed of her husband. Three scenes direct the siblings as if they were about to elope: (1) They will escape from paternal tyranny; (2) They will establish a new home; (3) They will always be together. These scenes preface Gradgrind's request to Louisa to marry Bounderby. Not Gradgrind's but Tom's previous arguments sway Louisa. They are Tom's 'marriage proposal'. After the marriage breakfast, Louisa is 'a little shaken' and not her usual 'reserved' self. She physically manifests her error. She cannot cling in her shaken condition to her legal husband; instead she clings to Tom (I:16, 83). Love misused and misdirected distorts reality.

Such love cannot be experienced verbally. It is expressed by the responses of the body. She blushes and becomes animated when Tom enters the room. That Harthouse tries to raise the same blush, stimulate the same animated response indicates that he understands their sexual nature. He wishes to replace her brother as her lover.

After she left Bounderby, Louisa explained her reasons for marrying him. Each concerns Tom: she could be 'useful' to him and express 'all the little tenderness' of her life (II:12, 166). Her tenderness arose, she explains, because she knew 'so well how to pity him'. If she does not exactly share the same kind of distress that Tom feels (compassion), she experienced the same matrix out of which he grew and so she wishes to help and comfort him (pity). If we catalogue the elements that compose the matrix, we have a classic condition for sibling incest: (1) a weak mother; (2) a father who is distant, physically or emotionally; (3) a sharing of a mutual condition; (4) a similar education; (5) a brother with no other female relationship. Brother–sister here, as it is so often, is equivalent to mother–son incest.[19] She comforts him and suffers for him as if he were her son and at the same time bestows her acts as if she were his wife – kisses him, offers tenderness to him, sells all she has to protect him (II: 7, 131), faints when he is in trouble (II:8, 139).

Sibling incest has a long history in literature. Dickens in *Hard Times* shifts its traditional use from explaining political corruption (e.g. Amnon–Tammar, 2 Sam. 13–19), exploring religious mores (e.g. Hartmann von Aue, *Gregorius*, 1195), and especially probing philosophical questions (e.g. Lope de Vega, *La fianza satisfecha*, 1614?), or just titillating the senses (e.g. Seneca, *Oedipus*) to the drama of its growth and expression. Dickens had frequently followed tradition. For example, he generally pictures sister–brother relationships as idyllic, an outgrowth of the Romantic notion of *amitié fraternelle* – love deepened by a knowledge of a blood relationship (e.g. Chateaubriand, *René*). In *Martin Chuzzlewit*, Tom Pinch and his sister Ruth set up house together after he – a pure knight in armour – rescues her from an intolerable position.[20] But in *Hard Times* all changes. He scorns the rebellious or philosophical use of sibling incest. More than this, he pictures the female side of sibling incest. Before him only Ford, in *'Tis Pity She's a Whore* (1633), and Defoe, in *Moll Flanders* (1722), had touched the female viewpoint. But neither considered the internal drama, for their brothers and sisters did not even grow up together. Dickens takes the theme and places it in the camp of what could happen and does to any ordinary brother and sister. Before Freud, Dickens demonstrated incest's mechanics in the capitalistic system.

That mechanism is fixed in the climactic bedroom scene. Louisa anxiously awaits Tom's return home after questioning by the police about the bank robbery (II:8, 144–6). While she waits, 'time lagged wearily', 'darkness and stillness ... thicken'. The gate bell rings for a moment. Tom has come home. Then, 'the circles of its [the bell's] last sound spread out fainter and wider in the air, and all was dead again' (II:8, 144). First, time is stopped, 'lagged wearily'. Next, space changes quality, 'thickens'. Lastly, waiting has charged Louisa's emotions; police questions have frayed Tom's nerves. A moment out of time is carefully constructed to permit a suspension of what usually governs conduct. Time and space, the sole matrix of norms, fade. The figures in the scene are no longer bound by their biographies; they are simply two humans, subject to one law – mortality. Louisa, entering his bedroom, tells Tom that she has come to him stripped not only of clothes but of identity. She is 'barefoot, unclothed, undistinguishable in darkness', exactly she says as will be 'through all the night of my decay until I am dust' (II:8, 145). She is not his sister, but a woman. She is not related (taboo), but mortal (like all others). In only her 'loose robe', she kneels beside Tom's bed. She draws his face to hers. Like a lover, 'she laid her head down on his pillow, and her hair flowed over him as if she would hide him from everyone but herself' (II:8, 145). Again a gesture takes the place of words, the letting down of the hair an ancient sign of female abasement and sexual availability.[21]

Louisa is overwhelmed by the wealth of the emotions both sensual and maternal that she hardly understands: 'in the energy of her love she took him to her bosom as if he were a child' (II:8, 145). An unspoken love binds her to him. The subconscious secret she holds in her heart parallels the conscious guilt Tom holds in his head. She begs Tom to verbalise what she suspects – his guilt in ravaging the bank vault.

The novel is filled with such distorted and perverted relationships, each conducted in a complex language of denial that pits desire against reality. The lower-class marriage follows the formula. Understandably, Blackpool has been misinterpreted, caught as he is in that uncharted territory between the drives of the psyche and the imperatives of society. On the psychic side, he has been condemned to facile appreciation as 'too good' or 'all good',[22] on the social side, to narrow evaluation as 'diagrammatic' or 'neutral'.[23] Blackpool is neither a reflection of some real working man, a figure the sociological critics have in mind when they castigate Dickens's characterisation and praise Mrs Gaskell's,[24] nor a one-dimensional allegory, the figure of Good in some medieval morality play. Blackpool is a complex prototype, a factory worker perplexed by ambient abundance and intelligence that results in depletion and injustice. What is mirrored in his character is what does not function in his society. For him the explanation of all problems is fixed in a single term 'muddle', a term that is the icon of his character and Dickens's explanation of his psychological state. Muddle and his name Blackpool are forms of the same idea, a denial of clarity – the muddying or blackening of a pool of water. The use of a word, muddle, that negates understanding defines his psychic state. When the social scene loses its laws – here of economic and family structure – language falters and perplexity follows. This is rather like the perplexity the Greeks must have felt about incest. It muddled their sense of order to such a degree that they had no single word for it, calling it by negations; for instance, 'the unmarriage marriage' (ἄγαμον γάμον). What must have been Blackpool's perplexity if scholars still debate the dynamics of early industrial England, one proving that capitalism bettered working conditions,[25] another that it brought psychological upheaval.[26]

Blackpool's temperament may be suggested by positioning his emotions on a map of fixed forms. Blackpool lives in a city, a 'kinetic structure', where activity takes place across the range of polarities from work to entertainment. But he must also face a system of norms, a 'social context' whose demands cut across mores and law, the rules of marriage and courtship and the regulations of employer and union. Where these intersect his personal desire, a 'human dimension' (these terms are adapted from Mandrou's historical psychiatry), the hidden self emerges.

The Blackpool captured in the kinetic structure reveals two things: Coketown mutilates human growth and reduces people to their economic function. Gradgrind annihilates 'the flowers of existence' (III:1, 169) and Sparsit exults that 'the harvest of her hopes' will be Louisa's moral decay (II:10, 156–7). In such a space, Blackpool is an oddity. However respected he may be, he is a loner in the mass of activity that defines the city: 'he had been for many years a quiet silent man, associating but little with other men, and used to companionship with his own thoughts' (II:4, 110). The city enforces isolation in its very structure. Streets are narrow; and true to the Victorian cityscape,[27] homes are a function of the shops to which they are attached. Jupe's home is on a narrow street, as is Blackpool's; and both working-class men live above stores (I:5, 21; I:10, 51). Whenever the worker's home is not tied to economics (the shop), it is tied to Death. Dickens weds death to the home in the image of the ladder – the counterpart to Sparsit's staircase that pre-dicts moral fall. Workers move with difficulty up the staircase of success, but with ease down the ladder that carries them to death. Though Blackpool's room was 'clean', its 'atmosphere was tainted' (I:10, 52), for it was a room to whose window 'the black ladder had often been raised for the sliding away of all that was most pre-cious in this world to a striving wife and a brood of hungry babies' (I:13, 63). The dirty outer city (Hermes) is contrasted with the clean inner room (Hestia); the space that holds a precious wife and chil-dren (Eros) is punctured by the black ladder that separates them (Thanatos). The room becomes the meeting place of life's polari-ties: Hermes–Thanatos and Hestia–Eros. Rather than a refuge, the home becomes a part of the muddle.

In this world of kinetic activity, work infects Blackpool's leisure time: 'Old Stephen was standing in the street with the old sensation upon him which the stoppage of the machine always produced – the sensation of its having worked and stopped in his own head' (I:10, 49). Even in his dream the loom at which he works becomes a machine that brings death (I:13, 66).

Set against the anxiety about dying are 'holiday' and 'honest dance' (I:5, 19), each a manifestation of fancy defined as entertain-ment that wards off work. So afraid is the bourgeoisie of entertain-ment that it must struggle on in 'convulsions' (I:5, 19). The workers did not belong to the churches of the city (I:5, 18). Rather they took 'opium' and 'drank'. Even worse they did 'low singing' and 'low dancing' in 'low haunts' (I:5, 18). All the 'lows' are the unvoiced but implied morality of the bourgeoisie. Entertainment is a mark of separ-ation, a mark of the suspicion of one class about another. We never see Blackpool entertained. He is the convulsed result of the fear of fancy. His only joy seems to be contact with Rachael, walking hand in hand with her and thereby feeling 'brightened' (I:10, 51). But even this activity is restricted by the morality of his world. For a married man to walk with an unmarried woman was scandalous (I:10, 50–1).

Examined from the standpoint of the 'social context', Blackpool becomes far more complex and tainted and his wife far less simple and malignant than is usually thought. In the social context, institu-tions designed to unify individuals and facilitate communication break down. Marriage and unionisation that should bring security at home and at work mirror each other in their futility.

What reduced the Blackpool marriage to an unholy alliance, one that causes each, in fact, to distort reality – she through drink and he through despair? How did the woman become a 'self-made outcast' (I:13, 64)? What made her 'drunken', 'begrimed', 'foul' (I:10, 52)? The marriage took place some eighteen or nineteen years before we meet them (I:11, 55; I:13, 67). Little is said of her background, but nothing indicates that she was unlike any other working-class girl. Indeed, she worked with and was a friend to Rachael (I:13, 64), which shows that at least she kept good company. Before marriage, Blackpool himself admits that as a girl she was quite 'pretty' and had 'good accounts of herseln' (I:11, 55). After marriage Mrs Gradgrind's head began to ache; after marriage, Blackpool's wife drinks. Blackpool professes that he was 'not unkind to her' (I:11, 55). But this is a negative response. When she began to go bad, he says that he tried to be 'patient' with her (I:11, 55). Again the word is significant, originating as it does in πασχω, to suffer. The word denies and reveals what he feels; he suffered her. Throughout the novel, she is not even called Mrs Blackpool. She is permitted no identity. She is a reflection of Blackpool's dilemma, the 'evil spirit of his life' (II:6, 119).

Marriage blackens his life. What seems to have happened to him is that as a youth he chose the flesh – the 'pretty' girl – and as a man he regrets his choice. Blackpool tries to escape the muddle, thinking even of suicide as a means: 'I ha' gone t' th' brigg [bridge], minded to fling myseln ower, and ha' no more on't. I ha' bore that much that I were owd when I were young' (I:11, 55). The last phrase emphasises that he has a sense of being cheated in his youth, cheated in his marriage, that he had grown old too soon, that he anticipated marriage to cure what he suffered in youth. He had married on Easter Monday (I:11, 55), a time of the year associated with freedom and rebirth – among the Hebrews Passover, a feast to celebrate the liberation from slavery in Egypt, among the Christians a feast to celebrate the resurrection of Christ. Could the anticipation of happiness meet the reality of marriage, especially in his changing world?

In his relationship to his work the same conditions prevail as in his marriage. The two are tied together by a 'promise' to Rachael. A pregnant ambiguity hides the exact wording of the promise in the same way as the wording of the commandment in his dream remains hidden and Mrs Gradgrind's final message has 'no meaning'. Each frustrates the expression of deep asocial desires. The promise is diverted from its particular impetus, found only in the Copy Proofs (after line 26 in I. 13. 68 and Textual Note 252), a promise to stem open anger against culpable bosses who passively accept industrial accidents, to its final form in the novel: an oblique pledge to refrain from passive violence (I:13, 68–9), the violence he felt for his wife. The substratum of pledge and promise is the same: to stem his rage. As a pledge against violence, the promise is one thing, but it becomes quite another when reattached to its original source – to stem open anger against bosses. Bounderby mocks Blackpool for having made no promise to the boss who paid his wages (II:5, 113). The snide remark condemns Bounderby but also undercuts a truth. Blackpool makes no promises to keep faith with any of the social forces around him, no promises to either boss or to union. He enforces his own isolation. The discontinuity between the man and the social context in which he moves is apparent in both his excommunication from the Union and his death in the industrial landscape.

But it is only in the third area, the 'human dimension', that we discover the extent of Blackpool's perplexity and the effect of economic conditions on his psyche. His dream stands at the centre of this dimension, splitting his asking for a divorce (or freedom) and his condemnation to a marriage (or imprisonment). The dream expresses elements floating in his daily life: (1) a desire for a 'new marriage' (I:12, 62) though he is already married – the dream impetus; (2) a symbolic murder and adultery – the dream thought; (3) a fusion of feelings about marriage and factory – the dream work; and (4) an obscure and haunting sensation of futility and death, personal mortality and meaningless existence – the dream 'navel',[28] a layer that goes so deep it is practically beyond perusal. Dickens exposes the tragic substratum of this 'navel' only later in the novel: 'Even Stephen Blackpool's disappearance was falling into the general way, and becoming as monotonous a wonder as any piece of machinery in Coketown' (III:5, 194). The dailiness of life dulls all feeling, whether noble or ignoble, with the indifference of the machine. In Blackpool's so-called 'ambiguous dream',[29] something of both the dilemma of this everyman of Coketown and of all men is captured.

Blackpool's state before the dream is dominated by thoughts of death on the one hand and marriage on the other. Both are brought out in his conversation with Bounderby – the figure of the father confessor. Death takes two forms, his own – suicide (I:11, 55); and his wife's – murder (I:11, 57). Marriage also takes two forms, his divorce from his wife and his desire for union with Rachael. The codes of law – not Church ethics – which he looks to for solutions bind him in every way. He may not flee his marriage nor 'hurt' his wife (I:11, 57); he may not commit bigamy nor 'live wi' Rachael (I:11, 57). Rachael then tries to calm him, first when his soul is compared to 'wild waters' and 'the raging sea' (I:12, 59) and then just before the dream when he will not let her touch him and has a 'violent fit of trembling' (I:13, 65). Again in this state his mood is dominated by death and marriage, but a new ingredient is added: a sense of injustice and hopeless existence. He hopes for a 'new marriage' that both he and Rachael want, but about which – in the typical technique of the book – they never speak. The hope is intermixed with the idea of 'home' and thus 'pleasure and pride' (I:12, 62). He thinks of Rachael seeing others marry while she may not and this thought 'smote him with remorse and despair' (I:12, 62). The injustice of all this is stressed by his seeing a light in the window of his small room, the window where the ladder of death had been, and thinking that ladder would carry away a good wife or child while his wife lived on. Again without words being used, without Blackpool saying anything, Rachael senses the intension of his heart: "'for that I,'" says Rachael, "know your heart, and am right sure and certain that 'tis far too merciful to let her [Blackpool's wife] die'" (I:13, 64). After this his eyes twice fall on the bottle of medicine that improperly drunk would poison. The first time he reads its letters he turns 'a deadly hue' (I:13, 64); the second time 'a tremble passed over him' (I:13, 65). Thoughts of murder and death are surrounded by a sense of hopelessness – 'the dreadful nature of his existence, bound hand and foot, to a dead woman, and tormented by a demon in her shape' (I:2, 62). The woman he married, the woman before him, has no being. She is like every other woman in this novel; she is an absence, a 'shape' that in this case has become demonic. This hopeless state, filled with thoughts of death and marriage – impossible opposites, the one to preserve what the other destroys – gives him the feeling of blowing up, of becoming bigger, different: 'Filled with these thoughts – so filled that he had an unwholesome sense of growing larger, of being placed in some new and diseased relation towards the objects among which he passed, of seeing the iris round every misty light turn red – he went home' (I:12, 63). Blackpool himself is now absent; his vision is blurred, his body lost, his sense of presence disrupted, his ability to act turned off by a 'red' light. He goes home; he goes to a shelter that provides no protection.

What he feels, he now dreams. His pre-dream state and his dream criss-cross. The dream also places him in a 'new diseased relation' to the world, and the dream also is composed of the same double layer of materials: on one side marriage, adultery and bigamy and on the other death. The dream confirms the hopelessness of human existence. In the dream, he had long set his heart on a woman – not Rachael but the 'pretty girl' who here, exactly as the wife in his daily life, is never named. Anticipation of joy and anxiety for the future mark his premarital state in the dream, again exactly as in his youth when he had also anticipated marriage. Suddenly as the marriage ceremony in the dream is being performed, his mental state is fixed in an image: 'a darkness came on, succeeded by the shining of a tremendous light'. Since the light burst forth from above in 'fiery letters' out of a line of the commandments and the burning words are dispersed all over the church, we may consider this written light to be the psychic expression for fatherly authority, for societal law. But what precisely are the words that the fiery letters spell out? Because he dreams of a marriage ceremony and because at this very moment in his waking life he is blocked from a divorce (I:11, 54–9), blocked from a 'new marriage' (I:12, 62), the words of the commandment must be: 'Thou shalt not commit adultery'. That is, his marriage is permanent. Permitted neither divorce by the codes of man nor adultery by the laws of God, his high hopes for marriage prove frivolous; his life is a dead end.[30] All turns dark in the dream, for marriage is self-murder. The dream scene now transforms from the space of hope to one of hopelessness. The someplace, the particular church that celebrates the prospect of joy, becomes a universal no-place, without extension, where 'if all the people in the world could have been brought into one space, they could not have looked ... more numerous' (I:13, 66). This is the place of the second death, the final judgement. Here all 'abhor' him, the counterpart of his avoiding in life all social contact. He feels condemned, persecuted by all and everything. His marriage and his life are both dead ends. The marriage ceremony and the last rites are one, administered by a single clergyman who links both scenes. Now a superimposition occurs, like a double-negative in photography; the no-place is overlayed with the most real place of all, the work place. In the same no-place, Blackpool stands under his looms and listens to the burial service. Neither marriage nor work supports him. His work, the loom that he works at, becomes the mechanism of his death. He looks up at it as if it were a noose, and then 'what he stood on fell below him'. The cloth looms here and throughout the novel remind us of the Fates, spinning out the cloth of life with no purpose but to destroy its makers. Marriage has become hanging; its ceremony of hope is a ceremony of death. Hearing the service read distinctly, he knows futility. Marriage and work, the twin foundations of his life – and of everyman's – lead but to the same end, to personal extinction.

With this manifestation, the final transformation in the dream takes place. Blackpool returns to familiar places but with the unfamiliar sense of condemnation, the same way he had previously felt 'filled' and in a 'diseased relation to the world'. The unnamed commandment in the first part of the dream is now mirrored in a 'nameless, horrible dread'. Dickens's rhetoric of exclusion is ever at the centre of his method. Blackpool is condemned to wonder without hope, to seek what cannot be known, and to cover what cannot be hid. The unnamed dread is caused by an unnamed 'shape'. Because all 'grew into that form', the 'shape' itself has no proper shape. The unnamed, the unshaped is of course the greatest negation of all those things sown into the imagery of the novel: death. Blackpool knows he is condemned to hopelessly wander in search of happiness, to never realise the beatific vision in a 'new marriage' with Rachael, to see all die and decay around him. His 'hopeless labour' is to prevent others from seeing the unnamed face of death. The very last words of the dream fix the image of death in an unnamed 'printed word' that infects the home, the 'drawers and closets', the cityscape, the 'streets', and work itself, the 'chimneys of the mills assumed that shape'.

Life is futile; marriage is hopeless. Condemned to 'miserable existence', 'aimless wandering', the marriage ceremony and the burial ceremony are one. Marriage is a reminder of mortality. The waking dream becomes a nightmare.

Blackpool tries to deal with his situation in the same way as the villains, Bounderby and Bitzer. Like them, he constructs a dream world in which to live. Bounderby and Bitzer build myths around themselves; Bounderby, the myth of his rise to success, Bitzer, the myth of his inevitably reaching the level of his idol Bounderby. One stage in the myth was to get rid of the mother and to deny family. Bounderby exiles his mother; Bitzer imprisons his in a workhouse. Both sever themselves from family ties. Blackpool tries to get rid of his wife. First, he paid her off to stay away from him and is proud that with her gone 'I ha' gotten decent fewtrils [trifles] about me agen' (I:II, 56). Next, he would divorce her, or as he puts it: 'be ridded o' this woman' (I:11, 56). Lastly, in a hypnopompic state he would murder her, passively doing nothing while his wife mistakenly poisons herself (I: 13, 66–7). He plunges into myth by fantasising that 'if he were free to ask her [Rachael, to marry him], she would take him' (I:12, 62). Forced into a purely symbolic marriage with Rachael, untouched by the carnal, he can experience neither fulfilment nor disappointment. The symbolic marriage deludes Blackpool into thinking he is free, no longer, as he puts it, 'bound' to 'a dead woman' (I:12, 62). But of course he is bound and only his death will free him.

To explore lower-class family life necessitated Dickens's reversing the roles of the typical husband and wife. Only by reversing the roles could he expose not only the female's but the male's need to love and sacrifice. This may be seen by contrasting Blackpool's marriage to a parallel working-class marriage, that of Mrs Dithridge in Collins' *Man and Wife* (1869). One mirrors the other. Blackpool supports a morally corrupt and psychologically abusive wife; Mrs Dithridge supports and eventually kills a physically abusive and drunken husband.[31] A husband could with impunity beat and rob his wife of her dowry, but the opposite was not permitted.[32] Blackpool plays the female role – allows his wife to take his property, allows her to dominate him sexually and financially.

Blackpool may not be a realistic description of the contemporary factory worker, but he is an effective symbol of the dilemma, psychic and social, which the working man of Coketown knew: the 'muddle'. Dickens is right: 'I have done what I hope is a good thing with Stephen, taking his story as a whole' (letter to Foster, 14 July 1854).

Only the circus family is uninhibited by the mores that bind and distort reality and thus the psychic condition of all the others.[33] Nevertheless, circus relationships have their own peculiarity. Contrary to the rest of the novel, circus folk live, at least metaphorically, in extended or multiple families.[34] Circus people marry within the circus family. Jupe marries a circus dancer. E. W. B. Childers marries Josephine Sleary. The diminutive, child-like Little Kidderminster, who once played Cupid, marries a widow, once a tightrope walker, now grown fat. It is as if the child were marrying his mother. Indeed, Mr Sleary remarks that she is 'old enough to be hith mother' (III:7, 213). Marriage here is endogamous, slightly incestuous by the nature of the tightly knit circus world.

Close to the end of the novel a clown at a circus performance tells a curious riddle, one which may serve for the novel's psychological icon; that is, the riddle like the novel is concerned with the structure of threes, the psychological stages of sowing, reaping and garnering, or youth, maturity, and old age. In attendance, Gradgrind, Louisa, and Sissy listen tensely awaiting the final solution to another riddle – the riddle of Tom and the bank robbery. Is he safe, what will become of him and of the family? The clown's story is the verbal equivalent to their psychological tension. It is 'about two legs sitting on three legs looking at one leg, when in came four legs, and laid hold of one leg, and up got two legs, caught hold of three legs, and threw' em at four legs, who ran away with one leg' (III:7, 212). The narrator calls this 'an ingenious Allegory' and solves it as 'relating to a butcher, a three-legged stool, a dog, and a leg of mutton' (III:78, 212). Allegory is deep layered, obliquely revealing what cannot be stated openly. It is a psychological map that followed correctly leads to the labyrinth of the mind. Behind the literal level of the butcher and the mutton there are others. This riddle belongs to a group called 'leg riddles', the most famous of which is the one the Sphinx poses to Oedipus. Her riddle opens with four but ends up with three legs. Almost all end with one leg less than they begin, either a leg disappears or, as in the clown's story, 'runs away'. The clown's allegory is in fact the classic form of an old and widespread riddle. In many cultures, both Eastern and Western, Primitive and Modern, leg and foot are freely employed as symbols for the penis. Oedipus' name, from οἰδάω (to swell) and πούς (foot) is not only appropriate for one who solves such a riddle but is also a reminder of the erect or swollen penis. In short, the clown's 'Allegory' and the Sphinx's riddle are the tame guises for the anxiety filled primal scene where the foot or leg, equalling the penis, 'runs away' into the vagina. The clown's riddle is worded exactly the same as one that Géza Róheim discusses: 'Two legs sat on three legs and ate one leg; / Then came four legs and took one leg from two legs; / Then two legs hit four legs with three legs; / So that four legs dropped one leg.' Róheim says that 'in yet another version [of the riddle], however, the object [dropped] is at last called by its right name [penis]. Two people lie in one bed. The observer first sees four legs (i.e. the father on all fours), the two outstretched legs of the mother, and finally one leg which, as in most variants, mysteriously disappears. We may suspect that the riddle of the Sphinx is concerned with the primal scene and the fact that her death coincides with its solution suggests that she is herself its object.'[35]

Whether or not it is simply a coincidence that Dickens chose a riddle with such implications to appear at the end of the novel is immaterial. The riddle encapsulises a psychic environment. All relationships in the novel are riddled by anxiety. Like the great riddle-giver herself, the Sphinx, the women here are anomalies, mysterious riddles. They are not only sexually neutralised, like the Sphinx whose lower body belies gender, but are intellectually destroyed, enigmas but never solvers, victims of the classic prejudice: Ῥᾷον ἐρωτᾶν ἥ ἀποκρίνεσθαί (Plato, *Republic* i. 336c). Taking up Oedipus' role as detective, males solve economic questions but are blind to themselves. The result is mutilated characters, stilted relationships, and biting tensions. Rather than comfort, the bells of the eighteen denomination churches of Coketown drive people 'sick' and 'nervous'. The people drink and take opium. They anaesthetise themselves to the relentless 'monotonous' work whose effect is expressed in a 'craving' for relief. They must 'vent' their emotions (I:5, 19). For the expression of emotion in language, they substitute a psychological rhetoric of exclusion. As a result 'Fancy' has to 'struggle' on in 'convulsions' (I:5, 19). Dickens's whole vocabulary is psychological, particularly when he deals with marriage. He speaks of 'suppression' (II:7, 127), 'alienation' (II:9, 150), and 'incompatibility' (III:3, 184). The people's favourite reading is significantly the bawdy and raucous Defoe (I imagine *Moll Flanders*, with its innocent incest), for what they are concerned with are the world of business, and the relationships of men, women, and children – with families and with 'human nature, human passion, human hopes and fears' (I:11, 57).

More than with social and economic problems, Dickens in *Hard Times* is concerned with the psychic effects of the new industrialism. A new personality type is evolving whose ideal is the lobotomised Bitzer. In this novel the genotype is not yet heroic.

The novel's end is structured as a final absence: to see in the present what we the readers will be like in the future, to see life as if our actions were to be judged from the grave. But the warning seems double-edged, for only Sissy among the characters seems to escape from the general dissolution of family life. Even the allusion to the Writing on the Wall at the end is to words whose meaning is elusive, names that may be seen but have no meaning – save to those with godly vision – and a warning about the degeneration of a family. The *mene, mene, tekel, parsin* that Daniel interprets for King Belshazar predicts his family's doom. Desire rather than fulfilment, thought rather than action, a language of absence rather than presence persists to the very end of the novel and is absorbed into a still greater pattern of absence. The book's three parts – as we have said – parallel its time sequence of spring, summer, fall. But the fourth season, the fourth temperament, is absent: winter. Winter, the dead season, is the unnamed destroyer. The final word of the novel is 'cold'.

From *Dickens Studies Annual*, 16 (1987), 61–94.

NOTES

[Richard Fabrizio proposes that, rather than being seen as a satiric portrait of industrialisation, *Hard Times* should be regarded as 'a keen description of the psyche forged out of socioeconomic conditions'. Victorian society, according to Furizio, glorifies such qualities as feeling – particularly in the male – whilst, paradoxically, at the same time denigrating emotion. This creates a context in which the position of the family is bound to be contra-dictory, and in which Dickens's own position is also complicated, as he has to 'describe a psychic condition with a vocabulary that itself was a symptom of the disease'. Fabrizio starts his essay with a brief consideration of the family in western society, paying particular attention to the roles as-signed to men and women in a changing capitalist economy. An aspect of this in *Hard Times* is the extent to which, in the patriarchal structure of the industrial society of the novel, sons deny their mothers. This leads Fabrizio to consider Mrs Gradgrind, who struggles to express something but dies before she can; Dickens refers to the 'figures of wonderful no-meaning' that she is attempting to articulate. The implications of this phrase are then pursued, Fabrizio working from a point Foucault makes about procedures of exclusion, that is to say, the structures society uses to avoid the expres-sion of what it does not permit – the prohibited. The focus of the essay, therefore, is simultaneously on the operations of language within the text and the larger social and ideological implications of what is detected in the language of the text. This involves a consideration of the domestic family and its intricate battle to survive under industrial capitalism. Fabrizio looks at how the family is welded together, how it thinks and loves, and, most importantly of all, how the family is perverted and dies. This essay stands, I think, as an approriate concluding essay for this collection for it combines many of the impulses of recent criticism: there is a deconstructive emphasis on the complex texture of the language of a text, an interest in gender, a psychoanalytic dimension in the discussion of the relationship between psy-chosexual issues and the larger operations of industrial society, and a New

Historicist concern with locating the text in a particular context of nineteenth-century Britain. But, far from letting such a weight of theoretical influences oppress him, Fabrizio uses theory as a platform for building a stunningly original sense of what is happening in *Hard Times*. In his discussion of 'the lobotomised Bitzer', for example, we gain an altogether new sense of the strange things that happen to the subject in an industrial society. References to *Hard Times*, cited by volume, chapter and page numbers, are from the Norton Critical Edition, ed. G. Ford and S. Monod (New York, 1966). Ed.]

1. Critics have rarely been interested in *Hard Times* as a psychological study and never as a portrait of the reciprocal relationship of social forces and family history: that is, with the development of the psyche (see for instance Leonard F. Manheim, 'Dickens and Psychoanalysis: A Memoir', *Dickens Studies Annual*, 11 [1983], 342). A typical formulation is that the novel's characterisation is so concerned with describing a 'system' that it lacks 'life' (Jenni Calder, *Women and Marriage in Victorian Fiction* [New York, 1976], pp. 76–7). Geoffrey Johnston Sadock (in 'Dickens and Dr Leavis: A Critical Commentary on *Hard Times*', *Dickens Studies Annual*, 2 [1972]) stresses the need to evaluate 'the breakdown of interpersonal communication under the stress of laissez-faire industrialism' (215) but does not do so. Only Benn, Lougy, Wilson, Johnson and Barickman have touched on the psychological nature of the work. Miriam J. Benn, 'A Landscape with Figures: Characterisation and Expression in *Hard Times*', *Dickens Studies Annual*, 1 (1970), 168–82, shows that the conflict in using both allegorical and human characterisation causes dullness; Robert E. Lougy, in 'Dickens' *Hard Times*: A Romance as Radical Literature', *Dickens Studies Annual*, 2 (1972), 237–54, that *Hard Times* should be read as a 'romance', in the sense that Northrop Frye defines the word in *An Anatomy of Criticism* (and therefore with psychological types), and adds that the work struggles between Eros and Thanatos; Angus Wilson, 'The Heroes and Heroines of Dickens', *Dickens and the Twentieth Century*, ed. John Gross and Gabriel Pearson (Toronto, 1962), that contemporary censorship forced Dickens to 'submerge' his 'sensuality' (p. 5); Pamela Hansford Johnson, 'The Sexual Life in Dickens's Novels', *Dickens 1970*, ed. Michael Slater (New York, 1970), pp. 173–94, that the characters were created to appeal to the ordinary Victorian family and thus are prim; R. Barickman, S. MacDonald and M. Stark, *Corrupt Relations: Dickens, Thackeray, Trollope, Collins and the Victorian Sexual System* (New York, 1982), that Victorian fiction expresses the 'tension' effected by patriarchal values (p. viii) and that the father's 'flawed sexuality' (p. 89) affected his children, particularly females.

Other critics of *Hard Times* fall into two groups, those concerned with the novel's bipolar structure or its artistry, and those concerned with its social, economic, and political implications. Among the many in the first group we may mention: F. R. Leavis, 'Hard Times: An Analytic Note', in The Great Tradition (New York, 1963), who finds the design and vision of the first two chapters carried out in a 'comprehensive' way (pp. 227–8); W. W. Watt, 'Introduction' to Rinehart edition of Hard Times (New York, 1958), who treats Dickens's 'symmetrical structure' (pp. xxiii–xxvii) and his 'symbolic method' (pp. xxx–xxxii), while acknowledging his concern with 'the evil practices of Victorian industrialisation' (p. 10); D. M. Hirsch, 'Hard Times and Dr Leavis', in the Norton edition of Hard Times (New York, 1966), pp. 366–72, who finds Leavis's view meaningless and thinks that the characters do not fulfil their symbolic potential nor can they be taken seriously; G. F. Sadock (see above), who finds that Leavis's appreciation is not criticism but simply 'preference' for 'organisational economy', an economy resulting in loss of 'richness of characterisation' (209); David Sonstroem, 'Fettered Fancy in Hard Times', PMLA, 84 (1960), who examines the work's imagery revolving around Fancy, concluding that Fancy means 'imaginative play' and 'fellow feeling' (520); Warrington Winters, 'Dickens' Hard Times: The Lost Childhood', Dickens Studies Annual, 2 (1972), 217–36, who finds the characterisation falters when the author's life and his characters are at odds; F. E. Smith, 'Perverted Balance: Expressive Form in Hard Times', Dickens Studies Annual, 6 (1977), who believes the balance of Fact and Fancy 'so carefully arranged' is 'false' (103); Catherine Gallagher, 'Hard Times and North and South: The Family and Society in Two Industrial Novels', Arizona Quarterly, 36 (1980), 70–96, who argues that the novel is organised on the metaphoric principle of social paternalism.

Among the many in the second group, we may mention: John Ruskin, 'A Note on Hard Times' (1860), in The Dickens Critics, ed. G. H. Ford and L. Lane (Ithaca, 1961), pp. 47–8), who finds the social criticism accurate; E. P. Whipple, 'On the Economic Fallacies of Hard Times', in the Norton edition of Hard Times (New York, 1966), pp. 323–7, who attacks Dickens for equating economic laws with their harsh effects on individuals, resulting in his failure to investigate the interior of such characters as Bounderby; George Bernard Shaw, 'Introduction to Hard Times' (1912), in The Dickens Critics, ed. Ford and Lane (Ithaca, 1961), pp. 125–35, who saw Dickens herein as a kind of Karl Marx aware of 'social sin'; George Orwell, Dickens, Dali and Others (New York, 1944), who summed up Dickens as a naïve 'moralist' and reduced Hard Times to preaching that 'capitalist ought to be kind not that workers ought to be rebellious' (p. 6); John Holloway, 'Hard Times: A History and a Criticism', in Dickens and the Twentieth Century, ed. Gross and Pearson (Toronto, 1962), who castigates the misconstruing of contemporary politics (pp. 159–74) and thus the failure to delve into the 'deepest levels' of human experience (pp. 167–74); Geoffrey Carnall, 'Dickens, Mrs Gaskell and the Preston Strike', Victorian Studies, 8 (1964), who attacks Dickens for deliberate historical distortion of both workers and unions, thus creating 'insulated

individuals' intent on giving vent to their lust for power (45–6); Robin
Gilmour, 'The Gradgrind School: Political Economy in the Classroom',
Victorian Studies, 11 (1967), 207–24, who argues against Holloway
and for the soundness of Dickens's view of utilitarian education;
Alexander Welsh, 'Satire and History: The City of Dickens', *Victorian
Studies*, 11 (1968), 379–400, who shows the way a journalistic approach helped to develop the metaphor of the city as a monster or
machine; K. J. Fielding, '*Hard Times* and Common Things', in
Imagined Worlds, ed. Maynard Mack and Ian Gregor (London, 1968),
pp. 183–201, who finds errors of fact and theory in Holloway and who
stresses the historical accuracy of Dickens's view of education; Sheila
Smith, *The Other Nation: The Poor in English Novels of the 1840s
and 1850s* (Oxford, 1980), who argues that the symbols of Coketown
are inadequate to describe correctly the lower class, particularly
Blackpool.

2. Lawrence Stone, *The Family, Sex and Marriage: England 1500–1800*
   (London, 1977), thinks that the 'restricted, patriarchal, nuclear family'
   dominated other types already by about 1750; Steven Ozment, *When
   Fathers Ruled: Family Life in Reformation Europe* (Cambridge, 1983),
   offers the opposite conclusion, that the Reformation was a time of liberation for women and for children, and that the family under
   Protestant impulse became humanised.

3. See W. K. Lacey, *The Family in Classical Greece* (London, 1972),
   pp. 9, 15–32, and James Buchanan Given, *Society and Homicide in
   Thirteenth-Century England* (Stanford, 1977), p. 42.

4. See Mikhail Bakhtin, *Rabelais and His World*, tr. H. Iswolsky
   (Bloomington, 1984), pp. 7–19; William Heywood, *Palio and Ponte*
   (1904; New York, 1969), pp. 1–23; and M. E. Whitmore, *Medieval
   English Domestic Life and Amusement in the Works of Chaucer*
   (1937; New York, 1972), pp. 192–247.

5. See David Levine, *Family Formation in an Age of Nascent Capitalism*
   (New York, 1977), p. 62, and Alan Macfarlane, *Marriage and Love in
   England: Modes of Reproduction 1300–1840* (Oxford, 1986), pp. 22
   ff. Over the course of history what constitutes a family – kin, degree
   and kind of kin, servants, inmates – has varied. Family here means no
   more than the economic unit composed of those who live in the same
   dwelling. We use the term without distinction of conjugal, extended, or
   multiple (see Peter Laslett, 'Introduction', *Household and Family in
   Past Times*, ed. P. Laslett and R. Wall [Cambridge, 1972], pp. 28–46).
   The functional aspect of the family seems to sit on safer grounds than
   its constitution. While the reproductive unit remains the same throughout history, a more complex kinship system exists within pre-industrial
   society (Jack Goody, 'The Evolution of the Family', in Laslett and Wall
   [above], p. 119). Although a simplification of structure or composition
   of the family occurs in industrial society, the size of the family is

subject to controversy. Laslett indicates that family mean size remains constant at about 4.5. Size in the long run may have decreased somewhat, but the size of Preston – a city Dickens knew – seems to have slightly increased during the nineteenth century (Michael Anderson, 'Household Structure and the Industrial Revolution: Mid-Nineteenth Century Preston in Comparative Perspective', in Laslett and Wall [above], pp. 232–3). The assumption of the extended family pre-dating the nuclear family is under attack, especially in England. Agricultural society in England seems to have functioned in the nuclear family, but that does not preclude a difference in the way it functioned.

6. See Peter Laslett, 'Mean Household Size in England Since the Sixteenth Century', in Laslett and Wall (eds), *Household and Family,* p. 146.

7. G. E. M. de Ste Croix, *The Class Struggle in the Ancient Greek World* (London, 1981), pp. 180–1.

8. Terry S. Reynolds, 'Medieval Roots of the Industrial Revolution', *Scientific American* (July 1984), 124.

9. Emotion seems to have coursed along a more direct route to expression in ancient literature. For example, during a violent battle, Paris flees the field for Helen's bed: 'Come on! Let's enjoy ourselves by going to bed and making love: for not even up to this moment has passion [eros] so entirely seized my senses [phrén]' (II. 3. 441–2). For an incisive summary of Foucault's position on Greek sexuality, see 'Le souci dela vérité', interview by François Ewald, *Magazine Litteraire* (May 1984), 19; and for his view of repression during the nineteenth century as the key to the sexualisation of women and everything else, see *La volonté de savoir,* vol. 1 of *Histoire de la sexualité* (Paris, 1976), p. 137 and passim.

10. See Michel Foucault, *L'ordre du discours* (Paris, 1971).

11. 'In pre-industrial England marriage came relatively late, and took place between people of about the same age. Therefore, the proportion of single persons was high on both sides' (Peter Laslett, 'Mean Household Size in England Since the Sixteenth Century', in Laslett and Wall [eds] *Household and Family,* p. 146).

12. Travers Twiss at Oxford in 1844 commented on the factory's power to reconstruct the psyche, rescuing workers of the old domestic handloom system from drink, sexual licence, and female exploitation (p. 65), and the factory's power 'to raise the condition of women' (p. 71). *Two Lectures on Machinery Delivered Before the University of Oxford in 1844* (Shannon, 1971).

13. *Dombey and Son,* Everyman edition (London, 1964), p. 616. *Martin Chuzzlewit,* Penguin edition (Harmondsworth, 1981), pp. 764–6. Ross H. Dabney, *Love and Property in the Novels of Dickens* (London, 1967), sees aggression and violence as the result of 'mercenary marriage' (pp. 70–1). David Sonstroem (see note 1 above) believes that the

'pervasive violence' of *Hard Times* cannot be accounted for by the 'action' but only by the 'imagery' (523). The point is that the violence is internalised, perceptible only in the paralinguistic code. In Sophocles' *Oedipus*, the code is externalised in expression: Oedipus and Tiresias curse and shout at each other freely, and when Oedipus learns what he has done he shatters the air with his lamentations.

14. Ancient states sometimes imposed penalties against bachelors (see Douglas M. MacDowell, *The Law in Classical Athens* [Ithaca, 1978], p. 86). Here both the bachelor and the spinster are norm. Dr William Ballantyne Hodgson, Dickens's contemporary, attacked the character of Bitzer by saying that economic science did not teach celibacy or filial cruelty (see Gilmour, *Victorian Studies*, II [1967], 221). That celibacy was a concern of the time is graphically illustrated by the subtitle of George Drysdale's 1854 anonymously published tract *The Elements of Social Science, or ... the only cure of the three primary social evils, poverty, prostitution and celibacy.*

15. An ancient comparison may be appropriate to show the radical shift in perspective. Hrethel feels the loss of a son only as a loss of honour and meaning given to life by inheritance and patronymics (*Beowulf*, 2435–70), very 'different from the usual responses to such tragedies today and they illustrate the central position of kingship obligations in Anglo-Saxon life' (Howell D. Chickering, 'Commentary', in *Beowulf*, tr. and ed. H. D. Chickman [New York, 1977], p. 263).

16. Otto Rank, *The Myth of the Birth of the Hero and Other Writings*, ed. Philip Freund (New York, 1964), p. 69.

17. *Dombey and Son*, p. 372.

18. Daniel P. Deneau, 'The Brother–Sister Relationship in *Hard Times*', *The Dickensian*, 60 (1964), 173–7.

19. See Karin Carlson Meiselman, *Incest: A Psychological Study of Causes and Effects with Treatment Recommendations* (San Francisco, 1978), pp. 263–77; Herbert Maisch, *Incest*, tr. Colin Bearne (New York, 1972), pp. 205, 214; and Susan Forward and Craig Buck, *Betrayal of Innocents: Incest and its Devastation* (Harmondsworth, 1979), p. 96.

20. *Martin Chuzzlewit*, p. 661.

21. See Numbers 5. 18. The degree to which this episode parallels one in Melville's *Pierre* is astounding: 'she [Isabel, Pierre's sister] fell upon Pierre's heart, and her long hair ran over him in ebon vines' (XXXVI, 362). A recent article on hair in Victorian literature discusses neither passage (Elizabeth G. Gitter, 'The Power of Hair in the Victorian Imagination', *PMLA*, 99 [984], 936–54).

22. See Leavis (note 1 above), p. 248 and F. E. Smith (note 1, above), 108.

23. See Raymond Williams, *Culture and Society* (New York, 1958), p. 93, and S. Smith, *The Other Nation*, p. 83.

24. See Carnall, *Victorian Studies*, 8 (1964), Gallagher, *Arizona Quarterly*, 36 (1980) and S. Smith, *The Other Nation*.

25. R. M. Hartwell, 'The Standard of Living', *Economic History Review*, 16 (1963), 135–46.

26. Eric Hobsbawm, 'The Standard of Living During the Industrial Revolution: A Discussion', *Economic History Review*, 16 (1963), 119–34.

27. H. J. Dyos and D. A. Reeder, 'Slums and Suburbs', in *The Victorian City: Images and Realities*, ed. H. J. Dyos and Michael Wolff, 2 vols (London, 1973), vol. 1, p. 360.

28. Sigmund Freud, *The Interpretation of Dreams*, tr. James Strachey, vols 4 and 5 of *The Standard Edition of the Complete Psychological Works* (London, 1955), vol. 5, p. 525.

29. See F. E. Smith, *Dickens Studies Annual*, 6 (1977), 108.

30. Warrington Winters, *Dickens Studies Annual*, 2 (1972), 229–30, believes the words are 'thou shalt not kill', and that the dream expresses Blackpool's guilt for an unexpressed desire to murder his wife. But he does express his desire with such clarity that Rachael realises it. To explain the second half of the dream by recourse only to this commandment seems doubtful.

31. Wilkie Collins, *Man and Wife*, Dover edition (New York, 1983), pp. 220–3.

32. Lee Holcombe, *Wives and Property: Reform of the Married Woman's Property Act* (Toronto, 1983), pp. 21–2.

33. For a discussion of the circus see Gallagher, *Arizona Quarterly*, 36 (1980), 76–7, and Joseph Butwin, 'The Paradox of the Clown in Dickens', *Dickens Studies Annual*, 5 (1976), who failing to note the words 'ingenious Allegory', calls the riddle discussed below 'an inane joke' (130). [The Gallagher essay, in the *Arizona Quarterly*, referred to in the course of this essay, is an earlier version of the essay included in this present volume. Ed.]

34. For definitions, see Peter Laslett, 'Introduction', *Household and Family*, pp. 29–32.

35. Géza Róheim, *The Riddle of the Sphinx or Human Origins*, tr. R. Money-Kyrle (1934; New York, 1974), p. 7.

Further Reading

This is a select, rather than comprehensive, reading list. I have not included many of the books and articles referred to in the essays and the Introduction. What I have concentrated on is providing a number of starting points for the reader who wants to look more closely at either Dickens or one of the two novels discussed in this New Casebook.

RECOMMENDED EDITIONS

Both *David Copperfield* and *Hard Times* are available in more than a dozen editions. In singling out the following, I have chosen editions with particularly good Introductions and Notes.

Trevor Blount (ed.), *David Copperfield*, Penguin Classics (Harmondsworth: Penguin, 1966).
Jerome H. Buckley (ed.), *David Copperfield*, Norton Critical Editions (New York: Norton, 1990). Incorporates almost 70 pages of extracts from critical essays, including Gwendolyn B. Needham on 'The Undisciplined Heart of David Copperfield'.
Nina Burgis (ed.), *David Copperfield*, Clarendon Edition (Oxford: Clarendon Press, 1981). The definitive edition, collating manuscript, proofs, and all editions published in Dickens's lifetime.
Nina Burgis (ed.), *David Copperfield*, World's Classics (Oxford: Oxford University Press, 1983).
David Craig (ed.), *Hard Times*, Penguin Classics (Harmondsworth: Penguin, 1969).
Terry Eagleton (ed.), *Hard Times*, Routledge English Texts (London: Methuen, 1987).
Paul Schlicke (ed.), *Hard Times*, World's Classics (Oxford: Oxford University Press, 1989).

BIOGRAPHICAL STUDIES

The standard biography of Dickens is still that by Edgar Johnson (available in Penguin paperback), but also recommended are Fred Kaplan's 1988 life and Peter Ackroyd's *Dickens*, a work which is just as imaginative and entertaining as one of Ackroyd's novels. Michael Slater's *Dickens and*

Women is a very useful source book for students wishing to look at Dickens and issues of gender.

Peter Ackroyd, *Dickens* (London: Sinclair-Stevenson, 1990).

Edgar Johnson, *Charles Dickens: His Tragedy and Triumph* (New York: Simon & Schuster, 1952).

Fred Kaplan, *Dickens: A Biography* (London: Hodder, 1988).

Michael Slater, *Dickens and Women* (London: Deutsch, 1983).

INTRODUCTIONS TO DICKENS

The six books listed below provide a solid introduction to Dickens's fiction. The outstanding volume is by J. Hillis Miller, who has been centrally involved in the development of poststructuralist criticism, in particular deconstructive readings of novels; his book on Dickens predates such work, but it continues to be a quite extraordinarily stimulating and helpful overview of Dickens's whole career as a novelist. Any student embarking upon sustained study of Dickens would be well advised to start with Miller.

A. E. Dyson, *The Inimitable Dickens: A Reading of the Novels* (London: Macmillan, 1970).

K. J. Fielding, *Charles Dickens: A Critical Introduction* (London: Longmans, 1965).

E. D. H. Johnson, *Charles Dickens: An Introduction to His Novels* (New York: Random House, 1969).

John Lucas, *The Melancholy Man: A Study of Dickens's Novels* (London: Methuen, 1970).

J. Hillis Miller, *Charles Dickens: The World of His Novels* (Cambridge: Harvard University Press, 1958).

Angus Wilson, *The World of Charles Dickens* (London: Secker & Warburg, 1970).

More recent criticism of Dickens gets under way with James Kincaid's book *Dickens and the Rhetoric of Laughter*. It would be nice to be able to add several other books offering a comprehensive overview of Dickens's output, but I get the impression that critics today are a bit reluctant to embark upon such a venture. There are plenty of books looking at, say, Dickens and education or Dickens and death, but a lack of general introductions. This might be because 'Dickens' is such a huge topic, but it also reflects a new spirit in criticism that recognises the impossibility of offering an authoritative overall view. Perhaps the last book of this kind on Dickens was John Carey's *The Violent Effigy: A Study of Dickens's Imagination* (an old-fashioned impressionistic piece of criticism, but packed with good ideas and insights). The best of the more recent books is Steven Connor's, which considers a number of Dickens's novels from a variety of critical and theoretical perspectives. Also highly recommended is Patricia Ingham's *Dickens, Women and Language*. Kate Flint's book does attempt an overall assessment of Dickens; the result is slightly disappointing, but it is, none the less, well worth reading as an introduction to up-to-date ways of looking at Dickens.

John Carey, *The Violent Effigy: A Study of Dickens's Imagination* (London: Faber & Faber, 1973).

Steven Connor, *Charles Dickens* (Oxford: Basil Blackwell, 1985).

Kate Flint, *Dickens*, Harvester New Readings (Brighton: Harvester, 1986).

Patricia Ingham, *Dickens, Women and Language* (London: Harvester Wheatsheaf, 1992).

James R. Kincaid, *Dickens and the Rhetoric of Laughter* (Oxford: Clarendon Press, 1971).

COLLECTIONS OF ESSAYS

David Copperfield was not included in the original Casebook volumes. *Hard Times* was, in a volume with *Great Expectations* and *Our Mutual Friend*. It includes an extract from Humphry House's 1941 *The Dickens World*, a 1957 essay by Butt and Tillotson on the problems of writing a weekly serial, and an extract from David Lodge's 1966 book *Language of Fiction* on 'The Rhetoric of *Hard Times*'. There are first-rate volumes on both *David Copperfield* and *Hard Times* in the Modern Critical Interpretations series. The *Copperfield* volume includes the essay by Robert Lougy, which is discussed in the Introduction to this New Casebook. The best collection on Dickens as a whole is that in the Longman Critical Readers series, edited by one of the contributors to this New Casebook volume, Steven Connor. Anyone browsing in a good library for material on Dickens should look at *Dickens Studies Annual* which, since its first appearance in 1970, has published much of the most exciting and original work on Dickens.

Harold Bloom (ed.), *Charles Dickens's David Copperfield*, Modern Critical Interpretations series (New York; Chelsea House, 1987).

Harold Bloom (ed.), *Charles Dickens's Hard Times*, Modern Critical Interpretations series (New York: Chelsea House, 1987).

Steven Connor (ed.), *Charles Dickens: A Critical Reader* (London: Longman, 1995).

Dickens Studies Annual: Essays in Victorian Fiction, 1– (1970–)

Norman Page (ed.), *Charles Dickens: Hard Times, Great Expectations and Our Mutual Friend*, Casebook series (London: Macmillan, 1979).

BOOKS AND ARTICLES ON *DAVID COPPERFIELD*

Specific page references are given for articles but, for the most part, I have not offered such precise information in relation to books; it seems fairly obvious that a book such as Buckley's on the *Bildungsroman* will deal with *David Copperfield* only for a certain number of pages, and that readers can be assumed to know how to use the contents page and index of the book to find the relevant sections. I have provided a brief comment on a number of the books and essays listed, but often the title gives sufficient indication of the nature of the item mentioned.

This first section covers a variety of material and approaches from the 1970s and beforehand. Much of the criticism, inevitably, has a liberal humanist orientation, but as the 70s progress there is, as structuralism begins to make an impact, an increasing emphasis on questions of form and narrative structure.

Janet H. Brown, 'The Narrator's Role in *David Copperfield*', *Dickens Studies Annual*, 2 (1972), 197–207.

Jerome H. Buckley, *Season of Youth: The Bildungsroman from Dickens to Golding* (Cambridge: Harvard University Press, 1974).

Felicity Hughes, 'Narrative Complexity in *David Copperfield*', *English Literary History*, 41 (1974), 89–105.

William T. Lankford, '"The Deep of Time": Narrative Order in *David Copperfield*', *English Literary History*, 46 (1979), 452–67.

Q. D. Leavis, 'Dickens and Tolstoy: The Case for a Serious View of *David Copperfield*', in F. R. and Q. D. Leavis, *Dickens the Novelist* (London: Chatto and Windus, 1970).

Sylvère Monod, *Dickens the Novelist* (Norman: University of Oklahoma Press, 1968). Includes nearly 100 pages on *David Copperfield*; a traditional discussion of the novel that considers its major themes and analyses Dickens's method of presenting David as a character with a rich emotional life.

Gwendolyn B. Needham, 'The Undisciplined Heart of *David Copperfield*', *Nineteenth-Century Fiction*, 9 (1954), 81–107. A landmark essay in traditional criticism of *David Copperfield*.

Harry Stone, *Dickens and the Invisible World: Fairy Tales, Fantasy, and Novel-Making* (Bloomington: Indiana University Press, 1979).

Norman Talbot, 'The Naming and the Namers of the Hero: A Study in *David Copperfield*', *Southern Review*, 11 (1978), 267–82.

Virginia Woolf, '*David Copperfield*', in *The Moment and Other Essays* (London: Hogarth, 1947).

Around the late 70s and early 80s, critics began to apply a variety of theoretical ideas and approaches to *David Copperfield*. The following items reflect this: there is Lougy's ground-breaking essay, and then, very soon afterwards names such as Lacan and Derrida begin to crop up in criticism. What tends to be lacking around this time, however, is any real sense of *David Copperfield* in its contemporary context. Quite a few of the essays, for example Hirsch's psychoanalytic rereading, look more original than is actually the case.

Gordon D. Hirsch, 'A Psychoanalytic Rereading of *David Copperfield*', *Victorian Newsletter*, 58 (1980), 1–5.

Robert E. Lougy, 'Remembrances of Death Past and Future: A Reading of *David Copperfield*', *Dickens Studies Annual*, 6 (1977), 72–101. Probably the first full-scale modern theoretical reading of the novel.

John P. McGowan, '*David Copperfield*: The Trial of Realism', *Nineteenth-Century Fiction*, 34 (1979), 1–19. Interesting on the different languages used by the different characters in the novel, in particular David's 'transparent style'.

Thomas Vargish, *The Providential Aesthetic in Victorian Fiction* (Charlottesville, University Press of Virginia, 1985).

Philip M. Weinstein, *The Semantics of Desire: Changing Models of Identity from Dickens to Joyce* (Princeton: Princeton University Press, 1984).
Barry Westburg, *The Confessional Fictions of Charles Dickens* (De Kalb: Northern Illinois University Press, 1977). One of the first critics to look at Dickens in the light of the ideas of Jacques Lacan; focuses on David seeing himself in mirrors.

As emphasised in the Introduction to this New Casebook, really interesting new work on *David Copperfield* begins to appear from around the mid-eighties. I have resisted the temptation to subdivide the following essays and books into separate categories (e.g. New Historicism, psychoanalytic criticism, feminism etc.) as the approaches so often overlap. There are also, of course, many critics who continue to think along traditional lines.

Murray Baumgarten, 'Writing and *David Copperfield*', *Dickens Studies Annual*, 14 (1985), 38–59.
David M. Craig, 'The Interplay of City and Self in *Oliver Twist, David Copperfield*, and *Great Expectations*', *Dickens Studies Annual*, 16 (1987), 17–38.
Edwin M. Eigner, '*David Copperfield* and the Benevolent Spirit', *Dickens Studies Annual*, 14 (1985) 1–15.
Edwin M. Eigner, 'Death and the Gentleman: *David Copperfield* as Elegiac Romance', *Dickens Studies Annual*, 16 (1987), 39–60.
Baruch Hochman and Ilja Wachs, 'Straw People, Hollow Men, and the Postmodernist Hall of Dissipating Mirrors: The Case of *David Copperfield*', *Style*, 24 (1990), 392–407.
John O. Jordan, 'The Social Sub-text of *David Copperfield*', *Dickens Studies Annual*, 14 (1985), 61–92. Lots of interesting parallels with the essay by Chris R. Vanden Bossche in this New Casebook.
David Kellogg, '"My Most Unwilling Hand": The Mixed Motivations of *David Copperfield*', *Dickens Studies Annual*, 20 (1991), 57–73. Kellogg starts with the proposition that 'we have come to understand *David Copperfield* not as a novel divorced from political concerns but rather as one with a deeply embedded social subtext'.
U. C. Knoepflmacher, 'From Outrage to Rage: Dickens's Bruised Femininity', in *Dickens and Other Victorians*, ed. Joanne Shattock (London: Macmillan, 1988), pp. 75–96.
Ned Lukacher, *Primal Scenes: Literature, Philosophy, Psychoanalysis* (Ithaca: Cornell University Press, 1986). A Freudian analysis of how the novel repeats the episode of Murdstone beating David, and David biting his torturer's hand.
Juliet McMaster, 'Dickens and David Copperfield on the Act of Reading', *English Studies in Canada*, 15 (1989), 288–304.
D. A. Miller, 'Secret Subjects, Open Secrets', *Dickens Studies Annual*, 14 (1985), 17–37. An unusual essay that confirms D. A. Miller's reputation as one of the critics who has done most to find a new direction for criticism after deconstruction.
Nicholas H. Morgan, *Secret Journeys: Theory and Practice in Reading Dickens* (Cranbury: Fairleigh Dickinson University Press, 1992).

Torsten Pettersson, 'The Maturity of David Copperfield', *English Studies*, 70 (1989), 63–73. A very traditional reading of the novel that, despite claiming to break new ground, returns to the idea of David as a coherent, unified self.

Dianne F. Sadoff, 'The Dead Father: *Barnaby Rudge, David Copperfield*, and *Great Expectations*', *Papers on Language and Literature*, 18 (1982), 36–57.

Natalie E. Schroeder and Ronald A. Schroeder, 'Betsey Trotwood and Jane Murdstone: Dickensian Doubles', *Studies in the Novel*, 21 (1989), 268–78.

Garrett Stewart, *Death Sentences: Styles of Dying in British Fiction* (Cambridge: Harvard University Press, 1984).

Stanley Tick, 'Dickens, Dickens, Micawber ... and Bakhtin', *The Victorian Newsletter*, 79 (1991), 34–7.

BOOKS AND ARTICLES ON *HARD TIMES*

This first section on *Hard Times* ranges from Leavis's enthusiastic, indeed lavish, praise to the kind of fault-finding exemplified by David Craig and others who criticise Dickens's politics in the novel. Perhaps the last critic to take this hostile line is D. W. Jefferson, who condemns *Hard Times* for its 'distortion of truth'; surprisingly, this essay appears as late as 1985. Jefferson seems quite unaware that the discussion might have moved on, that other critics are beginning to look at *Hard Times* in different ways.

Joseph Butwin, '*Hard Times*: The News and the Novel', *Nineteenth-Century Fiction*, 32 (1977), 166–87.

David Craig, 'Introduction', in *Hard Times* (Harmondsworth: Penguin, 1969), pp. 11–36.

Joseph Gold, '"Aw a Muddle": *Hard Times*', in *Charles Dickens: Radical Moralist* (Minneapolis: University of Minnesota Press, 1972), pp. 196–207.

Michael Goldberg, 'The Critique of Utility: *Hard Times*', in *Carlyle and Dickens* (Athens: University of Georgia Press, 1972), pp. 78–99.

David M. Hirsch, '*Hard Times* and Dr Leavis', *Criticism*, 6 (1964), 1–16.

John Holloway, '*Hard Times*: A History and a Criticism', in *Dickens and the Twentieth Century*, ed. John Gross and Gabriel Pearson (London: Routledge & Kegan Paul, 1962), pp. 159–74. Hirsch and Holloway emphasise faults in the novel, both as art and as social history.

D. W. Jefferson, 'Mr Gradgrind's Facts', *Essays in Criticism*, 35 (1985), 197–212.

F. R. Leavis, *The Great Tradition* (London: Chatto & Windus, 1948).

F. R. and Q. D. Leavis, *Dickens the Novelist* (London: Chatto & Windus 1970).

David Lodge, *Language of Fiction: Essays in Criticism and Verbal Analysis of the English Novel* (London: Routledge & Kegan Paul, 1966).

Robert Lougy, 'Dickens's *Hard Times*: The Romance as Radical Literature', *Dickens Studies Annual*, 2 (1972), 237–54.

Raymond Williams, *Culture and Society 1780–1950* (London: Chatto & Windus, 1958).

Alongside those critics who have concentrated on the politics of *Hard Times*, there have always been critics who have drawn attention to a variety of other aspects of the text.

John D. Baird, 'Divorce and Matrimonial Causes: An Aspect of *Hard Times*', *Victorian Studies*, 20 (1977), 401–12.
George Bernstein, 'Miscultivated Field and Corrupted Garden: Imagery in *Hard Times*', *Nineteenth-Century Fiction*, 26 (1971), 158–70.
Peter Bracher, 'Muddle and Wonderful No-Meaning: Verbal Irresponsibility and Verbal Failures in *Hard Times*', *Studies in the Novel*, 10 (1978), 305–19.
Michael Hollington, 'Ironic Infernos: *Bleak House, Hard Times*, and Ruskin's Conception of the Grotesque' in *Dickens and the Grotesque* (Totowa: Barnes and Noble, 1984), pp. 192–215.
Ian Ousby, 'Figurative Language in *Hard Times*', *Durham University Journal*, 74 (1981), 103–9.
Anny Sadrin, 'The Perversion of Desire: A Study of Irony as a Structural Element in *Hard Times*', in *Studies in the Later Dickens*, ed. Jean-Claude Amalric (Montpellier: Université Paul Valery, 1973), pp. 93–117.
Warrington Winters, 'Dickens's *Hard Times:* The Lost Childhood', *Dickens Studies Annual*, 2 (1972), 217–36.

As with *David Copperfield*, from around the mid-eighties critics began to look at *Hard Times* with different assumptions. This re-examination of the novel can be directly traced to new thinking about the language of literary texts, ideas which began to establish themselves with the advent of structuralism. The essay by Roger Fowler set the tone in trying to get beyond the old kind of approach, which in some ways came down to being either 'for' or 'against' the novel. By no means, however, do all of the critics included here automatically embrace these new assumptions; a number, as one might expect, continue to work along traditional lines, none the less producing valuable work that adds to our sense of the novel.

Diane Dewhurst Belcher, 'Dickens's Mrs Sparsit and the Politics of Service', *Dickens Quarterly*, 2 (1985), 92–8.
Jane Campbell, '"Competing Towers of Babel": Some Patterns of Language in *Hard Times*', *English Studies in Canada*, 10 (1984), 416–35.
Robert L. Caserio, 'The Name of the Horse: *Hard Times*, Semiotics, and the Supernatural', *Novel*, 20 (1986), 5–23.
Nicholas Coles, 'The Politics of *Hard Times*: Dickens the Novelist versus Dickens the Reformer', *Dickens Studies Annual*, 15 (1986), 145–79. A solid and substantial, traditional historicist reading of the novel.
David L. Cowles, 'Having It Both Ways: Gender and Paradox in *Hard Times*', *Dickens Quarterly*, 8 (1991), 79–84.
Terry Eagleton, 'Critical Commentary', in *Hard Times* (London: Methuen, 1987). An essay that, setting the novel in its historical context, hovers somewhat uneasily between a traditional condemnation of *Hard Times* for its confused stance and an illuminating explanation of the inevitability of such confusion on Dickens's part; particularly good on the relationship between the personal, the social and the sexual.

Roger Fowler, 'Polyphony and Problematic in *Hard Times*', in *The Changing World of Charles Dickens*, ed. Robert Giddings (London: Vision Press, 1983), pp. 91–108. Fowler was perhaps the first critic to read *Hard Times* in the light of modern critical theory.

Patricia E. Johnson, '*Hard Times* and the Structure of Industrialism: The Novel as Factory', *Studies in the Novel*, 21 (1989), 128–37.

K. Kearns, 'A Tropology of Realism in *Hard Times*', *English Literary History*, 59 (1992), 857–81.

Cynthia Northcutt Malone, 'The Fixed Eye and the Rolling Eye: Surveillance and Discipline in *Hard Times*', *Studies in the Novel*, 21 (1989), 4–26. An examination of the ideology of middle-class reform in *Hard Times*; one aspect of the disciplining of individuals is the sexual discipline carried out against Louisa.

Martha C. Nussbaum, 'The Literary Imagination in Public Life', *New Literary History*, 22 (1991) 876–910.

Alexander Pettit, 'Sympathetic Criminality in the Mid-Victorian Novel', *Dickens Studies Annual*, 19 (1990), 281–300.

Paul Schacht, 'Dickens and the Uses of Nature', *Victorian Studies*, 34 (1990), 77–102. A reading of *Hard Times* that sets the novel in a context of Victorian ideas about nature.

Grahame Smith, 'Comic Subversion and *Hard Times*', *Dickens Studies Annual*, 18 (1989), 145–60.

Stephen J. Spector, 'Monsters of Metonymy: *Hard Times* and Knowing the Working Class', *English Literary History*, 51 (1984), 365–84.

Notes on Contributors

Virginia Carmichael is a freelance writer in Missoula, Montana, and also teaches at the University of Montana. She is the author of *Framing History: The Rosenberg Story and the Cold War* (Minnesota, 1993), and is currently writing a book on US agriculture policy and practice.

Jean Ferguson Carr is Assistant Professor of English at the University of Pittsburgh. She co-edits the *Pittsburgh Series in Composition, Literacy and Culture* and has edited two volumes of *The Collected Works of R. W. Emerson* (Cambridge, 1979 and 1983). In addition to a number of essays on Dickens, she has written on cultural studies and curricular change, autobiography, and images of women. She is currently working on a book, *Learning to Be Natural: The Construction of American Literacy and Letters*.

Steven Connor is Professor of Modern English Literature and Director of the Centre for Interdisciplinary Research in Culture and the Humanities at Birkbeck College, London. He is the editor of *Charles Dickens: A Critical Reader* (London, 1995). Among his recent books are *Postmodernist Culture: An Introduction to Theories of the Contemporary* (Oxford, 1989), *Theory and Cultural Value* (Oxford, 1992) and *The Novel in History: 1950 to the Present* (London, 1994).

Simon Edwards is Principal Lecturer in English at Roehampton Institute. His publications include essays on Dickens, Disraeli and Scott. He is currently working on Scott's fiction and the revolutionary culture of the early nineteenth century.

Richard Fabrizio teaches courses in English and Comparative Literature and in the Classical Tradition at Pace University, New York. Among his articles is a study of the incest theme in Western Literature, in *A Dictionary of Literary Themes and Motifs* (New York, 1988).

Catherine Gallagher is Professor of English at the University of California, Berkeley. In addition to *The Industrial Reformation of English Fiction*, her publications include *The Making of the Modern Body: Sexuality and Society in the Nineteenth Century*, edited with Thomas Laquer (Berkeley,

263

1987) and *Nobody's Safe: Vanishing Acts of Female Authors in the Marketplace: 1670–1800* (forthcoming).

John Kucich is Professor of English Literature at the University of Michigan. He has published *Excess and Restraint in the Novels of Charles Dickens* (Athens, 1981), *Repression in Victorian Fiction* (Berkeley, 1987) and *The Power of Lies: Transgression in Victorian Fiction* (Ithaca, forthcoming).

Margaret Myers was educated in the UK at Birmingham University and in the US at Indiana University. She is now Associate Professor of Marketing at Northern Kentucky University. Her current research focuses on the portrayal of marketing institutions in nineteenth- and twentieth-century popular culture.

Mary Poovey is Professor of English at Johns Hopkins University, Baltimore. In addition to *Uneven Developments*, she is the author of *The Proper Lady and the Woman Writer: Ideology as Style in the Works of Mary Wollstonecraft, Mary Shelley and Jane Austen* (Chicago, 1984).

Chris R. Vanden Bossche is Associate Professor of English Literature at the University of Notre Dame. He is the author of the book *Carlyle and the Search for Authority* (Columbus, 1991), and articles on Dickens, Carlyle, Ruskin, Scott and Tennyson.

Index